Globalised Re/Gendering of the Academy and Leadership

The significance of higher education to national knowledge-based economies has made the sector the object of government policies, international monitoring and corporatisation. This radical global restructuring of higher education is gendered in its processes, practices and effects. Exploring how the reorganisation of the sector has redefined academic, management and professional roles and identities, this book considers the different impacts of structural change for men and women working at diverse levels of the academy.

Drawing from empirical studies undertaken in Europe, North America, Asia and Australasia, the contributions offer a range of theoretical and methodological perspectives, including large-scale comparative data and case studies. They inform what is a key policy issue in the twenty-first century – the repositioning of women in the academy and leadership. Despite a range of institutional equity strategies in which women learnt the 'rules of the game', this book shows that structural and cultural barriers – often conceptualised through metaphors such as sticky floors, glass ceilings, chilly climates, or dead-end pipelines – have not disappeared as might be expected as the academy becomes numerically feminised.

Each chapter provides an insight into how historical legacies, cultural contexts, geographic locations, modes of regional and institutional governance, and national policies are mediated and vernacularised through practice by localised gender regimes and orders. This book was originally published as a special issue of *Gender and Education*.

Jill Blackmore is the Alfred Deakin Professor in Education in the Faculty of Arts and Education, and the Director of the Centre for Research in Educational Futures and Innovation at Deakin University, Australia. She is also a Fellow of the Academy of Social Sciences, Australia. Her research interests include education policy and institutional governance from a feminist perspective, educational restructuring and organisational change and equity policy related to the work of education professionals. Recently, she has focused on disengagement with, and lack of diversity in, university leadership, international education and graduate employability. She is the author of *Educational Leadership and Nancy Fraser* (2016) and co-editor of *Mobile teachers and curriculum in international schooling* (2014, with Arber and Vongalis-Macrow).

Marita Sánchez-Moreno is a Professor in the Department of Teaching and School Organisation at the Universidad de Sevilla, Spain. Her research interests include gender and leadership in higher education, and the professional development of these leaders; and educational, cultural and organisational change, innovation and improvement.

She is a founding member of the *Network of Research on Leadership and Improvement in Education*, and takes part in the *International Successful School Principalship Project*, and the international Comenius Multilateral Project *Professional Learning through Feedback and Reflection* devoted to the training of school leaders.

Naarah Sawers is currently a Research Fellow in the School of Education, and teaches in the School of Communications and Creative Arts, at Deakin University, Australia. Her research spans the fields of children's literature, education and studies in higher education. Her most recent book is *Critical Fictions: Science, Feminism, and Corporeal Subjectivity* (2008). She has written for academic journals in cultural studies, literature and education.

Globalised Re/Gendering of the Academy and Leadership

Edited by
**Jill Blackmore, Marita Sánchez-Moreno
and Naarah Sawers**

LONDON AND NEW YORK

First published 2017
by Routledge

2 Park Square, Milton Park, Abingdon, Oxfordshire OX14 4RN
711 Third Avenue, New York, NY 10017

Routledge is an imprint of the Taylor & Francis Group, an informa business

First issued in paperback 2018

British Library Cataloguing in Publication Data
A catalogue record for this book is available from the British Library

ISBN: 978-1-138-23054-5 (hbk)
ISBN: 978-0-367-02996-8 (pbk)

Typeset in TimesNewRomanPS
by diacriTech, Chennai

Publisher's Note
The publisher accepts responsibility for any inconsistencies that may have arisen during the conversion of this book from journal articles to book chapters, namely the possible inclusion of journal terminology.

Disclaimer
Every effort has been made to contact copyright holders for their permission to reprint material in this book. The publishers would be grateful to hear from any copyright holder who is not here acknowledged and will undertake to rectify any errors or omissions in future editions of this book.

Contents

CONTENTS

Citation Information

The chapters in this book were originally published in *Gender and Education*, volume 27, issue 3 (May 2015). When citing this material, please use the original page numbering for each article, as follows:

CITATION INFORMATION

Chapter 6

Chapter 7

Chapter 8

Chapter 9

For any permission-related enquiries please visit:
http://www.tandfonline.com/page/help/permissions

Notes on Contributors

Sarah Jane Aiston is an Honorary Associate Professor in the Faculty of Education at the University of Hong Kong.

Mariana Altopiedi is a Professor in the Faculty of Education at the Universidad de Sevilla, Spain.

Jill Blackmore is the Alfred Deakin Professor in Education in the Faculty of Arts and Education, and the Director of the Centre for Research in Educational Futures and Innovation at Deakin University, Australia.

Marie Brennan is an Honorary Professor of Education at Victoria University, Melbourne, Australia.

Van Hanh Thi Do is based in the School of Education at the University of South Australia, Magill, Australia.

Johanna Hofbauer is based in the Department of Sociology and Social Research at the University of Vienna, Austria.

Jisun Jung is an Associate Professor in the Faculty of Education at the University of Hong Kong.

Katharina Kreissl is a PhD candidate and junior researcher in the Department of Socioeconomics at the University of Vienna, Austria.

Julián López-Yáñez is based in the Faculty of Education at the Universidad de Sevilla, Spain.

Rachel McNae is an Associate Professor of Educational Leadership at the University of Waikato, New Zealand.

Pat O'Connor is a Professor in the Department of Sociology at the University of Limerick, Republic of Ireland.

KerryAnn O'Meara is a Professor of Higher Education at the University of Maryland, USA.

Eugenie Samier is a Senior Lecturer and coordinator of the Doctor in Education programme at the British University in Dubai, United Arab Emirates.

Marita Sánchez-Moreno is a Professor in the Department of Teaching and School Organisation at the Universidad de Sevilla, Spain.

NOTES ON CONTRIBUTORS

Birgit Sauer is a Professor of Political Science in the Institute of Political Science at the University of Vienna, Austria.

Naarah Sawers is currently a Research Fellow in the School of Education, and teaches in the School of Communications and Creative Arts, at Deakin University, Australia.

Angelika Striedinger is a Researcher in the Faculty of Social Sciences at the University of Vienna, Austria.

Nelly P. Stromquist is a Professor of International Education Policy at the University of Maryland, USA.

Kerren Vali is the Pacific Project Officer for the Uniting Worlds Organisation, based in Suva, Fiji.

INTRODUCTION

Globalised re/gendering of the academy and leadership

Our purpose with this special issue has been to stimulate international scholarly and policy debates about how the social changes produced in the wake of late capitalism and emergent knowledge societies are affecting our research, theorising and practices about gender and leadership in higher education. The current processes restructuring the academy, while invoking the supposed needs of a global knowledge society, are clearly affecting the professional identities, the leadership roles and, consequently, the life and work of both men and women in the university globally. This issue explores these changes and its consequences through research informed by diverse theoretical perspectives grounded empirically and experientially from nine countries across five continents.

Together, these articles challenge dominant gendered binaries, discourses and assumptions. First, they draw on both qualitative methodologies involving in-depth interviews, observations and discourse analysis and survey data. This is indicative of the rise of mixed methods with the dissolution of the qualitative/qualitative divide that bedevilled many methodology debates within/against feminist research in the 1990s. Second, these papers trouble Global North/South and East/West binaries with contributions from Honk Kong, the UAE, Papua New Guinea, Vietnam, Australia, Spain, Austria, the USA and Ireland. All university systems are undergoing radical change informed by discourses about higher education as the driver of knowledge economies. But how seemingly similar globally mobile discourses and policies about knowledge economies articulate locally is made evident by these studies. Each case provides instances of how historical legacies; cultural contexts; geographic locations; modes of regional (e.g. European Union) and institutional governance as well as national policies are mediated and vernacularised through practice by localised gender regimes and orders.

Third, while the focus is on gender and leadership in higher education, the comparative perspective problematises a range of simplistic male/female binaries that characterise research around leadership and gender. Feminist scholarship has understandably focused on the slow progress of women gaining access to managerial and research leadership in higher education, particularly at the executive level, despite discourses about the benefits of diversity in and of leadership and the existence of nearly two decades of equal opportunity, affirmative action and gender mainstreaming policies in the Anglophone, North American and European university sectors, respectively. These papers take up and unpack this issue through large-scale comparative data (Aiston and Jung; Sánchez-Moreno, López-Yáñez, and Altopiedi), case studies (Blackmore and Sawers; O'Connor; McNae and Vali) and qualitative analysis of policy interventions (O'Meara and Stromquist; Kreissl, Striedinger, Sauer, and Hofbauer).

Western feminist research has focused, as have policies, on female academics and other subordinate groups, their experiences and perceptions, identifying the structural and cultural institutional barriers they confront. They tend to aim, as O'Meara and Stromquist indicate in their paper on the ADVANCE programme in the USA, on how women can work strategically to re/position themselves better through mentoring and networking; that is, 'learning the rules of the game'. But what remains evident from the papers collectively is that the structural and cultural barriers – often conceptualised through metaphors such as sticky floors, glass ceilings, chilly climates or dead-end pipelines – have not disappeared as could be expected as the academy becomes numerically feminised. Indeed, studies by Kreissl, Striedinger, Sauer, and Hofbauer in Austria, O'Connor in Ireland, and Blackmore and Sawers in Australia indicate that in the Western entrepreneurial university, these barriers have solidified if not been raised as universities seek to aggressively position themselves more favourably in global rankings, academic and student markets as 'world class'. Examining the changes in policy frames, Kreissl et al., refer to universities transitioning from 'local to global', from 'ivory tower to business' and from 'civil servant to excellence'.

Luke (2001) in her South Asia study identified the consequences of global transformations of the sector at the macro level (e.g. the increased casualisation, reduced funding and massification) on women's capacity to access and their experiences in formal leadership. She argued for greater attention to be paid as to how institutional micro-practices differ in culturally specific sites in ways that marginalise women. Luke lamented the lack of research regarding women and gender in higher education in Hong Kong, Thailand, Singapore and Malaysia compared to the body of literature in the global North and West. Likewise in 2014, Morley and Crossouard's report on Women in Leadership in South Asia (Afghanistan, Bangladesh, India, Nepal, Pakistan and Sri Lanka) identified the overwhelming lack of statistical data disaggregated by gender and academics as well as the lack of research on gender and leadership, or training of women for leadership positions. These papers go some way towards remedying this gap.

This issue continues to problematise what it means for women to be in formal positions of power. Feminist scholars can no longer talk about the unitary category of women, unifying value systems such as class, religion and race/ethnicity confuse such essentialising claims. Feminist post-structuralism pointed to the sense of contradiction, ambivalence and ambiguity many women leaders felt and the ways academic life and its reward systems produced the performative self-managing academic, in which we are and have been complicit. Women in formal positions in particular are seen to be powerful. While some do not necessarily feel powerful or exercise that power, others happily use their authority. While many of these studies reject meta-narratives of dominance and subordination of all women, they do indicate that women continue to lead in 'unequal regimes'. Particular to higher education are the gendered power/knowledge disciplinary hierarchies between 'hard/soft science' that position women differently across disciplinary fields, divides between managerial and research leadership, or as Blackmore and Sawers identify, between public and domestic roles in executive leadership.

This issue, including studies located in Vietnam, Hong Kong, Papua New Guinea and the UAE, adds to the growing body of literature on gender and leadership in higher education. It is indicative of issues for women in emergent university sectors now challenging Northern/Western dominance. These papers also confront any assumptions about the dominance of Western culture within the university sector. They point to the significance for women of socio-cultural belief systems ingrained into every aspect of domestic and institutional life in which women are expected to play particular (and usually subordinate) roles with regard to family, which extends to masculine authority within the academy as other workplaces. It is evident in how class, religious status, caste and kinship are significant in terms of how women gain formal leadership positions, but not necessarily in terms of how their leadership is perceived and received. Finally, these articles signal the effects of the assumed gender neutrality of Western/ised cultures underpinning discourses about quality, excellence, innovation, science, etc. which feed into academic cultures, and which are skewed towards particular ways of doing and valuing research. Collectively, these factors influence perceptions of leadership that are gendered rather than actual leadership practices.

These papers also raise significant questions, such as those posed by Morley and Crossouard (2014, 2) in their review of female leadership in the South Asian higher education sector:

> A key question resulting from our findings is whether women are being rejected or disqualified from senior leadership through discriminatory recruitment, selection and promotion procedures, gendered career pathways or exclusionary networks and practices in women-unfriendly institutions or indeed whether women are refusing, resisting or dismissing senior leadership and making strategic decisions not to apply for positions which they evaluate as unattractive, onerous and undesirable.

While they conclude it is a combination of these aspects, the question not asked is why higher education leadership positions are so undesirable not just for women, but as Blackmore (2014) found, for many men as well. What is it about contemporary university leadership that 'turns off' many academics, and who will take up these positions if that continues?

So what does this issue contribute to the above debates? First, it points to the consequences of global trends as they are vernacularised through situated institutional and individual practices. While policies of marketisation, academic capitalism and new managerialism dominate, their effects differ in each cultural context. All papers show the importance of symbolic, cultural and historic issues as factors mediating global policies and local practices, and how traditional values and practices re-negotiate, temper or resist policy (Do and Brennan; Samier; McNae and Vali). Samier suggests that Western values associated with discourses about globalisation are thus 'particularised'. The Austrian case study (Kreissl et al.) illustrates how some higher education systems, with all their paternalistic legacies and dispositions, are 'protected' from the harsher imperatives of neo-liberal policies, compared to Ireland (O'Connor) and Australia (Blackmore and Sawers). Independent of what type of formal position is undertaken, much of the power gained and utilised by women in developing university sectors was based on informal, local traditions and socio-cultural context. Do and Brennan clearly show that the role that Vietnamese women play in both organisations and the home as 'strong active, capable, independent, heroic and powerful' is deeply rooted in the history, culture and folklore of the nation. Likewise, McNae and Vali's demonstrate that women in PNG universities gain leadership skills through community organisations, sporting bodies or churches, indicating the importance of female networks outside the university in supporting their personal and professional lives.

While these papers indicate the significance of cultural difference, they do not ignore the universal persistence of gender inequality in its many forms – overt and covert (O'Meara and Stromquist; Aiston and Jung). The inequality mechanisms are quite varied including the greater feminine presence in the lower management position; a lower presence in key decision-making committees (O'Connor, Blackmore and

3

Sawers), bigger obstacles for getting scientific papers published (Aiston and Jung); and greater difficulties, both 'subjective' and of material nature, in finding a balance between familial life and academic work (McNae and Vali; Do and Brennan). While Aiston and Jung suggest that family-related variables, such a civil status, number of children in charge and caring responsibilities, did not have a negative impact on women's research productivity in their cross national study, they also recognise that survey data does not delve deeply into why this seems to be the case and how this impacts on access to leadership.

Interventions addressing gender inequality also work differently according to context. Both O'Meara and Stromquist, and Kreissl et al., report that the policies that promote gender equity in the academic field in their respective countries have had more failures than achievements. Interestingly, such failures can be attributed to failure to implement policy together with the traditional gender division of labour; the culture, symbols and values attributed to different disciplinary fields; predominant, patriarchal social relationships that permeate from the wider social order; different ways of understanding the academic work; and biased systems of assessment and promotion. While women leaders may be considered to have agency, they are restricted by normative images of leadership and male-dominated cultural values. Socio-cultural factors are ever-present. Gender discrimination is more evident in countries with developing higher education systems where discourses about women's traditional roles are more overtly mobilised (Do and Brennan; McNae and Vali). They illustrate how normative masculinities in leadership are both dominant and explicit. While defining or limiting women's roles overtly would no longer be acceptable in Western higher education institutions, discrimination is hidden by what O'Connor refers to as tacit 'invisibility laws' at the same time that policies and discourses about women being 'wasted talent' are mobilised.

So while, with modernisation, there are significant shifts in norms over time, some are retained, others disappear. These norms are informed by cultural, spiritual and religious belief systems which position women variously, often in contradiction to the modernisation thesis that women are the new source of leadership. Most obviously, as argued by Do and Brennan, while there has been greater emphasis on choice biographies in the Global North as gender roles have been challenged and as Western societies ramp up to enter the knowledge economies, we are increasingly aware of the instability of linear trajectories of career as institutions seek greater flexibility and the affordances available to women are fewer than for their male counterparts due to familial obligations and culturally framed social relations of gender.

A repeated theme emerging from the issue is the endurance of masculine dominance of executive leadership – both in management and research – with a horizontal division of labour. Most often, academic women managers are clustered horizontally in middle management positions which they only occupy for a limited period of time. Vertically, men take on the 'hard' issues of the management work (finances, bureaucratic administration, formal decision-making and resources seeking), whereas women in leadership are often in charge of the 'soft' domains including conflict intermediation, maintaining group cohesion, group well-being and caring for students, and not necessarily in the long term (Blackmore and Sawers; O′Connor; Sánchez-Moreno, López-Yáñez, and Altopiedi). At the same time, while perceptions about leaders are often filtered through a gendered lens, these studies reveal that the power basis (autocratic, technocratic, bureaucratic, ideological and political) used by both men and women academic managers is clearly similar. That is, there is no distinctive 'gender style' as all leaders use a range of practices to undertake leadership work required by the position, although informed by personal dispositions (Sánchez-Moreno, López-Yáñez, and Altopiedi).

The rarely mentioned background stories underpinning many of these papers are the processes of internationalisation of higher education over the past decades. These papers are written by or with white Western female academics located in Hong Kong, New Zealand or the UAE and their colleagues. Some have worked with their doctoral students, many have North American doctorates. Furthermore, a key aspect of Westernisation/globalisation is the expectation for fluency in academic English as publication is required in English language journals in order to be considered 'international' and as a result of the dominance of the global North in publication (USA, UK and Europe). European (in this instance Spanish and Austrian) academics as well as academics from the Middle East, Asia and Africa are expected to conform to English language norms of academic publishing. Internationalisation and academic capitalism are arguably tinged by new forms of colonialism.

The current structural and to some extent cultural reforms in the academy pose the necessity of keeping and intensifying our focus on such changes and its consequences from a gender perspective. Gender restructuring of the academic labour force continues. The scaling up of the university into a global multinational enterprise has become the game changer of the early twenty-first century. It has arguably stalled gender equity and policies seeking to redress female disadvantage with regard to leadership. These studies indicate there is no steady progress over the long term of women gaining executive leadership. While policies exist, there is little political will, sufficient resources or effective strategies that significantly improve the opportunities for women in seeking leadership. Indeed, knowledge economies have led universities to be harsher, where flexibility is less about women-friendly environments and more about entrepreneurial forms of leadership that revive modern/traditional but always unequal social relations of gender.

References

Blackmore, J. 2014. "'Wasting Talent'? Rethinking the Problematic of Leadership Disengagement in Entrepreneurial Universities from a Feminist Critical Policy Perspective." *Higher Education and Research Development* 33 (1): 83–96.

Luke, C. 2001. *Globalization and Women in Academia: North/West-South/East*. Mahwah, NJ: Lawrence Erlbaum Associates.

Morley, L., and B. Crossouard. 2014. *Women in Higher Education Leadership in South Asia: Rejection, Refusal, Reluctance, Revisioning*. Executive Summary. British Council. http://www.britishcouncil.in/sites/britishcouncil.in2/files/women_in_higher_education_leadership_in_sa.pdf.

Jill Blackmore
Deakin University

Marita Sánchez-Moreno
University of Seville

Naarah Sawers
Deakin University

Women academics and research productivity: an international comparison

Sarah Jane Aiston and Jisun Jung

Faculty of Education, The University of Hong Kong, Hong Kong SAR, China

In the prestige economy of higher education, research productivity is highly prized. Previous research indicates, however, a gender gap with respect to research output. This gap is often explained by reference to familial status and responsibilities. In this article, we examine the research productivity gender gap from an international perspective by undertaking a gendered analysis of the Changing Academic Profession Survey. We suggest that family is not, in all cases, operating as a form of negative equity in the prestige economy of higher education. In addition, we argue that an over-reliance on an explanatory framework that positions family-related variables as central to the research productivity gender gap might well be drawing our attention from significant structural and systemic discriminatory practices within the profession.

Introduction

Research related to the position, status and experience of women academics has increasingly attracted the attention of scholars in recent decades. Despite the increase in the numbers of women entering higher education as undergraduate students internationally (although this trend is far from universal[1]), women continue to fail to progress through the academic hierarchy in significant numbers and enter senior leadership positions. In 2012, in response to this situation, academics put forward a manifesto for change to increase women's participation in higher education leadership and research globally.[2]

How and why the academic gender gap is maintained is both complex and multi-faceted. The organisational culture and structures of the academy are regarded as both perpetuating and privileging masculine practices and norms (Husu and Morley 2000; Thomas and Davies 2002; Bailyn 2003; Harley 2003; Ozkanli et al. 2009). Academic gate-keeping, the process of selection, coupled with the allocation of resources, works to the disadvantage of academic women; either slowing down their career progression, or excluding them from the higher echelons of the academy (Husu 2004). The effectiveness of 'transparency' and 'accountability' measures in recruitment and promotion decisions is questioned (Van den Brink, Benschop, and Jansen 2010) and gender stereotyping in turn influences the roles academic women do undertake, positioning them as caretakers (Turner 2002; Schein 2007) or 'academic mommies'

(Ropes-Huilman 2000). Their work is different from their male colleagues and is generally viewed as unequal. Academic women are more likely to be heavily involved in pastoral care, committee work (but not necessarily decision-making bodies), teaching and the corresponding quality assurance and audit processes (Kjeldal, Rindfleish, and Sheridan 2006; Hughes et al. 2007; Morley 2007). Leadership is implicitly constructed as male (Madera, Hebel, and Martin 2009; Fitzgerald 2014) and a lack of mentors and networks further marginalises academic women (Baldwin 1985; Clark and Corcoran 1986; O'Leary and Mitchell 1990). And in the 'greedy' academy, women academics, in particular, face the challenge of how to negotiate work and family (Bailyn 2003; Probert 2005).

The aim of this article is to further contribute to our understanding of the academic gender gap from an international perspective. What factors or forces prevent women academics leading, rather than being led, within the academy? At this point the conceptual framework of the prestige economy is highly relevant, namely what is valued or prized most highly in higher education? (Blackmore 2012). What counts for, and what will gain, academic promotion? Answer: Research (Skelton 2005; Abreu et al. 2008; Postiglione and Wang 2009; Baker 2012; Macfarlane 2012; Fitzgerald 2014). As Morley notes, 'research performance is implicitly associated with the prestige economy in higher education, and is a pathway to academic seniority and indicator for promotion' (Morley 2014, 116).

In a comparative study, such as the one undertaken in this article, we may well ask, is the prestige economy universal in its application? One indication that a discourse of research excellence is dominant, particularly with respect to mature higher education systems in the developed world, is the increasing importance of global rankings; rankings that favour research-intensive universities (De Witte and Hudrlikova 2013). More specifically, the ranking organisations assess the research productivity of universities through statistics that aggregate quality and quantity of faculty publications (Hallinger 2014). The emphasis on international standing and the performativity audit culture of contemporary higher education demand tangible, measurable research outputs with an emphasis on both the quality and the quantity of academic publications (Baker 2012). Whilst partly initiated by Western new managerial-orientated doctrines and neo-liberalist ideologies, higher education institutions in Asia are also increasingly under pressure to compete internationally, particularly in measuring research performance and allocating performance-based funding (Deem, Mok, and Lucas 2008; Hallinger 2014). Take, for example, Korea's publish or perish culture (Lee and Lee 2013) or the introduction of the Research Assessment Exercise in Hong Kong (Postiglione and Wang 2009). Previous research confirms the gender gap in research productivity; women academics publish less on average than their male colleagues (Tower et al. 2007). The consequence of this gender gap in the prestige economy of higher education is highly significant in a promotion system that often favours research over teaching and service (Baker 2012).

The aim of this article is to further explore the issue of gender and research productivity from an international perspective, by undertaking an analysis of the Changing Academic Profession (CAP) survey data, with a focus on publications. There are a number of indicators to measure research productivity – number of publications, citation counts, doctoral students and competitive research funding (Litwin 2012), although there are differences between academic disciplines in terms of the importance attributed to these indicators (Becher and Trowler 2001). Nevertheless, the number of publications, particularly peer-reviewed journal articles, is the most widely used indicator of research productivity *across* academic disciplines (Toutkoushian and Bellas 2003; Horta, Dautel, and Veloso 2012; Shin et al. 2014) since it is the most important stimulant of career progression and also allows for comparative analysis (Litwin 2012).

The CAP survey

The CAP survey is an international survey that was conducted in 1992 and 2008. The most recent survey included 19 countries and is a 16-page closed questionnaire which contains items related to, for example, educational background, conditions of employment, academic role, university management and personal context. The survey, albeit not intentionally designed to consider the position of women as academics, can provide a large-scale insight into the working lives of academics, both men and women, internationally. To date, there have been few published studies that present specifically a gendered analysis of this survey; Bain and Cummings (2000) discuss the academy's glass ceiling in relation to the 1992 survey, whilst Aiston (2014) considers the situation of women academics in Hong Kong with respect to the 2008 data. The advantages of carrying out a gendered re-analysis of this survey data are three-fold. First, it provides the opportunity to explore comparatively the position of both men and women, thereby highlighting the extent to which the academy is gendered. Second, it enables an analysis of the position of women academics at a macro level in which we can observe large-scale trends. This provides an interesting comparison with respect to research that has largely drawn on interview data to uncover women's experiences (a point we will return to). Third, given the international dimension of the survey, we can also explore both the shared and divergent aspects of academic women's positions.

Five countries were selected for analysis on the basis of the following criteria. First, we considered the proportion of women academics in different countries, based on the Global Gender Index (Times Higher Education 2013). We selected a number of countries that varied with respect to the proportion of women academics and considered the representativeness of the CAP survey data compared to the proportion of women academics in each of these countries. Through this comparison, we narrowed down the scope of analysis to five countries: Japan, Hong Kong, Germany, the USA, and Finland. Table 1 shows the comparison between the Global Gender Index and the sample distribution of the CAP survey. Second, each of these five countries are economically advanced, with mature higher education systems, but also represent different forms of systems, for example, professional (Germany and Finland), market (the USA and Hong Kong) and state orientated (Japan) (Clark 1983; Shin and Harman 2009). In addition, each of these systems has different shapes of academic hierarchies (Bain and Cummings 2000). Finally, these five countries represent interesting different contexts with respect to the position and status of women in society in general. Finland, Germany and the USA rank relatively highly on a number of indicators with respect to gender equality – 2nd, 14th and 23rd, respectively (World Economic Forum 2013). By contrast, however, Japan is ranked 105th out of the 136 countries listed in the Global Gender Gap report. Hong Kong is not included in this report, however, culturally (as is the case with Japanese society), a premium is placed on women's role in society as wives, mothers and homemakers (Luke 2000).

Before moving on to consider the issue of gender and research productivity, Tables 2 and 3 present the rank and discipline composition of the sample. Across each of the five countries men outnumber women in both senior and junior academic

Table 1.   Percentage (%) of women academics.

	Global index (%)	CAP (%)
Australia	40–45	57
Finland	**40–45**	**45**
Canada	35–40	34
USA	**35–40**	**38**
Hong Kong	**30–35**	**35**
Norway	30–35	40
UK	30–35	46
Netherlands	30–35	40
Germany	**30–35**	**33**
Italy	30–35	32
China	<25	37
Japan	**<25**	**17**
Korea	No data available	18

Note: Global index: Times Higher Education (2013), http://www.
timeshighereducation.co.uk/story.aspx?storyCode=2003517

Table 2.   Gender and rank.

	Finland		Germany		Hong Kong		Japan		USA	
	Male	Female	Male	Female	Male	Female	Male	Female	Male	Female
Senior	245	132	374	89	288	76	1109	102	451	270
	(65.0)	(35.0)	(80.8)	(19.2)	(79.1)	(20.9)	(91.6)	(8.4)	(62.6)	(37.4)
Junior	438	557	438	238	238	180	155	23	209	205
	(44.0)	(56.0)	(64.8)	(35.2)	(56.9)	(43.1)	(87.1)	(12.9)	(50.5)	(49.5)
Total	683	689	812	327	526	256	1264	125	660	475
	(49.8)	(50.2)	(71.3)	(28.7)	(67.3)	(32.7)	(91.0)	(9.0)	(58.1)	(41.9)

Table 3.   Gender and discipline.

	Finland		Germany		Hong Kong		Japan		USA	
	Male	Female	Male	Female	Male	Female	Male	Female	Male	Female
Humanities/	207	279	214	126	287	162	321	63	343	285
social science	(42.6)	(57.4)	(62.9)	(37.1)	(63.9)	(36.1)	(83.6)	(16.4)	(54.6)	(45.4)
Science/	301	199	527	156	198	65	801	38	268	143
engineering	(60.2)	(39.8)	(77.2)	(22.8)	(75.3)	(24.7)	(95.5)	(4.5)	(65.2)	(34.8)
Total	508	478	741	282	485	227	1122	101	611	428
	(51.50	(48.5)	(72.4)	(27.6)	(68.1)	(31.9)	(91.7)	(8.3)	(58.8)	(41.2)

positions, with the exception of Finland at the junior level. As we can see, the gender gap is comparatively less significant amongst junior staff. However, what is striking is the small number of Japanese female academics at either level (see Table 2).[3]

With respect to the disciplinary composition of the sample (see Table 3),[4] unsurprisingly, the proportion of male academics in science and engineering is higher than that of female academics. This gap is particularly significant in the case of Japan, whereby 95% of male respondents indicated that they were in the science and engineering disciplines as apposed to only 5% of females. In Finland, this disciplinary gap is less significant with approximately 40%of female academics in science and engineering. Within this sample, women have higher representation in the humanities and social sciences.

Gender and research productivity

The CAP survey provides information on the number of scholarly contributions academics completed over a three-year period. Xie and Shauman (1998), in considering the extent to which self-reported number of publications is a valid measure of productivity, concluded that whilst we might acknowledge potential inaccuracies, consistency across multiple surveys suggests that this is an appropriate approach. The most significant output in the CAP survey, within a three-year period, is book chapters and journal articles (which are conflated into one item). Unfortunately, we have no indication of the status (e.g. peer-reviewed) or quality of these outputs, but nevertheless these data provide a significant insight into the issue of gender and research productivity.

As Table 4 shows, women academics on average published less over a three-year period. This gap in research output is particularly an issue for Asian women academics and strikingly so for Japanese female academics. By contrast, the discrepancy between male and female academics in the USA is marginal.

On further analysis by gender, rank and number of articles (see Table 5), we can see, particularly in the context of Germany, Finland and the USA, a more noticeable gap in output between senior male and female academics, as compared to the position of junior academics in those countries. How might we explain this? One hypothesis we might put forward is that these senior academic women are at a point in their lives when they have caring responsibilities – be it either childcare or care for elderly parents – which impact on their research output. For now, however, let us 'park' that thought.

When we go on to consider gender, discipline and number of articles (see Table 6), it is not surprising to see that women academics in engineering and the natural sciences fare less favourably in terms of their research output. Numerous studies have found that women publish at lower rates than men in the sciences (Kyvik 1990; Xie and Shauman 1998, Sax et al. 2002). This is statistically significant in all countries, except the USA. What is surprising, however, is that female academics in the humanities and social sciences in Germany, Finland and Hong Kong publish significantly less then male colleagues in the same field.

Table 4.   Gender and number of book chapters and articles.

	Male	Female
Germany	9.20	7.77
Finland	6.88	5.37
Hong Kong	9.69	7.36
Japan	8.56	3.60
USA	4.35	3.48

Table 5.   Gender, rank and number of book chapters and articles.

	Senior		Junior	
	Male	Female	Male	Female
Germany	12.58	10.38	5.81	5.16
Finland	10.0	7.52	3.75	3.22
Hong Kong	12.91	10.74	6.47	3.97
Japan	10.08	4.60	7.03	2.59
USA	5.60	4.15	3.09	2.80

Table 6.   Gender, discipline and number of book chapters and articles.

	Humanities/social science			Engineering/natural science		
	Male	Female	F (sig.)	Male	Female	F (sig.)
Finland	5.36	4.14	7.739**	6.69	4.98	7.071**
Germany	10.07	6.84	3.974*	8.29	6.28	12.067***
Hong Kong	6.43	4.61	9.462**	16.69	12.15	2.702*
Japan	4.22	2.95	1.187	11.50	5.10	9.396**
USA	3.39	2.85	1.543	6.67	5.48	0.283

Note: *$p < .05$, **$p < .01$, ***$p < .001$.

Research productivity: the gender gap

So far we have established within the context of this data that there is a gender gap with respect to research output. But the question then becomes what can account for this difference in research productivity? Previous research has attempted to explain this difference by placing a focus on family-related variables, particularly marriage and children (Sax et al. 2002). Family is seen as having a significant influence on academic women's career development, creating constraints and demands as they struggle and sacrifice more than men with respect to parenting and housework and negotiate the contradictory discourse of successful academic and good mother (Bhalalusesa 1998; Raddon 2010; Beddoes and Pawley 2013). It is a sacrifice which, research has indicated, leads to less investment in research, thereby impacting on research productivity (Bailyn 2003; Jons 2011; Beddoes and Pawley 2013).

Let us consider these variables within the context of this survey data. As Table 7 shows academic women overall are less likely to be married in comparison to their male colleagues (this finding supports previous research; see Baker 2012). In Germany and Finland, the marriage rate between male and female academics is marginal; however, in Hong Kong, the USA and particularly Japan this difference is more marked. Japanese male academics are twice as likely to be married than their female counterparts.

If we now consider our first family-related variable – marriage/partner – in terms of research output what do we find? Married academic women are *more* productive than single academic women on average. This is statistically significant in the case of Hong Kong and, even more so, for Finnish female academics. Marriage is not operating as a form of negative equity with respect to research productivity. As we can also see,

Table 7. Gender and marital status (%).

	Male	Female
Germany		
Married/partner	90.0	83.1
Single	10.0	16.9
Finland		
Married/partner	83.0	80.6
Single	13.6	13.8
Hong Kong		
Married/partner	83.5	65.5
Single	14.2	32.6
Japan		
Married/partner	91.7	52.8
Single	7.8	45.5
USA		
Married/partner	85.3	66.9
Single	7.3	13.7

marriage, or being in a partnership, also correlates positively with research productivity for academic men, and is statistically significant for Finnish, German and particularly Japanese male academics (Table 8).

The CAP survey also asks respondents to indicate if they had ever interrupted their employment in order to provide child or elderly care in the home (second family-related variable), along with if they have any children living with them (third family-related variable). As we might expect, academic women are far more likely to interrupt their academic careers to take up caring responsibilities (see Table 9). Finnish academic women and also Finnish academic men were most likely to have taken a career break. This is not surprising given the relatively high level of support provided by the Finnish state.[5]

So, of those academic women who have taken a career break, how has this affected their research output? Intuitively, and based on our knowledge, to some extent, of previous research, we would expect to see that women who have had a break in their careers would be less productive. However, as we can see (Table 10), these women, with the exception of women academics in Hong Kong, are *more* productive than those who have not taken a career break on average. The *t*-test shows that this is statistically significant in the case of Finnish and Japanese academic women.

On further analysis by discipline, female academics in the humanities and social sciences in Hong Kong and Japan who had taken career breaks were less productive than those women who had not taken career breaks. In the case of Japanese women, this difference is marginal, but for Hong Kong women academics the difference is substantive; female academics who had not taken a career break published on average 2.3 times more articles. Also, US female academics in science and engineering who had taken a career break were less productive.

With respect to children, more male academics had children than female academics across the five countries, however, as is shown this difference is variable. For example, only 31% of female academics, as opposed to 57% of male academics in Japan have children, whilst in the USA 31% of women and 36% of men have children (Table 11).

13

Table 8.   Gender and marriage status (*t*-test).

Married	Finland		Germany		Hong Kong		Japan		USA	
	Male	Female	Male	Female	Male	Female	Male	Female	Male	Female
Yes	9.15	6.62	6.71	4.43	11.09	7.98	10.05	4.63	4.91	3.93
No	5.03	6.12	3.93	2.71	8.19	4.51	5.39	3.77	3.93	2.56
Average number of articles	7.09	6.37	5.32	3.57	9.64	6.25	7.72	4.2	4.42	3.25
F (Sig.)	8.786*	1.356	5.651*	10.060**	0.473	4.633*	12.490***	1.870	1.437	3.221

Note: *$p < .05$, **$p < .01$, ***$p < .001$.

Table 9.   Gender and career break (%).

	Male	Female
Germany	4.3	23.8
Finland	12.3	39.3
Hong Kong	3.3	14.8
Japan	0.7	15.9
USA	4.7	27.2

Table 10.   Gender, career break and number of articles (*t*-test).

	Finland		Germany		Hong Kong		Japan		USA	
	Male	Female	Male	Female	Male	Female	Male	Female	Male	Female
Yes	7.62	4.97	8.83	7.73	6.09	7.07	8.08	5.89	3.96	3.67
No	6.06	3.75	8.88	6.16	10.88	7.24	9.72	4.01	4.87	3.57
F	3.973*	6.378*	0.031	0.648	2.427	1.273	0.462	8.581*	0.175	0.241

Note: *$p < .05$, **$p < .01$, ***$p < .001$.

Table 11.   Percentage of academics with children (within gender).

	Male	Female
Germany	449 (56.3)	127 (39.8)
Finland	353 (51.7)	319 (45.8)
Hong Kong	285 (57.1)	102 (47.0)
Japan	717 (57.3)	38 (31.4)
USA	237 (36.1)	145 (30.5)

And of those academic women who have children, how has this third family-related variable affected their research output? Again, with the exception of academic women in the USA, overall family is not operating as a form of negative equity in the prestige

Table 12.   Gender, children and number of articles (t-test).

	Finland		Germany		Hong Kong		Japan		USA	
	Male	Female	Male	Female	Male	Female	Male	Female	Male	Female
Yes	6.14	5.31	10.43	8	12.05	9.02	8.125	4.16	5.185	4.095
No	6.07	4.03	7.535	5.67	11.22	8.37	7.44	4.09	4.855	4.215
F	0.479	7.910**	3.183	4.638*	2.207	0.002	0.942	2.662	1.483	0.422

Note: $*p < .05$, $**p < .01$, $***p < .001$.

Table 13.   Gender, number of children and number of articles (correlation).

	Finland		Germany		Hong Kong		Japan		USA	
	Male	Female	Male	Female	Male	Female	Male	Female	Male	Female
Correlation	0.019	0.117**	0.128**	0.174	0.159**	0.010	0.040	0.027	0.032	0.020

Note: $*p < .05$, $**p < .01$, $***p < .001$.

economy. Female academics with children in Japan and Hong Kong are marginally more productive. Women in Germany, and particularly Finland, are more productive in a statistically significant way (see Table 12).

Again, on further analysis by discipline women with children in the humanities and social sciences in Finland and Japan, along with women in the sciences and engineering in the USA, were marginally less productive than those women without children. If we consider the linear relationship between the number of children academics have and their research output, we can see (Table 13) that having more children certainly does not have a negative affect on academic women and in the case of Finnish women actually correlates with a positive outcome

Possible explanations?

Thus far we have established within the context of this survey data that academic women are publishing fewer journal articles and book chapters. However, familial responsibilities are generally not adversely affecting this situation. Family is not in all cases operating as a form of negative equity in the prestige economy of higher education. There are a small number of studies that corroborate this finding, for example, Sax et al. in a survey of over 8000 academics in the USA concluded 'in short, family variables contributed little or nothing to the prediction of faculty research productivity' (Sax et al. 2002, 435, see also Kyvik 1990). This finding, however, is generally inconsistent with, and counter-intuitive given, our common understanding of this issue. Let us now consider, first, why this data seem so counter-intuitive and second, what therefore can account for the gender gap in research productivity.

As noted earlier, the CAP survey provides an interesting contrast to those studies that have largely drawn on interview data to explore the position, experience and opinions of academics. Our tentative explanation, as to why our findings seem counter-intuitive, is the power of both 'narrative' and discourse in positioning family-related variables as a significant factor impacting on research productivity. Narrative models of analysis can provide us with an insight into how human beings understand and enact their lives through stories, how interview respondents explain their situations and how researchers can seek out causes to explain an end outcome by considering critical moments (Sandelowski 1991). What if academic women are explaining, or even taking individual responsibility, for their apparent 'failure' to compete in the prestige economy of higher education by appealing to factors (e.g. family-related) that first, do not account fully for the gender gap in research productivity and second, are factors that the academy could, but often does not, take into account in assessing performance? For example, in a qualitative study of the experiences of female academics in a US research-intensive university, Monroe et al. (2008) found that a number of women did not judge balancing work and childcare as relevant to the university. Rather, such issues were seen as the responsibility of the individual. Similarly, Grummell, Devine, and Lynch (2009) found that the language interviewees used about balancing childcare and work responsibilities in a study of senior appointments in Ireland was significant. Caring was assumed to be a woman's problem see Aiston (2011) for a fuller discussion of this point).

In addition, to what extent is there a discourse operating which conveniently attributes, be it unintentionally, responsibility for the research productivity gender gap to factors perceived to be largely beyond the influence of the academy? For example, the following quotation from a respondent in Morley's study on women in the global academy illustrates this point:

> A woman in Japan has to take care of her children, as well as both her parents, and sometimes even her husband's parents, beside the domestic duties on daily life. They do not have enough time to concentrate on doing research. (Morley 2014, 122)

As we have seen from the CAP data, however, Japanese academic women with familial responsibilities are not particularly at a disadvantage in terms of research output.[6] Similarly, interview data from Baker's study (2013) also provide an insight on this issue. The following quotation describes a young female academic's dilemma with respect to having a second child:

> We're feeling – well [child's name] is so great maybe we would like to have a second one … but one of the big things is for me feeling like this has had a big impact on publishing career. (Baker 2012, 110)

It is critical to bring to the fore research which questions, or problematises, the link between academic women, family-related variables and research productivity for a number of reasons. First, an explanatory framework that over-relies on family-related variables to account for the gender gap in research productivity may well be distracting us from other, equally relevant or more significant explanations. Second, the widely held assumption that family responsibilities compromise a woman's academic career affects both the recruitment and the retention of women within the profession (Sax et al. 2002, Van Anders 2004; De Welde and Laursen 2011).

Before moving on to consider other potential factors that could account for women producing less than their male colleagues, let us reflect on how women with familial responsibilities might maintain competitive levels of research productivity. Hamovitch and Morgenstern's (1977) study of child-rearing and women academics' research productivity hypothesised that women with children attempt to do more with their limited time and take time out of other activities, particularly their own free time (Hamovitch and Morgenstern as discussed in Sax et al. 2002). And for those women who interrupt their careers for caring responsibilities, is it the case that these women continue to work, particularly on their research, during this 'break'? Given the entrepreneurial nature of research, stopping work completely may be unrealistic, as the following reflection by a British academic on maternity leave suggests:

> Not only will a research-active academic find it difficult to extricate herself from her career for the full 12 months to which she is legally entitled, in all likelihood she will also not really want to be out of the loop for so long – no more than a small business holder would countenance closing her shop for a year. (Braun 2014)

There are a number of important factors that we might consider in exploring further explanations for the research productivity gender gap. One factor is allocation of time. The CAP survey asks respondents to detail how many hours a week they typically spend on a number of activities (e.g. teaching, research, service and administration[7]). Table 14 shows the average number of hours per week spent on research by academics when classes are in session. The analysis indicates that the difference in time spent on research between men and women is statistically significant in the context of junior women academics in Hong Kong and the USA: women spend less time on research. However, we can also observe some interesting differences in the case of Hong Kong, Japanese and US senior women academics when looking at the weekly average hours spent on research.

If women academics, particularly women academics in the USA, Hong Kong and Japan, are spending less time on research, where is their time being spent? Junior and senior academic women in the USA are spending more time on administration than their male colleagues (this is statistically significant in the case of junior women).[8] Senior women in Hong Kong are spending 10%, whilst junior Hong Kong women are spending 17% more of their time on teaching in contrast to their male colleagues[9] and senior Japanese women are spending 41% more of their time on teaching in contrast to their male colleagues.[10] It would not therefore surprise us to see that women academics in Hong Kong and Japan have the lowest research output. This may suggest that there are workload allocation issues. Kjeldal, Rindfleish, and Sheridan (2006) found evidence of male academics using male networks to negotiate more favourable workloads, whilst Barrett and Barrett (2011) highlight how workloads can disadvantage women. Institutions therefore need to be pro-active with respect to workload allocation:

Table 14. Gender and time allocation – research.

	Senior			Junior		
	Male	Female	t-test	Male	Female	t-test
Finland	12.81	11.27	2.416	17.56	17.59	5.125
Germany	13.87	14.02	3.539	17.33	16.32	0.387
Hong Kong	17.32	14.81	1.727	17.34	13.01	13.318***
Japan	17.02	13.12	1.383	16.44	16.32	0.377
USA	13.60	10.92	3.348	14.00	10.23	9.175**

Note: *$p < .05$, **$p < .01$, ***$p < .001$.

Departments need to be keenly aware of any gender bias in the allocation of work: are women more likely to be assigned heavy teaching and administrative loads and pastoral care, thereby limiting their research capacity? (Aiston 2011, 288)

A second factor to consider with respect to the research productivity gender gap is the process itself: 'As much of the research-based prestige economy relies on peer review, this raises questions about gender bias and discrimination in the process itself' (Morley 2014, 116). Publication rates relate to disciplinary context and area of specialisation and tend to be lower in the humanities and social science, where more women academics are located. In addition, a lower value is awarded to feminist scholarship or research related to women. Male colleagues are less likely to read women's research, which in turn leads to women's lower visibility as productive academics and collaboration with male colleagues (Baker 2012). For women academics in the sciences and engineering, this is particularly an issue: there are relatively fewer women, thereby placing them at a disadvantage because it is more difficult for them to find collaborations (Bentley 2003 discussed in Tower et al. 2007). Women are also less likely to be journal editors and sit on editorial boards. For example, in the 12 major medicine journals, only 25% of editors and 17% of board members were women (Kennedy, Lin, and Dickstein 2001); out of 12 management journals, women accounted for less than 10% of the editorial boards (Metz and Harzing 2009) and in the political sciences only 18% of women were editors when an analysis of 50 journals was undertaken (Stegmaier, Palmer, and Assendelf 2011). The manifesto for change calls for editorial boards, which play significant gate-keeping roles, to be more transparent in their selection processes and policies on gender equality.

Conclusion

Before stating our conclusions, it is important to discuss what we are *not* suggesting. First, we are not denying that women academics struggle more than male academics with work–family balance, that they sacrifice more and that this struggle is significant (Neale and Ozkanli 2010; Baker 2012; Beddoes and Pawley 2013). Those women with familial responsibilities who continue to be productive are clearly 'overextended' (Sax et al. 2002). On the basis of this survey data, we are not arguing against the 'motherhood penalty' (Baker 2012) and suggesting that being married and having children gives academic women 'credits' as opposed to 'penalties'. Second, leading on from this point, we are not promoting a hetero-normative model of social organisation, in which the nuclear family is more enabling with respective to research productivity and that those academic women (or men) who transgress this traditional family structure are less productive as a result.

Within the context of the CAP survey data, we also have no indication of the extent to which women have support with their domestic lives. However, without further research, we would exercise caution in suggesting that the women academics in this sample, who are married, have taken career breaks and/or have children are productive because they have access to a level of domestic support which enables them to be so. In addition, nor are we denying that the academy should strive to introduce policies to support work–family life and performance assessment structures that take into account the gendered dimension of care work.

We are also not privileging the aforementioned CAP survey data above the extensive qualitative research that is more likely to indicate, in contrast to the findings within this study, that the link between gender, family-related variables and research productivity is significant. What we have done is to explore what might account for this apparent tension.

What we *are* suggesting, however, is the importance of bringing to the fore research that does question, that does challenge, the link between women's academic research productivity and their familial context. Within this comparative study, we have seen that family is not in all cases operating as a form of negative equity in the prestige economy of higher education. An over-reliance on an explanatory framework which positions family-related related variables as central with respect to the gender research productivity gap has the potential to draw our attention away from other, equally as significant structural and systemic discriminatory practices. These are practices within the profession, which we might more strongly advocate to change. Examples are workload allocation – a critical issue upon which institutions have the capacity to take direct action – and the research production process. The comparative aspect of our research has strengths in that we have been able to explore the common experiences of academic women with respect to research productivity. By looking at academic women in different cultural settings, our research has also highlighted that women academics in Japan and Hong Kong particularly face challenges with respect to this aspect of their academic role. This may be an indication of a wider Asian problem that would benefit from further investigation.

Disclosure statement

No potential conflict of interest was reported by the authors.

Notes

1. See Leathwood and Read (2009). This research highlights both the global differences in the participation and achievement of women students' in higher education, along with the gendered stratification of subject choice.
2. The manifesto was an outcome of a workshop, *Absent talent: women in research and academic leadership in East Asia*, organized by the British Council held in Hong Kong in September 2012.
3. In the CAP survey, senior and junior academics are classified as follows in each country: Finland: Senior (Senior researcher, Principal lecture, Professor, other senior) and Junior (Researcher, Lecture, Assistant professor, Other junior, Assistant) Germany: Senior (Professor) and Junior (Junior professor, other academic position above entrant position, other academic position on typical entrant position) Hong Kong: Senior (Professor, Associate professor) and Junior (Assistant professor, Lecture, others) Japan: Senior (Professor, Associate professor) and Junior (Lecture, Research Associate, other) USA: Senior (Professor, Associate professor) and junior (Assistant professor, Lecture, other).
4. We classified academic disciplines as follows: Humanities and social science – to include teacher training and education science, humanities and arts, social and behavioural sciences, business and administration, economics, law Science and engineering – to include life sciences, physical sciences, mathematics, computer sciences, engineering, manufacturing and construction, architecture, agriculture, medical sciences.
5. The Finnish government guarantees 105 days maternity leave, 158 days parental leave, 18 days paternity leave and bonus leave for fathers (Ministry of Social Affairs and Health 2006).
6. We acknowledge that the CAP survey does not provide data with respect to *ongoing* parental care.
7. Teaching (preparation of instructional materials and lesson plans, classroom instruction, advising students, reading and evaluating student work) Research (reading literature, writing, conducting experiments, fieldwork) Service (services to clients and/or patients,

unpaid consulting, public or voluntary services) Administration (committees, department meetings, paperwork) Other academic activities (professional activities not clearly attributable to any of the categories above).

8. Senior academic women spent on average 9.50 hours a week on administration (male senior colleagues spent 8.29). Junior academic women spent on average 6.49 hours a week on administration (male junior academics spent 4.98). The *t*-test indicated this as significant (10.495***).

9. Senior academic women spent on average 19.23 hours a week on teaching (male senior colleagues spent 17.41). Junior academic women spent on average 23.47 hours a week on teaching (male junior colleagues spent 20.06).

10. Senior academic women spent on average 28.32 hours a week on teaching (male senior colleagues spent 20.08).

References

Abreu, M., V. Grinevich, A. Hughes, M. Kitson, and P. Ternouth. 2008. "Universities, Business and Knowledge Exchange." Council for Industry and Higher Education, and Centre for Business Research.

Aiston, S. J. 2011. "Equality, Justice and Gender: Barriers to the Ethical University for Women." *Ethics and Education* 6 (3): 279–291.

Aiston, S. J. 2014. "Leading the Academy or being Led? Hong Kong Women Academics." *Higher Education Research & Development* 33 (1): 56–69.

Bailyn, L. 2003. "Academic Careers and Gender Equity: Lessons Learned from MIT." *Gender Work & Organization* 10 (2): 137–53.

Bain, O., and W. Cummings. 2000. "Academe's Glass Ceiling: Societal, Professional-Organisational and Institutional Barriers to the Career Advancement of Academic Women." *Comparative Education Review* 44 (4): 493–514.

Baker, M. 2012. *Academic Careers and the Gender Gap*. Toronto: UBC Press.

Baldwin, G. 1985. *Women at Monash University*. Monash: Monash University.

Barrett, L., and P. Barrett. 2011. "Women and Academic Workloads: Career Slow Lane or Cul – de –Sac." *Higher Education* 61 (2): 141–155.

Becher, T., and P. R. Trowler. 2001. *Academic Tribes and Territories: Intellectual Inquiry and the Culture of Discipline*. Milton Keynes: SHRE/Open University Press.

Beddoes, K., and A. L. Pawley. 2013. "Different People Have Different Priorities': Work–Family Balance, Gender, and the Discourse of Choice." *Studies in Higher Education*. doi:10.1080/03075079.2013.801432.

Bentley, J. T. 2003. *Gender Differences in the Careers of Academic Scientists and Engineers: A Literature Review*. Arlington, VA: National Science Foundation, Division of Science Resource Statistics.

Bhalalusesa, E. 1998. "Women's Career and Professional Development: Experiences and Challenges." *Gender and Education* 10 (1): 21–33.

Blackmore, P. 2012. "Academic Motivation: Exploring Prestige Economies." *Practice*, 28: 1–4.

Braun, R. 2014 "No Kidding: Research is as Demanding as a Newborn." http://www.timeshighereducation.co.uk/features/no-kidding-research-is-as-demanding-as-a-newborn/2/2010631.article.

Clark, B. R. 1983. *The Higher Education System: Academic Organization in Cross-National Perspective*. Los Angeles, CA: University of California Press.

Clark, S. M., and M. Corcoran. 1986. "Perspectives on the Professional Socialization of Women Faculty: A Case of Accumulative Disadvantage?" *Journal of Higher Education* 57 (1): 20–43.

Deem, R., K. H. Mok, and L. Lucas. 2008. "Transforming Higher Education in Whose Image? Exploring the Concept of the 'World-Class' University in Europe and Asia." *Higher Education Policy* 21: 83–97.

De Welde, K., and S. L. Laursen. 2011. "The Glass Obstacle Course: Informal and Formal Barriers for Women Ph.D. Students in STEM Fields." *International Journal of Gender, Science and Technology* 3 (3): 571–95.

De Witte, K., and L. Hudrlikova. 2013. "What about Excellence in Teaching? A Benevolent Ranking of Universities." *Scientometrics* 96 (1): 337–364.

Fitzgerald, T. 2014. *Women Leaders in Higher Education: Shattering the Myths*. Abingdon: Routledge.

Grummell, B., D. Devine, and K. Lynch. 2009. "The Careless Manager: Gender, Care and New Managerialism in Higher Education." *Gender and Education* 21 (2): 191–208.

Hallinger, P. 2014. "Riding the Tiger of World University Rankings in East Asia: Where are we Heading?" *International Journal of Educational Management* 28 (2): 230–245.

Hamovitch, W., and R. D. Morgenstern. 1977. "Children and the Productivity of Academic Women." *Journal of Higher Education* XLVII: 633–645.

Harley, S. 2003. "Research Selectivity and Female Academics in UK Universities: From Gentleman's Club and Barrack Yard to Smart Macho?" *Gender and Education* 15 (4): 377–92.

Horta, H., V. Dautel, and F. M. Veloso. 2012. "An Output Perspective on the Teaching-Research Nexus: An Analysis on the US Higher Education System." *Studies in Higher Education* 37 (2): 171–187.

Hughes, C., L. Clouder, J. Pritchard, and J. Purkis. 2007. "Caring Monsters? A Critical Exploration of Contradictions and Ambiguities." In *Challenges and Negotiations for Women in Higher Education*, edited by P. Cotterill, S. Jackson, and G. Letherby, 131–147. Dordrecht: Springer.

Husu, L. 2004. "Gate-keeping, Gender Equality and Scientific Excellence." In *Gender and Excellence in the Making*, edited by D. Al-Khudhairy, N. Dewandre, and H. Wallace, 69–76. Brussels: European Commission.

Husu, L., and L. Morley. 2000. "Academic and Gender: What has and had not Changed." *Higher Education in Europe* XXV (2): 137–138.

Jöns, H. 2011. "Transnational Academic Mobility and Gender." *Globalisation, Societies and Education* 9 (2): 183–209.

Kennedy, B. L., Y. Lin, and L. J. Dickstein. 2001. "Women on the Editorial Boards of Major Journals." *Academic Medicine* 76 (8): 849–851.

Kjeldal, S., J. Rindfleish, and A. Sheridan. 2006. "Deal-making and Rule-breaking: Behind the Façade of Equity in Academia." *Gender and Education* 17: 431–37.

Kyvik, S. 1990. "Motherhood and Scientific Productivity." *Social Studies of Science* 20 (1): 149–60.

Leathwood, Carole, and Barbara Read. 2009. *Gender and the Changing Face of Higher Education. A Feminized Future?* Berkshire: McGraw-Hill, Open University Press.

Lee, H., and K. Lee. 2013. "Publish (in International Indexed Journals) or Perish: Neoliberal Ideology in a Korean University." *Language Policy* 12: 215–230.

Litwin, J. 2012. "Who's Getting the Biggest Research Bang for the Buck." *Studies in Higher Education* 39 (5): 771–785.

Luke, C. 2000. "One Step Up, Two Down: Women in Higher Education Management in Southeast Asia." In *Academic Work and Life: What it is to an Academic and how this is Changing*, edited by M. Tight, 285–305. Bingley: Emerald Group.

Macfarlane, B. 2012. *Intellectual Leadership in Higher Education: Renewing the Role of the University Professor*. London: Routledge.

Madera, J. M., M. R. Hebl, and R. C. Martin. 2009. "Gender and Letters of Recommendation for Academia: Agentic and Communal Differences." *Journal of Applied Psychology* 94 (6): 1591–1599.

Metz, I., and A. Harzing. 2009. "Gender Diversity in Editorial Boards of Management Journals." *The Academy of Management Learning and Education* 8 (4): 540–557.

Ministry of Social Affairs and Health. 2006. *Gender Equality Policies in Finland*. Helsinki: Ministry of Social Affairs and Health.

Monroe, Kristen, Saba Ozyurt, Ted Wrigley, and Amy Alexander. 2008. "Gender Equality in Academia: Bad News from the Trenches, and Some Possible Solutions." *Perspectives on Politics* 6 (2): 215–33.

Morley, L. 2007. "The Gendered Implications of Quality Assurance and Audit." In *Challenges and Negotiations for Women in Higher Education*, edited by P. Cotterill, S. Jackson, and G. Letherby, 53–63. Netherlands: Springer.

Morley, Louise. 2014. "Lost Leaders: Women in the Global Academy." *Higher Education Research and Development* 33 (1): 114–128.

Neale, Jenny, and Ozlem Özkanli. 2010. "Organisational Barriers for Women in Senior Management: A Comparison of Turkish and New Zealand Universities." *Gender and Education* 22 (5): 547–63.

O'Leary, V. E., and J. M. Mitchell. 1990. "Women Connecting With Women: Networks and Mentors in the United States." In *Storming the Tower Women in the Academic World*, edited by S. Stiver Lie, and V. E. O'Leary, 58–74. London: Kogan Page; New York: Nichols/GP.

Özkanli, O., M. L. Machado, K. White, P. O'Connor, S. Riordan, and J. Neale. 2009. "Gender and Management in HEIs: Changing Organisational Andmanagement Structures." *Tertiary Education and Management* 15 (3): 241–57.

Postiglione, G. A., and S. Wang. 2009. "Hong Kong: Governance and the Double-Edged Academy." In *Changing Governance and Management in Higher Education*, edited by William Locke, W. Cummings, and D. Fisher, 343–368. Dordrecht: Springer.

Probert, B. 2005. "'I Just Didn't Fit in': Gender and Unequal Outcomes in Academic Careers." *Gender, Work & Organization* 12 (1): 50–72.

Raddon, A. 2010. "Mothers in the Academy: Positioned and Positioning within Discourses of the 'Successful Academic' and the 'Good Mother'." *Studies in Higher Education* 27 (4): 387–403.

Ropes-Huilman, B. 2000. "Aren't You Satisfied Yet? Women Faculty Members' Interpretations of their Academic Work." In *What Contribute to Job Satisfaction among Faculty and Staff: New Directions for Institutional Research*, edited by L. Hagedorn, 27 (1), 21–32. New York: Jossey-Bass.

Sandelowski, M. 1991. "Telling Stories: Narrative Approaches in Qualitative Research." *Journal of Nursing Scholarship* 23 (3): 161–166.

Sax, L. J., L. S. Hagedorn, M. Arredondo, and F. A. Dicrisi III. 2002. "Faculty Research Productivity: Exploring the Role of Gender and Family-Related Factors." *Research in Higher Education* 43 (4): 423–446.

Schein, V. 2007. "Women in Management: Reflections and Projections." *Women in Management Review* 22 (1): 6–18.

Shin, J. C., and G. Harman. 2009. "New Challenges for Higher Education: Global and Asia-Pacific Perspectives." *Asia Pacific Education Review* 10 (1): 1–13.

Shin, J. C., J. Jung, G. A. Postiglione, and N. Azman. 2014. "Research Productivity of Returnees from Study Abroad in Korea, Hong Kong and Malaysia." *Minerva* 52 (4): 467–487.

Skelton, C. 2005. "The 'Self-Interested Women Academics: A Consideration of Beck's Model of the 'Individualised Individual'." *British Journal of Sociology of Education* 26 (1): 5–16.

Stegmaier, M., B. Palmer, and L. Assendelf. 2011. "Getting on the Board: The Presence of Women in Political Science Journal Editorial Positions." *PS: Political Science & Politics* 44 (4): 799–804.

Thomas, R., and A. Davies. 2002. "Gender and New Public Management: Reconstituting Academic Subjectivities." *Gender, Work and Organization* 9 (4): 372–397.

Times Higher Education. 2013 "Global Gender Index." http://www.timeshighereducation.co.uk/story.aspx?storyCode=2003517.

Toutkoushian, R. K., and M. L. Bellas. 2003. "The Effects of Part-time Employment and Gender on Faculty Earnings and Satisfaction: Evidence from the NSOPF:93." *Journal of Higher Education* 74 (2): 172–195.

Tower, G., J. Plummer, and B. Ridgewell. 2007. "A Multidisciplinary Study of Gender-Based Research Productivity in the World's Best Journals." *Journal of Diversity Management* 2 (4): 23–32.

Turner, C. S. V. 2002. "Women of Color in Academe: Living with Multiple Marginality." *Journal of Higher Education* 73 (1): 74–93.

Van Anders, S. M. 2004. "Why the Academic Pipeline Leaks: Fewer Men than Women Perceive Barriers to Becoming Professors." *Sex Roles* 51 (9/10): 511–521.

Van den Brink, M., Y. Benschop, and W. Jansen. 2010. "Transparency in Academic Recruitment: A Problematic Tool for Gender Equality?" *Organization Studies* 31 (12): 1–25.

World Economic Forum. 2013. *Global Gender Gap Report: 2013*. Geneva: World Economic Forum.

Xie, Y., and K. A. Shauman. 1998. "Sex Differences in Research Productivity: New Evidence about an Old Puzzle." *American Sociological Review* 63 (6): 847–870.

Will gender equality ever fit in? Contested discursive spaces of university reform

Katharina Kreissl[a], Angelika Striedinger[b], Birgit Sauer[b] and Johanna Hofbauer[a]

[a]Department of Socioeconomics, Vienna University of Economics and Business, Vienna, Austria; [b]Institute for Political Science, University of Vienna, Austria

Similar to other European countries, the introduction of non-academic, especially managerial, criteria in higher education has shaped and altered Austrian universities since over a decade. This paper presents the results of a frame analysis of Austrian higher education debates from 1993 until 2010. It outlines how reforms in higher education were prepared and enhanced by a new policy discourse, with a special focus on the way gender equality is framed in reform debates. Our article describes three core frames: 'from local to global', 'from ivory tower to business' and 'from civil servant to excellence'. We cluster these three frames around imaginations of space that are embedded in the normative foundations of academia, and discuss how this links up with arguments for gender equality. We furthermore propose to analytically separate two conceptions of the university: the 'entrepreneurial' and the 'managerial' university.

1. Introduction

So what do we want to achieve? – We want our universities to be world class [...]. We want to increase international competitiveness, we want to create flexibility and free spaces, the university needs to establish itself as an active institutional agent. (Parliamentary Enquete 2001)

This is how then Austrian minister of education, Elisabeth Gehrer, outlined the main goals for the most radical reform project of Austrian universities in the past three decades. Similar to European developments, the Austrian higher education system has been undergoing regular reforms since the beginning of the 1990s. The core of the reforms was a re-structuring of the higher education landscape according to the principles of new public management (NPM). This new organising principle promised to de-gender university structures and procedures (Flicker, Hofbauer, and Sauer 2010), and at the same time gender equality policies were changed and expanded, shifting their focus away from women's advancement towards processes of gender mainstreaming (Kucsko-Stadlmayer 2007).

For proponents of gender equality in universities, the reforms provide both chances and pitfalls, and the literature on NPM and gender equality paints an ambivalent picture. On the one hand, the new organisational principles proved not to suffice in abolishing the very persistent phenomenon of gender inequality in academia. Twenty years after the start of the higher education reforms, gender inequalities continue to exist in universities despite well-established gender equality agendas: While numbers indicate an increase in women's participation along all steps of the academic career, in higher positions these numbers are still far off parity. Between 1993 and 2011, the share of women in assistant positions doubled from 22% to 44%, and the share of women among full professors increased from 3% to 17%. However, in 2014 women still represent just over a fifth (22%) of full professors (uni:data 2014). Furthermore, personnel statistics also confirm a horizontal gender segregation, with the share of women among full professors between a quarter and a third in the arts, humanities and social sciences, and well below 20% in medicine, agriculture, natural sciences (10%) and technical sciences (5%) (uni:data 2014). On the other hand, strategic discursive alliances between proponents of university reforms and gender equality agents emerged, which might be useful in tackling persistent gender inequalities in academia. However, as we will highlight, there are limitations to those alliances and overlaps of frames and discourses about strategic aims of university reforms.

In order to take a more detailed look at the dominant frames of the higher education reform and how they link up with gender equality arguments, this article investigates political debates between 1993 and 2010. It outlines how reforms in higher education were prepared and enhanced by a new policy discourse on academia and universities, with a special focus on the way gender equality is framed in reform debates about the Austrian university. Using the method of critical frame analysis (Bacchi 2009; Verloo 2005), we analyse powerful interpretative schemes, revealing political intentions and patterns of legitimation for university reforms. We show how the intrusion of market into academia is legitimised and how managerial hierarchies are justified.

Our article describes three core frames that dominate the political reform debate, indicating a triple shift of Austrian universities: 'from local to global' concerning the context of knowledge production, 'from ivory tower to business' regarding the organisation of university and 'from civil servant status to excellence' referring to the academic subject. We cluster these three frames around imaginations of space that are embedded in the normative foundations of university and academia. These frames are guided by two conceptions of university, which are usually not analytically separated: the 'entrepreneurial' (Clark 1998) and the 'managerial' university. Despite the compatibility of these concepts, we propose this distinction since it facilitates more poignant descriptions of the university as an ('entrepreneurial') actor and the ('managerial') inner life of the university.

The restructuring of academic space, as we will show, makes it possible to reframe gender in the academic landscape. Hence, we ask: How does gender equality fit in this framing of a triple shift towards an entrepreneurial and managerial university? Neither the idea of the entrepreneurial, nor that of the managerial university legitimised by the observed triple transformation of Austrian higher education openly oppose equality goals. However, these new spaces and concepts of universities are firmly grounded in ideas of academic performance and quality which, as other studies have shown, include a strong gender bias (e.g. Beaufaÿs 2003; Brink and Benschop 2012). When forming (strategic) discursive alliances to further the equality agenda, gender equality agents engage with elements of those dominant concepts. In doing so, as we will discuss, they might run the risk of contributing to a discourse which barely allows for a more fundamental critique of core concepts, such as (international) competition and academic excellence.

In this ambivalent situation, equality agents need to carefully develop their strategy and argumentation. Through our frame analysis and, in particular, our analytic distinction between the concepts of the 'entrepreneurial' and the 'managerial' university, we hope to provide a more differentiated description of the main points of reference in university reforms. By analysing how these frames and concepts link up with gender equality arguments, we aim to contribute to and thereby strengthen the strategic capacity of gender equality agents in universities.

This article begins with a general introduction to the Austrian higher education reforms (Section 2), followed by an outline of our methodological approach, the material we used and how we analysed our data (Section 3). After a short overview of relevant actors in the Austrian policy network (Section 4), we then elaborate on the three frames and the embedded concepts of university, as well as the respective gender equality arguments (Section 5). Finally, the conclusion (Section 6) discusses possible chances and pitfalls of (strategic) alliances between reformers and gender equality promoters.

2.   Reforming the Austrian higher education landscape: outline and classification

Changes in the higher education landscape are not exclusive to Austrian universities, but can be observed across Europe since the 1990s. Austria's situation is however unique, because after a long period of stagnation, the country became a model student for university managerialism in Europe at a very accelerated pace. The core of the reform of Austrian higher education is the University Act (UG) 2002, which re-structured academic governance mechanisms according to the principles of NPM. First steps towards this change had already been made almost a decade earlier, in the course of the university reform in 1993 (University Organisation Act [UOG] 1993). Some analyses highlight that the 1993 university reform was motivated by the intention to overcome organisational stagnation due to the then-prevalent system of academic self-governance (Hüther 2010; Pechar 2004; Schimank 2000, 2005); others see in the reform a first adaptation of the Austrian university landscape to ideas of NPM, motivated by the intention to create political legitimacy through adherence to a 'global model' of governance (Hüther 2010; Lorenz 2012). However, the original proposal from the early 1990s, which strongly reflected the ideas of NPM, was toned down in the course of political compromise and negotiation between a socialist-conservative government coalition, opposition parties and higher education interest groups (Titscher et al. 2000). Under a conservative-right wing government coalition since 2000, many elements of the original 1993 proposal entered into law in the UG 2002 against loud protests of parliamentary opposition, higher education stakeholders and students.

In 2002 universities became full legal entities entitled to take their own decisions on budget spending and on personnel, with far-reaching autonomy from state authorities. Also, democratic decision-making competencies of academic self-governing bodies were reduced, and replaced by centralised management structures. The financing of universities was redesigned from an input- to an output-based concept, through performance agreements with the ministry for higher education. These agreements are to be broken down within the universities and handed on to faculties, departments and individual professors. The UG was again amended in 2009 by a government coalition of social democrats and conservatives, mostly in the spirit of the preceding reforms (Novak and Perthold-Stoizner 2010). Parallel to the reforms of university structures, the personnel structures were changed fundamentally at the beginning of the new millennium. The 2001 reform of the civil servant law (Dienstrechtsnovelle 2001) abolished the civil servant status of university employees, and the traditional Austrian tenure model was replaced by fixed-term contract models for junior academics and assistant professors. Although a tenure track model was established in the following years, which re-opened a perspective of permanent employment for the next generation of academics, universities are hesitant in implementing this new career model. The employment structure in Austrian universities remains highly dualised, with a shrinking group of 'insiders' who are permanently employed, and a growing group of 'semi-outsiders' who have only very limited chances to ever become insiders (Pernicka 2010).

Managerial university reforms have been thoroughly discussed in the academic literature. These analyses offer on the one hand a wide array of criticism of NPM in academia, focussed in buzzwords such as 'academic capitalism' (Slaughter and Leslie 1997) or 'McUniversity' (Parker and Jary 1995). The critique highlights an increase in managerial power at the expense of professional autonomy, and a higher emphasis of universities on marketing and business. According to these critiques, the reforms lead to an 'encroachment of the profit motive into the academy' (Slaughter and Leslie 1997, 9). On the other hand, a more positive light is shed on these reforms by Clark's (1998) elaborations on the 'entrepreneurial university': The relationship between the state and the university is reformulated from micro-management towards context management; students take the role of customers that evaluate the knowledge transfer provided to them; and, overall, criteria of commodification and rationalisation become important for academic activity. Rather than pointing out a possible detrimental nature of these orientations for academia, Clark uses the term 'entrepreneurial' in a more empowering sense, aiming to depict the deliberate, innovative and risk-taking organisational character of university transformation. His description of the 'entrepreneurial university' has become a point of reference for a number of studies and discussions in the field of higher education, both affirmative and critical towards the observed changes (e.g. Barry, Berg, and Chandler 2006; Brink and Benschop 2012; Gumport 2000; Münch 2010; Philpott et al. 2011; Whitley and Gläser 2014). While certainly providing rich descriptions of the new role of universities, Clark's elaborations do not offer rigorous examination of the internal workings of the university. In order to grasp this aspect of university reform, we build on another term offered in academic literature: the 'managerial university' (Lea 2011; Saravanamuthu and Filling 2004). This term describes an ideological shift in universities that privileges corporate organisation models. We use it in this paper to contrast the above-discussed term of the 'entrepreneurial university'. Although these two conceptions are highly symbiotic and usually appear in combination, we propose this analytical distinction, since it facilitates more poignant and specific descriptions of the observed phenomena: While the concept of the 'entrepreneurial university' includes references to the role of the university in the knowledge economy and society, and is grounded on the principle of competition between universities, we apply the term 'managerial university' when we describe the 'inner life', the management, planning and decision-making processes within universities.

In this paper, the policy discussions around the outlined reforms of university structures represent our main focus. However, we embed our analysis in developments of gender equality programmes and legislation in higher education. A number of gender equality measures were introduced at Austrian universities in the past two decades. The core legal framework is the federal law for equal treatment, which came into effect in 1993. Its main aim consists in raising the percentage of women in all personnel categories to 40%. At the beginning of the 1990s, first grant programmes for women were created, and 10 years later, fFORTE was founded, a comprehensive programme for financial support of female scientists. Since 1992, working groups for equal treatment monitor recruitment procedures, with the aim to abolish gender discrimination on all academic levels. In the early 2000s, gender mainstreaming[1] became an important element in university governance and, since the UG 2002, is part of the task of university leadership. The amendment of the UG in 2009 introduced a gender quota of 40% in the rectorate, university council and all collegial bodies including search committees for professorships.

Studies that analyse whether, how and under which conditions NPM in higher education provides service or disservice to gender equality concerns do not conclude by offering generalised estimations (see, for example, Flicker, Hofbauer, and Sauer 2010). Especially when analysing governance structures in universities, most studies lead to contingent conclusions: Reforms can be beneficial for the equality agenda under certain conditions and constellations. These conditions include on the one hand power relations within universities, and on the other hand the meanings attached to dominant patterns of argumentation. In this paper, we focus on the latter point. This requires a detailed analysis of the higher education reform discourse, which is informed by the above-outlined analyses on the entrepreneurial and the managerial university. We do notice that some analyses implicitly refer to – and implicitly mash up – a number of different dimensions of higher education change. These dimensions include both the relevance of knowledge and innovation in our societies, as well as organisational elements of universities, and the role of individual academics. While these elements are obviously tightly interrelated, we attempt to analytically separate these dimensions through our use of the terms 'entrepreneurial university', 'managerial university' and 'entrepreneurial academic in the managerial university'. In doing so, we aim to improve our understanding of the character of higher education reforms and how it impacts on gender equality.

3. Research approach: methodology and data analysis

Our article is based on a critical frame analysis of policy documents. The critical frame analysis investigates how university reform was prepared through policy discourse. Based on Goffman's (1977) metaphor, the method of frame analysis was developed in the context of Social Movement Theory (Benford 1997; Benford and Snow 2000), Policy Theory (Bacchi 2009), and Gender Studies (Verloo 2005). Frame analysis aims at tracking interpretative schemes, which structure statements and organise political ideas and goals. It is based on the assumption that political discourse is shaped by patterns of meaning. According to Verloo, policy frames are 'an organising principle that transforms fragmentary or incidental information into a structured and meaningful policy problem, in which a solution is implicitly or explicitly enclosed' (Verloo 2005, 20). Our analysis of policy documents on higher education reforms aims at identifying patterns of meaning, which not only reflect the dominant understanding of university but also might take a strong role in determining legal frameworks. Our research design includes three elements: dimensions of space, concepts of entrepreneurial and managerial organisation, as well as gendered frames and frames of gender equality.

Our material consists of 44 documents from 1993 to 2010, clustered around the three university reforms outlined above, the UOG 1993, the UG 2002, and the amendment to the UG in 2009. The documents include parliamentary debates and enquetes, government agendas, statements and press releases of higher education stakeholders, as well as documents by the education ministry such as agendas for women's advancement, gender reports, performance agreements and university reports. In the first step we identified the main actors in the field who are given voice and say on the issue of university reform. In the second step we analysed the documents according to sensitising questions including problem diagnosis, prognosis, goals, norms and concepts of the university, the academic subject and gender equality (Verloo 2005).

In the third step we organised main lines of argumentation around problems and possible solutions. Based on these lines of argumentation, we created frames, that is, patterns of argumentation which construct a problem and suggest a solution. The framing of the higher education landscape clusters around the metaphor of space, the creation of borders, the dissolution of borders and the intrusion of logics, that is, of a market logic into the sphere of academia. Spatial shifts, relocations and overlaps of spaces are embedded in the normative conceptions of university and academia. This spatial perspective on the frame analysis, first, highlights the dynamic of the debate in binary terms such as constriction-extension, limitation-delimitation, incorporation-extrusion; and, second, carves out power relations and hierarchies represented in the discourse through images of proximity-distance, centre-periphery, inside-outside and above-below. This perspective furthermore allows us to analyse the role of gender in the frames of higher education reform, by drawing attention to doing space at universities – both in terms of opening and closing spaces, as well as in terms of hierarchical organisation.

4.   Actors and lines of distinction in the higher education discourse

A first look at the relevant actors and their positions in the discourse shows two lines of distinction: The first concerns differences between the ideological orientation of political parties and the different government compositions. The reforms of the UG 2002 were pushed by a conservative-right wing government[2] but opposed by a left wing opposition of socialists and the Green Party. Stakeholder organisations associated with or close to the political parties generally follow the argumentation of the respective parties. These clear-cut distinctions were blurred both in the 1990s and from 2007 onwards, when a grand coalition of socialists and conservatives required joint argumentation from both parties, at the same time raising criticism from both left- and right-wing opposition parties. The 2002 debate, therefore, provides a clear picture of distinct pro- and counter-reform camps, with ideologically backed arguments on both sides. The policy debates around the 1993 and 2009 reforms, on the other hand, present a more complex picture: Proposals were tempered and packaged to make them compatible with the agenda of the partners in the respective mixed alliances. However, rather than simply returning to the arguments and discourse elements of the 1990s, the debate around the 2009 reform is clearly moulded by the more radical discussion of the early 2000s. New arguments and points of reference that were introduced in that period continue to be relevant and re-define the discursive field of higher education reform.

The second line of distinction runs between, on the one hand, politicians and, on the other hand, experts, including stakeholders of university personnel groups and leadership, members of the science council, labour and industry groups, as well as representatives from business and economy. The discourse of stakeholders and experts is characterised by a higher degree of differentiation and a limited use of political slogans. This diverse composition of actors leads to a variety of particular interests represented in the discourse.

Although the policy debate over almost 20 years is characterised by heterogeneity and diversity of actors we were able to identify shifts in the dominant patterns of meaning, which shape the problems identified and solutions proposed in the course of reforming higher education.

5. Framing university reforms: restructuring spaces of reference and power

In the following we describe three core frames used in the policy debates.[3] We structure our findings along three levels: the macro-level of knowledge production, the meso-level, that is, the organisational level of universities, and the micro-level of individual researchers. Our frame analysis shows how dimensions of spatial organisation interact with concepts of managerialism and entrepreneurialism, and how shifts in the discourse on gender and equality are embedded in these frames. Table 1 provides an overview of the problem diagnosis, the proposed concept of the university as well as the compatible arguments for gender equality for each of the three levels.

5.1. *From local to global – the context of knowledge production*

The first shift in framing refers to the context of knowledge production and includes a massive increase of the referential space, which is identified as relevant for universities.

Table 1. Frames in the Austrian higher education discourse.

Frame	From local to global	From ivory tower to business	From civil servants to excellence
Problem diagnosis	Protected space of national state shelters universities from international competition	Protected space created by the Higher Education Ministry's coordination preserves ivory tower	Protected space of long-time security employment fosters idleness and mediocrity
Concept of university	Internationally competitive university with marketable academic products	Efficient managerial structures with less academic self-governing bodies	Standardised performance indicators and short-term contracts serve as incentive
	→ entrepreneurial university	→ managerial university	→ entrepreneurial academic in managerial university
Gender	Human resource argument (international competition)	Claim for more transparency through managerial instruments	Performance orientation instead of gender stereotyping

In the early 1990s the state provides the main point of reference for the higher education discourse across all political parties. Universities are held accountable to the taxpayers in their duty to educate and develop society. Their social responsibility concerns tasks such as the promotion of democracy, education of the youth 'oriented on external requirements for professions' and academic diversity (Government Agenda 1990). This justifies the financing of universities by the public, that is, the citizens:

> Today and tomorrow, the universities carry a huge societal task, and are therefore accountable for the many billions which society invests in them. I believe in the service character of the universities for the working population, which bears the financing of universities. (Parliamentary Debate 1993, Member of Parliament, Conservatives)

In the higher education reform debate around the UG 2002, the space of reference for higher education expands the borders of the nation state. This spatial delimitation of the higher education landscape was initiated by the Bologna Process and the Lisbon Strategy of the European Union, which challenged the identity and the structure of Austrian universities. A powerful pattern of meaning entered the discourse, structuring this expanded space: the argument of international competition. In the parliamentary expert discussions, this idea is referred to as an 'element of movement' (president of the German rector's conference, Enquete 2001), creating a new basis of justifying reforms.

The idea of international competition is now recognised as most important by almost all relevant higher education agents, be it government or opposition, experts or politicians. It 'is reality, whether we like it or not', the Minister for Sciences, Elisabeth Gehrer stated (Enquete 2001). Knowledge is perceived as a core resource in the international competition for economic power. The shift in referential space from the nation state to international competition – from local to global – is based on a distinctive problem diagnosis by supporters of a fundamental reform of Austrian universities: Universities, they argue, were a protected space, sheltered from international competition and therefore lacked the incentive to improve their academic output. Stakeholders such as the Federation of Austrian Industries demand for a 'de-provincialisation of Austria' (Press release 2002). Also voices within universities criticise the proclaimed withdrawal to a national arena:

> The times are over when universities operated with the strategy of 'proud to be on our own'. Individualistic national approaches should be abruptly stopped when the comparison [...] with the best of the field points at decades of homegrown deficiency. (Parliamentary Enquete 2001, full professor)

To become effective international actors in the production of knowledge, Austrian universities need to leave this safe space of the national framework and must enter the international knowledge arena and unlimited market, a process which entails both 'a space of freedom and a space of responsibility' (Parliamentary Enquete 2001, full professor). This framing is expressed by an invited expert and former rector at a parliamentary enquete on the university reform in April 2001:

> After all, we know without doubt: Universities do not want to, and should not be an ivory tower. But this also entails that they have to *subordinate* themselves to the conditions which are completely *natural* in the society which surrounds them. (Parliamentary Enquete 2001, former rector; accentuation by the authors)

The recognition of international competition as an unchangeable, external condition for Austrian universities also frames the debate on knowledge production in an economic way. The international fight for the 'best brains' (e.g. Parliamentary Enquete 2001) and the acquisition of financial and institutional resources represent the crucial element on the way to the best, that is, most marketable, scientific products.

In the discussions preceding the UG amendment 2009, the idea of social responsibility of universities regained prominence in the political higher education discourse, however, in a redefined way. It no longer refers to the frame of the nation state, but to the international arena. The core of social responsibility is no longer the promotion of democracy, education of youth and academic diversity, but universities' contribution to the international competitiveness of the country, which in turn is portrayed as the precondition for economic prosperity and the persistence of the welfare state: 'Science and research is the basis for the creation of employment, for the sustainability of our competitiveness, for economic growth and, finally, for social security' (Government Agenda 2007). This argument is further strengthened with reference to the economic crisis during the later years of the new millennium's first decade: 'Particularly in times of economic challenges, the focus should be put on fields which are the basis for innovation: Engineering and natural science, mathematics and informatics' (Austrian Economic Chamber of Commerce, Press Release 2009). Competitiveness concerns both Austria's academic profile in international rankings and the recognition in the international research arena, as well as the universities' placement in the international economic competition. In both cases, 'Austria should advance from the group of "followers" to the group of "innovation leaders"' (Government Agenda 2008).

An analysis of the political debate further shows the discursive connection between the paradigm of competition and gender equality: Opening universities up to international competition is accompanied by the demand to open up gendered spaces, that is, safe spaces of male networks and homosocial communities in Austrian universities. An optimised use of human resources, which is imperative for guaranteeing competitiveness in the international arena, can only be achieved if science no longer misses out on the potential of women. High-quality science is 'not possible without female excellence', a professor at the University of Vienna and promoter of the reform argued (Parliamentary Enquete 2001), because universities without women 'necessarily fall into mediocrity' (Parliamentary Enquete 2001). In 2007, the government states: 'People and their development opportunities are the greatest RTI resource[4] and should be particularly promoted: The promotion of young talent, mobility and women are central to this' (Government Agenda 2007). Proponents for gender equality policies similarly draw up links between gender equality and the openness of Austrian universities towards an international sphere and standard, which requires the optimum use of human resources. This strategic framing with the aim of strengthening the demands of gender equality refers to the established frame of the political discourse, namely international competition.

These descriptions on the roles and responsibilities of universities for society, further accentuated in the combination of gender equality and competition, clearly express core ideas of entrepreneurialism: Universities are competing with each other, they have to actively seek for avenues to prove themselves and use the resources available to them in the most efficient way possible. In our analysis of this first frame, the context of knowledge production, we clearly find a reflection of Clark's (1998) understanding of the entrepreneurial university as a wilful, risk-taking, initiating and agentic organisation. We also observe that an entrepreneurial understanding of the role and purpose of a university provides argumentative grounds for gender equality, since discrimination prevents universities from making full use of the human resources available. However, if such an approach to gender equality predominates, other bases of legitimation for gender equality – such as the idea of social justice – become less discursively relevant not only in the arguments of university reformers, but also in those of proponents for gender equality.

5.2. *From ivory tower to business – the organisation of university*

A second frame redefines organisational borders of universities within and towards the outside. Again, closed and so-called state-protected spaces are depicted as a problem. In 1993, the then conservative minister of science Erhard Busek explained the necessity to release Austrian universities from the state's custody and grant them autonomy: 'I believe that legally forcing universities to develop inner-organizational rules is an important process in order to teach them to take responsibility for themselves' (Parliamentary Debate 1993, Minister of Science). This frame suggests that universities need to be forced into a state of responsibility by a sort of 'parental' or paternalist legislative assertiveness in order to emancipate themselves from statehood. While the state represents the domestic home, universities now need to prove themselves in the 'outside world', the international knowledge market. In the course of the years following the UG 2002, a stronger implementation of this culture of responsibility is demanded. Universities should be held accountable for what they achieve or do not achieve – and accordingly, they should bear the full consequences. Performance indicators, for example, should be implemented as a management tool to foster competition: 'If there are no losers, there are no winners either, and the system doesn't work' (Parliamentary Enquete 2008, President of the Research Council).

This demand for competitiveness led to a re-evaluation of organisational and institutional needs.

> The current system is not fit for granting the needs of performance oriented university management – neither in terms of finances, nor in terms of personnel structure and space arrangements. This is in great parts due to centralism, bureaucratism and party political interventionitis.[5] (Parliamentary Debate 1993, Member of Parliament, Freedom Party)

Quite similarly, the programme document outlining the government's agenda at the beginning of the 1990s stated: 'Increasing the financial means for higher education in the coming ten years can only be argued for if universities are organised efficiently, and if performance evaluation and focal points are established' (Government Agenda 1990). In this context, reformers pushed for a concept that gained significance during the 1990s: the university as service company, managed on business terms, where students are redefined as customers. Rather than the above-outlined idea of an entrepreneurial university, we here identify the concept of a 'managerial university' (Lea 2011; Saravanamuthu and Filling 2004). Managerial structures become essential quality markers for a well-functioning and output-oriented university, summarised in catchwords such as 'world class', 'modernity' and 'efficiency' (e.g. Parliamentary Debate 2002).

One of the core elements of the university reform in 2002 was the introduction of 'performance agreements' between the higher education ministry and the universities, with consequences for the university budgets depending on the achievement of these agreements. These agreements are to be handed down within the universities to sub-units such as departments and institutes – to be documented in university internal 'target agreements', and further to individual academics – to be discussed and documented in the course of annual personnel talks between academics and their respective supervisors.

The managerial and economic character promoted in the course of the 2002 reforms was subject to heavy criticism, which led to a discursive reformulation in the course of the debate around the amendment of the UG in 2009. Now the government emphasised that universities are not merely business models, but institutions sui generis. However, also this debate was dominated by core principles of the managerial university: Academic and business-administrational spaces are considered deeply intertwined, since 'there is a price tag attached to every academic decision', as an invited expert claimed (Parliamentary Enquete 2008).

These developments severely shaped power relations and hierarchies: Both sceptics among the opposition in parliament as well as members of the (non-professorial) academic staff suspected that the growth of management's space might limit the space for participation in decision-making for representatives of the academic profession:

> This proposed law shows a clear tendency to establish a professionally inappropriate hierarchy, to move decision-making powers towards individuals who are outside of democratic control. [...] Overall, this law is a backlash against democracy, without offering even the smallest indication for an actual increase in efficiency. (Parliamentary Debate 1993, Member of Parliament, Liberal Party)

While democratic principles were an important point of reference in the discussions around the reform proposals in the early 1990s, this normative argumentative pattern lost its interpretative authority during the turn of the millennium. However, in the policy debates around the 2009 amendment, the idea of democracy reappeared in a new framing: Here, democracy was mentioned predominantly as a means to increase the output of knowledge production by motivating academics and stimulating their performance potential:

> It is bad to give up on the resources, the intelligence, the creativity of the majority of not only early career academics, but the majority of those who do academic research and teaching, those who do not hold a professorship, to demotivate them by excluding them from important processes of the dialogue: Where is the university going? What should be the focal points? (Parliamentary Enquete 2008)

In the political debate on restructuring the university's organisation in a managerial way – from ivory tower to business – gender equality was also negotiated on new terms. Along with the demand for opening up universities towards society and economy appeared the call to open up university administration towards the societal issue of gender justice, and hence gender equality policies. In the early 1990s, gender equality was usually regarded as a 'women's concern' (Parliamentary Debate 1993, Member of Parliament, Green Party): The target group of equality policies was limited to women in need of advancement through individual support programmes such as scholarships or counselling. Family responsibilities and persistent gender stereotypes were identified as primary reasons for unequal gender relations at universities. While these frames and policy instruments implied that the roots for discrimination lie outside of the university, the debates in the late 1990s focused on the relational aspect of gender issues and put attention on academic discrimination structures and practices within universities and the academic profession: This frame resulted in demands for structural changes via 'gender-democratic measures' (University report 2002) which include women's advancement, gender equality policies and equal treatment, as well as gender mainstreaming programmes. The responsibility for universities – including gender relations – now, at least in part, lies within the organisation, rather than outside.

The entrepreneurial frame discussed in the previous section provides a new basis of argumentation for gender equality – the necessity to make full use of female human resources. The managerial frame provides a similar argument for equality measures: Gender equality experts strategically expand the managerial frame and argue that university management should not only transfer knowledge into society, but should also transfer societal needs into the university and hence foster gender equality in internal processes and academic careers. If the university 'is not gender-equal based on a real commitment to equality, then let's at least use our damn intellect: male networks no longer pay off' (Parliamentary Enquete 2001, full professor).

This strategic frame of a convergence of interests led to an alliance between those who strove for stronger managerial influence and control at universities, and those who aimed to achieve gender equality in higher education. The performance agreements between universities and the state, for example, are pushed as a tool for negotiating and controlling a university's output from a mangerialist point of view. However, promoters of gender equality also welcome the new instrument: 'That's something I really reckon as a big chance when it comes to gender equality […], when this tool, used with consistency, also focuses on equality objectives' (Parliamentary Enquete 2002, assistant professor). For gender equality agents, strong management processes provide a helpful basis to further their agenda, if they manage to include gender equality elements in these processes. And for university managers, gender equality agents can be a useful alliance partner in extending the zones of managerial control. While these discursive alliances and coalitions provide effective grounds of argumentation and legitimation to gender equality agents, there are strings attached: By referring to the idea of the managerial university, proponents of gender equality simultaneously strengthen this frame. In doing so, they contribute to a discourse which legitimises underlying concepts such as output orientation and performance evaluation, and de-legitimises feminist critique concerning the gender bias inherent to these underlying concepts, as well as a more justice-oriented argumentation for gender equality.

5.3. *From civil servants to excellence – the academic subject*

Notions of academic excellence, efficiency and marketability resulted in attempts to reframe the idea of the academic subject and to restructure the requirements placed on the academic subject. Reformers therefore call for fundamental changes in the personnel structure of Austrian universities. In the traditional tenure model (until the reform of the civil servant law in 2001), the 'habilitation' (achievement of the venia docendi) entitled university employees with a fixed-term contract to get a permanent position in their university. In the new model (since 2009), a large amount of junior academics on fixed-term contracts compete for a very limited number of tenure track positions, and tenure is dependent on the achievement of performance goals, such as the number of papers published or the amount of external funding acquired.

The 'old system', this frame suggests, had fostered an atmosphere of mediocrity and idleness as academics did not need to compete for positions and, hence, there was no incentive for excellence: The tenured staff, the president of the German rector's confer-ence argued in one of the parliamentary expert discussions, created a 'protected area [...], far away from a competitive spirit and performance orientation directed by elites. The slogan [...] used to be: Everybody is equal, everybody is a professor [...]. All soldiers become officers' (Parliamentary Enquete 2001). Again, the protected space is identified as the main cause of deficiency. To delimit this protected space of mediocrity and to open it towards excellence, evaluative procedures should be implemented to assess quality through objective criteria. Scientists should permanently self-monitor their performance in constant competition for positions and resources, aiming to advance from mediocrity to the elite. After all, it must be 'ensured, that the automatic character of the career ladder is replaced by performance orientation' (Parliamentary Enquete 2001, full professor).

In the 'world class universities' (Government Agenda 2000), performance orien-tation and elite are interlinked in the term 'excellence'. This concept is connected with a social-Darwinist rhetoric of evolution, referring to the need for selection. In order to achieve excellence, it is necessary to introduce mechanisms of 'negative selec-tion', as a participant in the enquete claimed; competition for good research needs 'a kind of "sorting out"' (Parliamentary Enquete 2001, full professor): One of the main questions for university reform therefore should be: 'How do I keep the good, respect-ively the best ones, and how do I get rid of the bad ones?', as another expert put it (Parliamentary Enquete 2001). The demand for excellence results in clear borders between different performance groups – those who are excellent and those who are only mediocre – and regulations of access to the sphere of excellence.

One dominant theme in this argument concerns work contracts: Security of employ-ment conditions is portrayed as an impediment to excellent performance of academics. In contrast, terms such as 'freedom', 'flexibility', 'mobility' and 'responsibility' are put forward: 'Good science can only be nurtured in a climate of individual freedom and personal responsibility' (Parliamentary Enquete 2002, full professor). Hence, this frame suggests that fixed-term contracts and precariousness of employment conditions for junior researchers will create incentives for efficient, high-quality knowledge pro-duction. In this argument we see a new conceptualisation of the ideal academic, which is compatible with the two frames discussed above: the entrepreneurial academic in the managerial university.

This discourse on performance indicators not only affects the working conditions of academics, but also influences the content of research, especially those areas of science, whose results cannot immediately be transformed into economic profit. Discussions around this issue are marked by inconsistencies: The right to a protected space for basic research is explicitly mentioned even by proponents of university reforms, while at the same time research is always connected to economic output. We found competing frames: While the Humboldtian ideal of the university – the unity of teach-ing and research, and the focus on broad education rather than professional training – still has some authority, economic profitability should nonetheless be a deciding factor. One example might be the debate around the so-called 'orchid subjects', studies without an immediately profitable output (like the flower: nice to look at, but useless): These subjects should be abolished or combined and thus make universities 'more focused, parsimonious and at the same time more effective', as the president of the Austrian Academy of Science put it (Parliamentary Enquete 2001).

This shift in perspective of the 'good' academic gave room for gender equality argu-ments: The demand for transparent, rational decisions in the distribution of resources and career opportunities for academics is put forward both by higher education reformers and by promoters of gender equality. Both aim to limit space for traditional homosocial male communities and to open spaces for women by breaking up the protected space of male dominance: In the entrepreneurial university, the protected space 'beyond any consideration for competitiveness and elitist performance' should be limited (Parliamentary Enquete 2002, assistant professor), while equality promoters want to limit the space for discrimination and unequal treatment based on gender stereotypes. As a gender equality officer of an Austrian university expresses it pointedly: 'First class professors do not necessarily appoint other first class professors! And even if they do, they do so in exactly the way I'm saying it now: Men promote men' (Parliamentary Enquete 2008).

Therefore,

> excellent female academics need excellent and intelligent autonomous structures, where they can be discovered, formed, coached, supported and challenged in order to compensate their gendered discrimination. [...] [T]he university must develop its personnel resources towards excellent quality in an autonomous and gender-equal way. (Parliamentary Enquete 2001, full professor)

Discursive coalitions can be found here: This statement involves elements of the entrepreneurial university, such as autonomy from the state as a precondition to participate in international competition, or academic staff as crucial resources. Also, the term 'excellence', which is used twice, draws from the framing of the entrepreneurial academic. At the same time, these powerful patterns of meaning promote gender equality.

When forming those kind of alliances, gender equality advocates are bound to argue on the basis of the dominant frame's core concepts such as performance orientation and competition. In doing so, they need to leave aside a critical reflection on the gender bias of those normative foundations, because such a critical stance lies outside the discourse coalition: Since the idea of performance is such an important element of the higher education reform discourse, a critical discussion of its normative conception lies outside of what is debatable. We hardly found any statements critically questioning the core concepts of the reform efforts, which indicates that critique is beyond the universe of what is debatable. We only found one critical statement, brought forward by a gender expert in the course of the 2009 discussion: 'We have to start scratching the shiny surface of our belief in quality criteria, in order to answer the question why we have not managed to bring a significant number of women into middle and higher positions' (Parliamentary Enquete 2008).

6. Discussion: spatial delimitation and intrusion. Ambivalences of gender equality in the entrepreneurial and managerial university

Our analysis shows that the 'protected space' of Austrian universities is identified as a main problem in the framing of the reform discourse since the 1990s. Paternalistic state universities are seen as discouraging Austrian academics from entering the international arena of competition. On the meso level of university organisation, state governance is discredited as preserving the ivory tower character of universities, closed towards the society. On the micro level, long-term employment security and a lack of performance incentives promoted idleness and research topics which society and economy are not in need of. These diagnoses are contrasted with an image of the 'real life out there': international competition, the need for profitability of academic products, and the focus on excellence and individual performance measurements.

The Austrian debate suggested three major prognostic frames, that is, solutions for the identified problems. First, the entrepreneurial university refers to the context of knowledge production and international competition: the university is portrayed as an agentic, wilful, innovative organisation. Second, the managerial university is organised by a powerful university leadership as the main driver of organisational change processes. Third, these solutions need entrepreneurial academics, who proactively pursue their careers at their own risk.

Gender equality agents engage with elements of these dominant concepts and form (strategic) discursive alliances. Within the entrepreneurial conception, universities need to be market-competitive through the most efficient use of their resources, including their academic staff. Here, gender equality promoters point to the crucial connection between academic excellence and the full use of the female academic workforce. In the managerial framing, which pushes for efficient management structures and business instruments, gender equality advocates seek to implement equal opportunity objectives in the core of management processes.

As we have shown, the problem diagnosis of protected space does not only serve reformers in their political struggle for legitimation. It also allows promoters of gender equality to push their agenda by putting closed spaces of masculinity under pressure: Fraternalist networks of male academics, which dominate informal negotiations behind closed doors, are blamed as detrimental for optimal capitalisation of female academic potential, which is a necessary precondition for excellence. The room for discrimination and unequal treatment should be strongly constricted through formalisation of recruitment procedures and increased importance of quantitative performance indicators. Those so-called objective performance standards, the argument goes, provide a higher level of transparency and enable accountable decisions on the grounds of individual performance, or at least facilitate interventions from gender equality agents within the university. Through this (partly strategic) reference to important elements of the entrepreneurial and managerial concepts (human resources, managerialist instruments), gender equality advocates want to effectively push for their agenda.

While this can provide a solid foundation for promoting gender equality policies, certain elements of gender critique are clearly incompatible with the dominant frames that structure the debate on higher education reforms (for similar observations on EU gender equality policies, see Stratigaki 2004). As our results show, this discourse does not allow for a critical reflection on the gendering effects of its tools and concepts, specifically on the gendered images that underlie the normative conception of academic performance. Such a critique would fundamentally question core concepts, such as performance orientation, excellence and quality control, and is therefore not part of the higher education reform discourse. Hence, (strategic) alliances between gender equality agents and advocates for the entrepreneurial or managerial university appear to be a double-edged sword: By promoting instruments based on those normative foundations, their alleged gender neutrality is legitimised.

We therefore conclude that an important precondition for effective gender equality work in universities is an awareness of the possible ambivalence of frames used to legitimate and strengthen the gender equality agenda. Our aim was to provide a more differentiated picture of these frames: the entrepreneurial university, the managerial university and the entrepreneurial academic within the managerial university. We further discussed how gender equality proponents use these concepts to give more weight to their own arguments. In doing so, we hope to make a contribution to the development of effective and refined strategies for gender equality work in universities.

Disclosure statement
No potential conflict of interest was reported by the authors.

Funding
This research was supported by the Austrian Science Foundation FWF – Der Wissenschafts-fonds [grant number I 727-G22].

Notes
1. Definition of gender mainstreaming: 'Gender mainstreaming is the (re)organisation, improvement, development and evaluation of policy processes, so that a gender equality per-spective is incorporated in all policies, at all levels and at all stages, by the actors normally involved in policy-making' (Council of Europe 1998, 15).
2. Consisting of the conservative Austrian People Party (ÖVP) and the right-wing Austrian Freedom Party (FPÖ).
3. An earlier version of the three frames can be found in Kreissl et al. (2013).
4. Research, technology and innovation (comment by the authors).
5. The neologism 'interventionitis' points to the fact that too much intervention is seen as an illness.

References
Bacchi, C. L. 2009. "The Issue of Intentionality in Frame Theory: The Need for Reflexive Framing." In *The Discursive Politics of Gender-equality: Stretching, Bending and Policymaking*, edited by Emanuela Lombardo, Petra Meier, and Mieke Verloo (Hg.), 19–35. London: Routledge.

Barry, J., E. Berg, and J. Chandler. 2006. "Academic Shape Shifting: Gender, Management and Identities in Sweden and England." *Organization* 13 (2): 275–298.

Beaufaÿs, S. 2003. *Wie werden Wissenschaftler gemacht? Beobachtungen zur wechselseitigen Konstitution von Geschlecht und Wissenschaft* [How are Scientists Made? Observations of the Co-Constitutions of Gender and Science]. Bielefeld: Transcript Verlag.

Benford, R. D. 1997. "An Insider's Critique of the Social Movement Framing Perspective." *Sociological Inquiry* 67(4): 409–430.

Benford, R. D., and D. A. Snow. 2000. "Framing Processes and Social Movements: An Overview and Assessment." *Annual Review of Sociology* 26: 611–639.

Brink, M. van den, and Y. Benschop. 2012. "Gender Practices in the Construction of Academic Excellence: Sheep with Five Legs." 19 (4): 507–524.

Clark, B. R. 1998. *Creating Entrepreneurial Universities: Organizational Pathways of Transformation*. Oxford: Pergamon Press.

Council of Europe. 1998. "Gender Mainstreaming. Conceptual Framework, Methodology and Presentation of Good Practices." EG-S-MS (98) 2 rev. Accessed March 2, 2015. http://www.gendermainstreaming-planungstool.at/_lccms_/downloadarchive/00003/Europarat.pdf.

Flicker, E., J. Hofbauer, and B. Sauer. 2010. "Reforming University, Re-gendering Careers. Informal Barriers to Women Academics in Austria." In *Gender Change in Academia*, edited by Birgit Riegraf, Brigitte Aulenbacher, Edit Kirsch-Auwärter, and Ursula Müller (Hg.), 123–136. Wiesbaden: VS Verlag für Sozialwissenschaften.

Goffman, E. 1977. *Rahmen-Analyse. Ein Versuch über die Organisation von Alltagserfahrungen* [Frame Analysis: An Essay on the Organization of Experience]. Frankfurt am Main: Suhrkamp.

Gumport, P. 2000. "Academic Restructuring: Organizational Change and Institutional Imperatives." *Higher Education* 39: 67–91.

Hüther, O. 2010. *Von der Kollegialität zur Hierarchie? Eine Analyse des New Managerialism in den Landeshochschulgesetzen* [From Collegiality to Hierarchy? An Analysis of New Managerialism in Provincial University Laws]. Wiesbaden: VS Verlag für Sozialwissenschaften.

Kreissl, K., A. Striedinger, B. Sauer, and J. Hofbauer. 2013. "Gleichstellung in der unternehmerischen Hochschule? Diskursive Verschiebungen in der hochschulpolitischen Landschaft Österreichs" [Gender Equality at the Entrepreneurial University? Discursive Transformations at Austrian Academia]. In *Die unternehmerische Hochschule aus der Perspektive der Geschlechterforschung: Zwischen Aufbruch und Beharrung* [Entrepreneurial Universities from a Gender Perspective: Between Euphoria and Inertia], edited by B. Kubicek, L. Weber, C. Binder, and A. Rozwandowicz, 20–21. Münster: Westfälisches Dampfboot.

Kucsko-Stadlmayer, G. 2007. "Gleichstellung von Frauen und Männern an vollrechtsfähigen Universitäten" [Equality of Women and Men at Autonomous Universities]. *Zeitschrift für Hochschulrecht* 7 (6): 8–17.

Lea, D. R. 2011. "The Managerial University and the Decline of Modern Thought." *Educational Philosophy and Theory* 43 (8): 816–837.

Lorenz, C. 2012. "If You're So Smart, Why Are You under Surveillance? Universities, Neoliberalism, and New Public Management." *Critical Inquiry* 38 (3): 599–629.

Münch, R. 2010. "Der Monopolmechanismus in der Wissenschaft. Auf den Schultern von Robert K. Merton" [Monopoly in Science. On the Shoulders of Robert K. Merton]. *Berliner Journal für Soziologie* 20: 341–370.

Novak, M., and B. Perthold-Stoizner. 2010. "Die österreichische Universitätsreform 2009. Zentrale Inhalte und Angelpunkte" [Austrian University Reform 2009. Central Themes and Core Issues]. *Wissenschaftsrecht* 43: 151–183.

Parker, M., and D. Jary. 1995. "The McUniversity: Organization, Management and Academic Subjectivity." *Organization* 2 (2): 319–338.

Pechar, H. 2004. "The Changing Academic Workplace: From Civil Servants to Private Employees. Country Report Austria." In *The International Attractiveness of the Academic Workplace in Europe*, edited by J. Enders and E. De Weert (Hg.), 32–51. Frankfurt am Main: GEW.

Pernicka, S. 2010. "Professur oder (r)aus? Widersprüche der Personalpolitik an Universitäten" [Professorship or Good-Bye? Contradictions of Human Resource Policy at Universities]. *Unilex – Informationen zu universitätsrechtlicher Theorie und Praxis* 1–2: 20–25.

Philpott, K., L. Dooley, C. O'Reilly, and G. Lupton. 2011. "The Entrepreneurial University: Examining the Underlying Academic Tensions." *Technovation* 31: 161–170.

Saravanamuthu, K., and S. Filling. 2004. "A Critical Response to Managerialism in the Academy." *Critical Perspectives on Accounting* 15: 437–452.

Schimank, U. 2000. "Welche Chancen und Risiken können unterschiedliche Modelle erweiterter Universitätsautonomie für die Forschung und Lehre der Universität bringen?" [Chances and Risques of Different Models of University Autonomy for Research and Teaching?]. In *Universitäten im Wettbewerb. Zur Neustrukturierung österreichischer Universitäten* [Universities in Competition. The Re-structuring of Austrian Universities], edited by S. Titscher, G. Winckler, H. Biedermann, H. Gatterbauer, S. Laske, R. Moser, F. Strehl, F. Wojda, and H. Wulz (Hg.), 94–147. München und Mering: Rainer Hampp Verlag.

Schimank, U. 2005. "New Public Management' and the Academic Profession: Reflections on the German Situation." *Minerva* 43: 361–376.

Slaughter, S., and L. L. Leslie. 1997. *Academic Capitalism: Politics, Policies, and the Entrepreneurial University*. Baltimore, MD: Johns Hopkins University Press.

Stratigaki, M. 2004. "The Co-optation of Gender Concepts in EU Policies: The Case of 'Reconciliation of Work and Family'." *Social Politics* 11 (1): 30–56.

Titscher, S., G. Winckler, H. Biedermann, H. Gatterbauer, S. Laske, R. Moser, F. Strehl, F. Wojda, and H. Wulz. 2000. *Universitäten im Wettbewerb. Zur Neustrukturierung österreichischer Universitäten*. München und Mering: Rainer Hampp Verlag.

uni:data. 2014. "Datawarehouse Hochschulbereich des Bundesministeriums für Wissenschaft, Forschung und Wirtschaft" [Datawarehouse University by the Ministry of Science, Research and Economy]. Accessed November 17, 2014. https://oravm13.noc-science.at/apex/f?p=103:36:0::NO:::.

Verloo, M. 2005. "Mainstreaming Gender Equality in Europe. A Critical Frame Analysis Approach." *The Greek Review of Social Research* 117: 11–34.

Whitley, R., and J. Gläser. 2014. "The Impact of Institutional Reforms on the Nature of Universities as Organisations." *Research in the Sociology of Organizations* 42: 19–49.

Sources of quotes for the frame analysis

Austrian Economic Chamber of Commerce, Press Release, June 12, 2009.

Dienstrechtsnovelle 2001.

Federation of Austrian Industries, Press Release, November 4, 2002.

Government Agenda SPÖ/ÖVP 1990.

Government Agenda ÖVP/FPÖ 2000.

Government Agenda SPÖ/ÖVP 2007.

Government Agenda SPÖ/ÖVP 2008.

Parliamentary Debate, October 20, 1993.

Parliamentary Debate, July 11, 2002.

Parliamentary Enquete 'Die Universitätsreform'/'The university reform', 2001.

Parliamentary Enquete "Der Weg zur vollen Rechtsmäßigkeit der Universitäten'/'The path towards full legality of universities', 2002.

Parliamentary Enquete "Novelle des Universitätsgesetzes 2002'/'Amendment of the University Act 2002', 2008.

University Report 2002.

Emirati women's higher educational leadership formation under globalisation: culture, religion, politics, and the dialectics of modernisation

Eugenie Samier

Institute of Education, The British University in Dubai, Dubai, United Arab Emirates

The United Arab Emirates (UAE) is a small state transitioning from traditional communities into a modern society. This is a complex process: it involves instilling a national identity over tribal structures; modernising and technologising while retaining Islam; ensuring a high level of security while allowing for a liberal and relatively free society; preserving culture while building one of the largest and most multicultural societies, albeit mostly expatriate; and providing one of the safest countries in the Arab world for women. This paper presents an expatriate female academic's position in relation to the emergent literature on the contradictory positioning of women in different Arab cultures. It reviews the literature in the light of anecdotal evidence drawn from the author's doctoral students' experiences as women leaders within the wider socio-cultural context of the UAE and the emergent higher education system that is considered central to its nation-building exercise. The discussion recognises the implications of different contexts for Emirati women moving into leadership positions and calls for further research in the field.

Introduction

Among the many developments and changes in the Middle East over the last 40 years, both constructive and destructive, is the changing role of women, whose opportunities have ebbed and flowed with the social and political transformations and disintegrations that have taken place. The consequences for women of political crises such as the civil war in Algeria, devastation in Iraq, repeated bombings of the Gaza, and the current destruction of Syria have been dire. Moghadam (2008) identified a number of other factors that have affected societies and women's place in them: the post-oil boom stagnation; authoritarian states in a number of countries; and patriarchal Islamicist movements that have taken hold or have strong influence in many countries. The prospects for women in these countries are very different from those in the Western countries that have most contributed to educational administration (primarily the USA, the UK, Australia, and Canada). The concerns and analyses in the field of women's issues in these Western countries are slight when compared to the unforgiving and relentless conditions that many women in the Middle East face. However, there are

41

also positive developments, even in countries that are currently in disarray and which may be poised on the brink of civil war, such as Egypt.

In these contexts, the theories and models pertaining to Western countries may not hold. This is true even in the Arabian Gulf states where there is relative peace, and a rapid expansion of women's education and societal roles. While there is considerable scholarship on the economy and strategic affairs of the Gulf states, there are few academic writings on changing social and cultural structures and processes (Ramakrishnan and Ilias 2011). Little in Western scholarship in educational administration builds upon an Islamic worldview. The long and rich tradition of Arab culture, and Islamic intellectualism that the West benefitted from in all disciplines during the 'Renaissance', the unique structures of social institutions, the ever-present security issues, and the transitional characteristics of modernisation in the Gulf states, including the United Arab Emirates (UAE), are largely ignored.

Western scholarship in many fields does not generally cover Middle Eastern conditions. This is in part due to the secularisation of social science disciplines (Hirschkind 2011; Volpi 2011). The literature that does exist suffers from overgeneralisations, misrepresentation, negative stereotypes, and demonisation (Cole 2009; Nader 2013; Shaheed 1999), often reflecting what is projected in the media (see Esposito and Kalin 2011; Flood et al. 2012; Lean 2012; Zempi and Chakraborti 2014). There is a confusion of Islam with Islamism (Badran 2001) and the neglect of the historical role of women, many of whom have been rulers of Islamic states from the early Islamic to the modern period (e.g. Bennett 2010; Mernissi 1993). Much Western literature also assumes that in national development, the Western models of the state and its social institutions are appropriate to ex-colonial parts of the world (Chatterjee 1993). These models include not only institutional and organisational structures and processes, but also roles and role construction that affect identity construction. Chatterjee's postcolonial nationalism critique also points to important bifurcations that were formed in most colonies. These include separating the material levels of the economy, including science and technology associated with the West and its colonising powers from the spiritual levels, including cultural identity. One of the questions this article asks is whether Emirati women who are creating and entering leadership roles in higher education are re-integrating the material and spiritual.

There are other misrepresentations of Muslim women in Western scholarship. Sonbol (2006) identifies the essentialist approach to defining women in only Islamic terms as if they are only 'religious creatures', an approach that excludes many social, cultural, and historical experiences, and which portrays Islamic history as 'backward and patriarchal' with enlightenment only brought by imperialist missionaries. Sonbol questions the assumption that the future for Muslim women must reside in Western programmes and models (see also Shaheed 1999). She also questions the frequent attribution of limitations and punishments of women to Islam, when in most of these cases culture and the state are the sources of these practices and are not confined to Muslim women. In fact, provisions for women's education, as Sonbol explains, are very different from the negative stereotype that prevails. Women are equally recognised in the Qur'an as having rights to learn, debate, attend educational organisations, and hold positions in education and other sectors (Lootah 2006). And as Al Oraimi (2011) points out, some elements of women's rights are embedded in Islamic concepts of social justice, particularly in Islam's call for education as a 'religious duty incumbent on all Muslims, male and female … without discrimination or exception' (85), which distinguished Islam as an early force for women's rights (see also Schvaneveldt,

Kerpelman, and Schvaneveldt 2005). Women's participation actually dropped off significantly when education was institutionalised during modern state formation (Sonbol 2006), a situation that has been significantly reversing in many countries more recently.

Similar arguments are made by Moghadam (2008) who explains how different views of Islam contribute to a misunderstanding of its nature and role in women's lives. The Western view of Islam as having a primary responsibility for limiting and suppressing women is contrary to the view that it is a 'source of women's rights and empowerment' (425). Her argument rests on a socio-political and economic approach that recognises both the differences across Islamic states and across the 'diverse and heterogeneous' roles of women in them, influenced by a 'country's social structure and stage of development, as well and the nature of the state and its economic, social, and cultural policies' (426). The degrees of neopatriarchy, where religion is integrated into the power and state structures and where the family is a major social institution within which the individual functions, varies considerably across the Middle East and North Africa (Shaheed 1999; Sharabi 1988). The patriarchal domination of women is often attributed in the West to Islam and Arab culture. However Sharabi (1988) argues that Western modernisation forces in the Middle East bring with it the subjugation of women that is practised in capitalism. Despite a number of problems for women, itemised in the UN report (1994) from a meeting of women's organisations in Arab countries, the picture is not solely a bleak one. By the 1960s, as Moghadam explains, women were increasingly occupying high-status professions in law, medicine, and universities, including serving as judges in many states. They had the vote, ran for parliament, and were appointed to senior government positions. They were also forming social movements to increase their participation, in many countries shifting from state feminism programmes to civil society feminism in the 1990s, and participating in the 'Arab Spring' that spread across the Middle East and North Africa regions from 2011 (see Olimat 2013; Syeed and Zafar 2014).

An important point made by Sonbol (2006) that holds today, particularly under globalisation, is that the very patriarchal values and practices of Western systems, which Western women work against, is transmitted through imperialism and, now, globalisation. While there are many definitions of globalisation in the literature, Held and McGrew's (2002) work is seminal and covers aspects of the phenomenon that is relevant here. It builds upon the work of Hirst (1997) and Hoogvelt (2001), and portrays globalisation as part of the neoliberal project that aims at an Anglo-American capitalist hegemony with significant cultural influence on receiving countries including commodified education. Similarly, Stiglitz (2003) has identified the economic subjugation of developing countries. In addition to the economic sphere and the commodified export of education and other cultural goods, globalisation has had a profound effect on governance and policy in developing countries (Coleman 2012). Politically, globalisation is the spread of neo-liberalism that aims at 'unmitigated marketplace relations' against which no other political economic system can stand (Teeple 1995, 143).

One of the aims of this paper is to describe the role-making processes that a number of Emirati women are engaged in. These women are self-reflectively aware of the tensions, contradictions, and dynamics they are a part of, as they ascend to senior positions in higher education. One question asked is whether Emirati academic women are experiencing the 'shock of civilisation' that Bourdieu found in Algeria:

> This society ... which was constituted through a totality of indissociable elements that
> were all expressions of the same original 'style,' suffered [*a subi*] the shock of another

civilization that did not make itself felt in a piecemeal or targeted fashion but in totality, rupturing not only the economic order but also the social, psychological, moral, and ideological [*spheres*]. (translation in Silverstein and Goodman 2009, 15)

In other words, is it a *habitus clivé*, or 'split habitus' (Bourdieu and Sayad 1964), that compromises a society's ability to 'reproduce' itself through authentic and intact social institutions? These dynamics are also the result of what Said (1993, 2003) refers to in 'Orientalism' as the negative stereotypes that consciously and unconsciously are embedded in many Westerners' worldview and which inform their conceptual constructions (see Burney 2012).

Women are increasingly assuming senior roles in higher education organisations in the UAE. Many of these roles are being created as the Emiratisation policy, which aims to replace many expatriates with nationals. Given the short history of higher education in the UAE and the recent availability of Emirati women with higher degrees, this is a case of 'gendering' rather than 'regendering' the academy. The following sections provide a profile of UAE, and the socio-cultural and economic conditions that affect the conditions and roles for women, and a description of Emirati women's status in UAE society, including their participation in higher education.

Country profile of UAE

The UAE is a small state in the Arabian Gulf. It is a relatively new nation-state, formed in 1971 as it emerged from colonisation. Oil and gas wealth has enabled a desert state to build from subsistence level to one with a high GDP (O'Sullivan 2008) and an extremely fast modernisation. As in other countries, this has been associated with urbanisation, industrialisation, and internationalisation with evidence of materialism and secularisation in the large commercial and retail tourism venues. It is facing many challenges as it transitions from traditional communities into a modern society. These include instilling a national identity over tribal structures; modernising and technologising while retaining Islam; preserving culture while building one of most multicultural societies, albeit mostly expatriate (Atiyyah 1996; Omair 2011); and maintaining its security in the Middle East while allowing for a liberal and relatively free society and providing one of the safest countries in the world for women (see Findlow 2000; Kazim 2000).

Due in part to its traditional tribal values of tolerance and hospitality (Rugh 2007) and adherence to Islamic values of tolerance, fairness, and equity (Hasan 2007; Hashmi 2002; Kamali 2002; March 2009), the UAE is highly successful, not only economically, but in creating a society that is stable and tolerant (O'Sullivan 2008). It reflects Islamic principles of justice and social obligations and equity which govern social relations in everyday life (e.g. An-Na'im 2010; Mannan 2005; Rosen 1989, 2000). These include those Islamic principles that protect a woman's right to education, ownership of property, participation in the economy, and political rights in voting and holding office. These principles are contained in the Qur'an and Sunnah rather than in exegesis, which often contains influences of culture (Engineer 2004) and the cultural, economic, and political subjugation practices that do not follow authentic Islamic principles (Barlas 2002; Jawad 2002).

The UAE is experiencing an intense nation- and institution-building phase in its development, which is unique due to the high level of non-citizens (over 80%), with a distinctive political system and culture (Heard-Bey 2005). It is in the early stages of establishing a higher education system that is negotiating a number of dimensions: creating a system unique to the UAE to meet its needs (Al Farra 2011; Fox 2008); managing a highly cross-cultural workforce with a broad range of foreign institutional configurations and practices; constructing professional roles that are culturally appropriate; building up the intellectual and social capital of its citizens to play a stronger role in governance and administration; and preserving its unique cultural and societal heritage (Al-Ali 2008; Rugh 2007). An important consideration in these dynamics is the UAE's position as a receiver of neoliberal globalisation that is exported predominantly from the USA and the UK (Donn and Al Manthri 2010). Dubai, in particular, has had one of the highest Globalisation Indices of the region in the economic, cultural, and social spheres, all of which place pressure to conform to the demands of globalisation in political, economic, and cultural institutions, thus creating cultural threats to Emirati society (Lootah 2006).

Despite the many foreign influences that under globalisation can be termed colonising processes, Emirati culture is still strong in most parts of the country. One measure of this is the continuation of devout Muslim daily and seasonal practices that help maintain traditional social structures. However, there are also unintended changes occurring through the influence of Western media, foreign travel and goods, which have strong influences on culture as part of the general development of the Gulf states. Mandaville (2011) describes hybrid countries that are mergers of traditional societies with modern technology, oil production, and security systems. Most institutions and organisations, including those in higher education, operate along foreign principles, mostly American, British, and Australian. While the more severe colonising features that Bourdieu (and Sayad 1964) witnessed and recorded in Algeria – 'rupture, alienation, de-culturation, disaggregation, and uprooting' (Silverstein and Goodman 2009, 13) – do not exist, there is a more benign destructive influence on social and cultural structures on a values and symbolic level, which are consistent with the post-colonial critiques of Said (2003) and Burney (2012), and the dialectics of modernisation and neo-colonialism (Henry and Springborg 2001).

Women's status in the UAE

Traditionally, women in the Arabian Gulf, like those in many traditional and pioneering societies, contributed substantially to the economy through agricultural work, marketplace activity, trade, investing their inherited money in businesses, and running and supporting families, often alone when men did not return from the sea or skirmishes (Maestri 2011). Al Oraimi (2011) describes the society as one where women were 'social agents' and where economic activity was not assigned by gender but through the structure of a family production unit where roles were assigned primarily on the basis of 'natural capacities' (80). As Schvaneveldt, Kerpelman, and Schvaneveldt (2005), explain, women's role in the economy and working outside the home is not forbidden by Islam, providing that it does not compromise family responsibilities. Education is not only schooling but apprenticeship in traditional societies, where women played a strong role in maintaining learning in the socio-cultural and economic spheres. Most women in the UAE still live in traditional community and extended family guided heavily by custom and Islam, which define life and shape their opportunities. These, as will be discussed below, are not wholly in opposition to modernisation and women's higher education. The tendency in the literature is to present cultural and religious values as 'resistances' to modernisation, for example, in Maestri (2011) or 'hindrances' in Ramakrishnan and Ilias (2011), displaying a 'Western' bias in dealing with traditional cultures in other parts of the world, and limiting the discussion of education to that of 'schooling' and Western models. However, in many Muslim countries, like the UAE, and contrary to much Western literature as Raghavan and Levine (2012) argue, there has been considerable reform in women's rights.

The UAE is a state that exemplifies many of the best virtues of Islamic and Arab culture. In many ways it is unique in the organisation of its social institutions and, in particular, in the rights and opportunities provided for women. In the UAE life expectancy is very high for women and exceeds that of many other Arab states (AbouZeid 2010). Contrary to the assumptions made in the West, Emirati women drive vehicles, have a strong presence in the economy, in government and in the professions (law, medicine, engineering) as ambassadors, judges, and representatives in the Federal National Council (see Bristol-Rhys 2010), with the UAE having the highest number of women appointed to these positions in any Arab country (Al Oraimi 2011). Women also play a large role in the workforce in banking, business, medical, corporate, and construction sectors (Augsburg, Claus, and Randeree 2009). The demand from women to receive services from women is driving much of the economic and public-sector development and creating employment opportunities for women (Maestri 2011). In countries such as Egypt and Jordan Emirati women have recently succeeded in rising to senior and sensitive positions in government, the private sector and in non-profit organisations (Yaseen 2010). While data collected during the 2000s suggested that culture and religion were seen as barriers to women's higher participation in the workforce (e.g. Gallant and Pounder 2008; Metcalfe 2006), by 2012, according to Government of Dubai (2012) official figures, this picture has changed with 41% of Emirati women being in the workforce.

The educational and professional status that Emirati women enjoy was not possible without the political vision and supports that were established by Shaikh Zayed Al Nahyan when the country was founded. His vision encompassed women taking senior roles in all sectors, evidence not only of acute political perception but also of Islamic principles with respect to women:

> The means to develop a country and modernise its infrastructure is a magnificent burden that should not be taken up by men only. ... It would lead to an unbalanced rhythm of life. Hence, women's participation in public life is required and we must be prepared for it ... . Nothing could delight me more than to see woman taking up her distinctive position in society. Nothing should hinder her progress. Like men, women deserve the right to occupy high positions, according to their capabilities and qualifications. (Augsburg, Claus, and Randeree 2009, 29–30)

This vision and political will, staunchly supported by the ruling families, has resulted in extensive building of school systems, universities, programmes, and foundation grants enabling a very large number of Emirati women to pursue higher education in the UAE and outside it (Soffan 1980), as well as many other government-sponsored initiatives (see Marmenout and Lirio 2014).

A further note must be made about Islam's position with respect to women in education and the workforce, and in leadership positions. Much of the negative stereotyping regarding women in Muslim countries is based on practices that issue from politics and culture, having little relationship to the rights and roles of women in Islam represented in the Qur'an and Sunna (Soffan 1980). Abuses and marginalising of women, as Augsburg, Claus, and Randeree (2009) argue, have been misattributed to

Islam, where in contrast women have rights to property, businesses, in choosing leaders, to education, inheritance, and independent wealth (see also Bristol-Rhys 2010), rights that were revolutionary at the time of the establishment of Islam, including the right of women equally to education (Soffan 1980). The UAE constitution and laws respect and implement these rights, described by Shaikha Fatima below:

> This support for women [by the government] stems from the teachings of the Islamic religion and the heritage and traditions of the UAE as well as the prudent view of President His Highness Sheikh Zayed bin Sultan Al Nahyan. It gives women the opportunity to reach the highest echelons of education, penetrate all fields of work, establish a foothold in society and asserts their belief in their own abilities and justify the faith of the society in them. (in Augsburg, Claus, and Randeree 2009, 31; see also Soffan 1980)

Gallant and Pounder (2008) record the many initiatives the UAE government has taken in supporting women's employment including legal provisions for equal pay and benefits as well as national strategies and frequent statements of support. Yaseen's (2010) results from a study on men's and women's leadership styles in the UAE demonstrated that the differences that existed were much more due to culture than religion. Yaseen found that culture produced stronger transformational characteristics in women in contrast to transactional characterisitcs in men. Women were also more proactive in addressing problems before they developed to a serious level.

This paper reflects on anecdotal evidence gained from teaching many Emirati women from most of the Emirates and supervising their research. These were women who exemplified a confidence in their abilities to succeed at high levels, while at the same time regarding this as a responsibility to Islam and as their duty to their country as part of its nation-building progress. These women comprise the pool of potential leaders within the current modernisation process.

Government policies supportive of Emirati men and women in the workforce have resulted in high participation levels in higher education and the workplace (Omair 2010). For example, the Emiratisation policy has had some influence by setting quotas for the hiring of Emiratis (Mashood, Verhoeven, and Chansakar 2009), although the representation of Emirati women in senior positions is still low due in part to men's unwillingness to share power. This is attributable more to the social system and particularly the new patriarchy that arose with modernisation than with the traditional system (AbouZeid 2010; Al Oraimi 2011; Sharabi 1988). However, these views are changing (e.g. Abdalla 1996; Mostafa 2005; Omair 2011) as is evident in a significant increase in women's appointments to senior positions, which has accelerated in the last two years (Augsburg, Claus, and Randeree 2009).

The attitudes of young Emirati women university students are also changing. In a recent survey Augsburg, Claus, and Randeree (2009) found that only 1% planned to stay at home, with 65% planning on working. Schvaneveldt, Kerpelman, and Schvaneveldt (2005) found similar results, while Bristol-Rhys (2010) found the age of marriage rising. These indications are doubly significant in a young country that has developed most of its social institutions in the last 20 years, and is still in the process of nation-building. A strong feature of the employment pattern in the UAE for Emiratis is a preference for the public sector, where salaries and working conditions are often better, even though it has come close to 'saturation point' in many fields with up to 66% of government organisations consisting of women (Williams, Wallis, and Williams 2013), with 30% of these in senior decision-making positions (*The National* 2014).

There is an additional consideration in examining women's leadership roles in a society that is still quasi-traditional, and where modernisation may, in fact, reduce women's influence. As Peterson (1989) notes of traditional Arab societies, family and politics are not separate spheres, and women and their networks carry strong leadership roles. If examined through a Western lens far more used to a differentiated society where power and authority are located in a formal political role, much of what women achieve is not captured. This has an impact on Emirati women currently who have to navigate a career path through a complex society that is part traditional, part modern, and in organisations that may be dominated by foreigners, many, if not most of whom can be non-Arab and non-Muslim. Additionally, if power and authority are assumed to reside in a particular repertoire of expressive styles, the quiet and tenacious quality of Emirati women can be easily overlooked, where traditionally 'family honor and dignity' rest in part upon women's code of modesty affecting dress and interaction with men who are not family members (Williams, Wallis, and Williams 2013, 140; also Peterson 1989).

The traditional dress that Emirati women wear, the abaya (cloak) and shayla (head-scarf), and for some the niqab (veil), has taken on an important symbolic value in expressing national identity. Women are fully aware of the way dress represents their nationality (Omair 2011), 'because traditional and modest clothing makes her appear as a true Emirati lady' (Alsumaiti 2014, 135). The values attached to traditional clothing are tribal values that emphasise reputation, generosity, hospitality, courage, modest appearance, and proper behaviour (see Rugh 2007). For Emirati women, it is also associated with their rights and achievements. This is even more important in a country that is now predominantly occupied by foreigners, with figures for locals varying from less than 10–20% (dubaifaqs.com), although if the non-nationals (not included in the census figures) and the many visitors are taken into account it is clear that Emiratis are a very small minority. Traditional dress not only symbolises nationalism and religious observance, but is also is a means 'to avoid sexual harassment and to gain sexual neutrality in managerial work' (Omair 2011, 156).

Women in the UAE, as in many parts of the Middle East, have benefited from their institutionalised advancement in education over the last 30 years, particularly in education and health where literacy rates, enrolment in secondary and higher education, have increased substantially since the 1970s, although gender disparities still exist (AbouZeid 2010). Women's educational attainment levels in the Gulf Cooperation Council (GCC) countries compare well with Western countries, even outranking the USA and Switzerland, although workplace participation is still much lower (Marmenout and Lirio 2014). In Moghadam's (2008) survey, in many states more than 50% of college students were women, with more than 40% in many others, and women were entering professions usually associated with men such as engineering, law, mathematics, commerce and finance, IT, and medicine. Even in some authoritarian states, such as Iraq and Egypt, women were supported in making advancements in higher education as part of modernising and reform programmes, with the women in Iraq showing the least participation due to the American invasion (Moghadam 2008).

Employment figures also show dramatic increases for women. Over the 1960–2000 period, the 548% increase for women in the UAE was not atypical in the region (Omair 2011). There was a significantly increasing participation in the labour force, including the publishing field, in the Arabian Gulf countries, including the UAE. In even conventionally predominantly male occupations like policing and the military, women have made significant progress in the last few years with 1500 women police in Dubai and 93 of these in senior positions, and 3 female judges and 17 female prosecutors in Dubai (Dubai Women Establishment 2012). In the UAE, women now hold 66% of public-sector jobs with 30% in decision-making positions despite the existence of organisational mindset barriers. In 2014, the UAE ranked number one in the Middle East for women in the Social Progress Index of the World Economic Forum (2014).

In the Gulf region, secondary and higher education systems have only been systematically developed over the last 30–40 years. According to Lootah (2006), the expansion of schooling during the 1950s, 1960s and 1970s contributed to a politicisation of Emiratis in resisting colonisation and creating the federation of the UAE. The establishment of universities and higher colleges of technology greatly contributed to education for women, due largely to the high level of support by the UAE government for women's education (Gallant and Pounder 2008). Lootah presented a striking trend in the numbers of female versus male students attending university and graduating. Even by 2003, at United Arab Emirates University women far outnumbered men with 11,872 registered in comparison with 3728, and of those graduating from universities, women again outnumbered men 4611–1910 (239). More recently, Al Oraimi (2011) found Emirati women represented 70% of the graduates from higher education, which can be attributed in part to the government's public policy on gender equality.

This trend has to be placed in the context of national development; many young women are entering higher education from families where large percentages of older generations did not enter or finish high school (Schvaneveldt, Kerpelman, and Schvaneveldt 2005). Comparatively speaking, the large numbers of Emiratis, particularly the women, in higher education represent a speed of development that Western countries did not experience, and whose development models are not well suited to regional conditions.

For Emirati women there are additional benefits perceived by them and the many fathers and extended families that support their advanced education and careers (Williams, Wallis, and Williams 2013). Women's achievements are supported by the principles of Islamic social justice, which the UAE applies through equality in social services and other public programmes as well as in their legal rights (Al Oraimi 2011). The areas that constrain women are social and cultural values. For example, in some families women are not allowed to travel unaccompanied (Gallant and Pounder 2008), and sometimes women themselves, as Al Oraimi (2011) pointed out, have difficulty identifying with Western (and secular) conceptions of feminism and gender, conceptions that are highly individualistic and do not transfer well to a collective-based family and tribal society (see Alhaj and Van Horne 2013). While men can exert significant influence over women and can hold them back (see Maestri 2011), the converse is also true. It is common for fathers and brothers to support women in pursuing higher education and jobs even against the wishes of women in the family (Al Rasbi 2012). Hertz-Lazarowitz (2005) found similarly in her study on women in traditional Muslim families. As with Muslim women from 'traditional, male-dominant Muslim families', interviewed by Hertz-Lazarowitz (165) in Israel, many Emirati women in Al Rasbi's study were highly motivated to pursue higher education and professional careers, and were able to maintain their family relationships while negotiating a path between traditional and non-traditional modern values.

The UAE has also provided important female role models, although in research conducted by a number of my Emirati women doctoral students (e.g. Al Naqbi; Al Rasbi), many Emirati women also look to male role models, especially Shaikh Zayed Al Nahayan, the founder of the country who died in 2004, who embodies for most locals the qualities of a good leader and of Islamic principles, and quite often their fathers (Alhaj and Van Horne 2013; Harold and Stephenson 2008). Augsburg, Claus, and Randeree (2009) profiled female role models who were most often referenced by Emirati women, including Shaikha Fatima bint Mubarak and Shaikha Lubna Al Qasimi.

Shaikha Fatima bint Mubarak is the wife of Shaikh Zayed and mother of the current Crown Prince of Abu Dhabi, Shaikh Mohammed bin Zayed, who has exercised considerable influence in the development of public policy (Peterson 1989). Shaikha Fatima, shortly after the formation of the country in 1971, established the first women's organisation and strongly supported education for women as part of nation-building activities. She was instrumental in women's political participation in the country's national council and their influence in the development of personal law (Peterson 1989). She also became heavily involved in regional and international development and humanitarian projects. Similarly, Shaikha Lubna Al Qasimi has been a critically important role model in the public sector, serving as Minister of Economy and Planning and as Minister of Foreign Trade, previously working in IT positions as a technician and manager, and also serving as a model as a women advancing in higher education to the masters level.

What is clearly evident in one doctoral student participant's experience is a strong sense of reintegrating the material and spiritual, although this finding cannot be generalised to all Emirati women. This participant applied her background knowledge and interpretation of data to her own situation. Similar results, though, were found by Alsumaiti (2014) and Al Rasbi (2012), both Emirati doctoral students who were also on career trajectories and found in their own research strong self-awareness of national and Islamic identity formation. However, it is too early in the advancement of Emirati women to leadership positions in higher education to draw firm conclusions, as women are only just now advancing into these positions in any numbers. There is a need for further research in this area.

Several questions arise. Do the assumptions and experiences that pertain to the 'West' actually apply here, and what possible negative stereotypes of Arab and Islamic cultures (see Croft 2012; Nader 2013) may get in the way of an authentic understanding of the professional lives of Emirati women in higher education? What kind of leadership identity for women can be both modern and maintain the country's Arab and Islamic character (see Al Farra 2011)? Fakhro (2009) argues that modernisation in the Gulf needs to be 'Arab-specific' by ' … revising and reconstructing heritage on the one hand, and selecting and assimilating important aspects of the modernity of foreign societies, on the other' (291). By 2013, a number of women had risen to senior administrative positions in higher education, including Dean of Education at United Emirates University, Dean of Student Services in the HCT system, and President of Zayed University in Abu Dhabi (*The National* 2013). Beginning in mid-2014, the Emiratization policy of the country was applied to the higher education sector, targeting many senior positions through the public higher education organisations as being for Emiratis only. Given that the majority of Emiratis in higher education degrees are women who earn the majority of qualifications, most of these positions will be filled by women.

Creating educational leadership roles is also, in part, an identity formation process for Emirati women. They are embedded in a multifaceted identity formation and maintenance dynamic (Beech 2008), which consists of being Muslim, being Emirati, being a woman, and achieving a managerial or leadership role organisationally. According to Beech (2008), and the theories of Alvesson and Willmott (2002), Creed and Scully

(2000), and Sveningsson and Alvesson (2003), identity construction in the organisational context is a performative process, grounded in interactions with others. All modes of image and presentation have meaning attached to them, and are interpreted. However, when placed into a foreign context such as the UAE where a strong Western influence is experienced by Emirati women, there can be a conflict of values and custom. In modernising organisations Emirati women are required to mediate between cultures in order to create leadership roles that are consistent with Emirati culture and Islam, while at the same time meeting the needs of organisations with non-Muslim Westerners in senior positions. In these contexts, creating a leadership identity is difficult.

Comparisons of the advances of women in a country such as the UAE with that of other countries, particularly Western countries, must take into consideration differences of religion, culture, social institutions, and conceptions that women themselves hold. Fox, Mourtada-Sabbah, and Al-Mutawa (2006) raise a fundamental question about development and globalisation in the Gulf region that relates to issues of post-colonial critiques, recolonisation, and intellectual imperialism. They contend that the strong cultural and religious values and patterns of life have created a distinctive form of globalisation, that is, the market forces and societal and cultural norms that it brings with it, 'cushions' indigenous society from many of its effects, although Westernising pressures still exist. Dubai in particular they cite is a world leader in many economic fields. The role and values of kin, religious values, traditional leadership roles, and a different mode of capitalism has reshaped many of the foreign influences. For example, in the UAE in particular, capital has been used for infrastructure building and the benefit of citizens.

In relation to Emirati women moving into leadership positions, there are a number of critiques that pertain particularly to the UAE. One is national identity formation (Alsharekh and Springborg 2008), another is negotiating a form of internationalised higher education that incorporates Islamic values and Islamic intellectual, legal, and administrative traditions (Bennett 2010; Fox, Mourtada-Sabbah, and Al-Mutawa 2006; Moghadam 1994). Yet another approach that is relevant, given the way that Emirati women posit the roles they are constructing, is Anderson's (1991) model of 'imagined communities', which examines how 'nation' is a constructed concept through actual and imagined shared experience of its members, shaping and shaped by its political and cultural institutions. In this case, opposition to colonial powers often ensures that the identity constructed is separate from that of other nations. Said (1993) criticises Anderson's representation of institutions as being too linear, and Chatterjee (1993) views Anderson's model as limited by its exclusion of the diversity of other nations. However, the model can be extended, that is indigenised, into non-Western settings and made more permeable to the differences of culture, religion, and social institutions. Chatterjee (1993) argues that colonisation limits imagination, a major problem of globalised, imported education. However, a counter-imagining through indigenised curriculum and other authentic nation-building processes is achievable, and, it could be argued, necessary for Emirati women who have to construct leadership roles that preserve Islamic and cultural values.

Related to this limited imagining is the polarised view of tradition versus modernisation, which regards tradition as a barrier, a hindrance. To become legitimate states do not necessarily have to follow a trajectory towards the 'Westphalian' state model and economic system that dominates in the West, as if this were a necessary historical norm (Ilias 2011; Ramakrishnan and Ilias 2011). Neither does Emirati women's success in leadership roles need to be evaluated by Western standards. An underlying assumption in such an evaluation is that living a traditional life is somehow not meaningful or fulfilling, a view that Berman (1981) brought into question in his *Disenchantment of the World*, which was influenced by Weber's 'iron cage' critique in finding that differentiated modern societies lacked many of the meaningful characteristics of integrated societies.

What does this mean for the development of educational curriculum that will support Emirati women in achieving a culturally authentic leadership in higher education? First, it cannot be dominated by Western (mostly USA, UK, and Australian) material to the degree it is, nor can it assume that Western scholarship is virtually the exclusive source of knowledge, problem-solving, teamwork, creativity, and communication skills. It is problematic also in its high degree of individualism and secularism, which excludes Islamic and cultural values that inform the social bonds, structures, and practices that binds the society (e.g. Maestri 2011). Much more work needs to be done to indigenise the curriculum in order to support institution building that is appropriate to an Arab Muslim state, while combining this with a broader international literature. This requires the use of the rich Islamic intellectual tradition, which to a large extent forms the foundation for the Western tradition (see e.g. Morgan 2007; Saliba 2011), and Shari'a, which is the constitutionally preferred legal tradition, and of studies and material from the region.

Even the research methods usually taught in developing countries can be problematic, or, in the case of behaviourist-informed positivistic methods diametrically opposed to Islamic conceptions of the human being. Research informs the very nature of social institution building and the leadership roles that guide them (e.g. Chilisa 2011; Kovach 2010; Moore-Gilbert 2009; Reagan 2005; Smith 2012; Walter and Andersen 2013). There is a recent development of indigenised research methods that are suitable to both non-Western and some Western contexts that should be promoted.

Given the discursive nature of this article, it ends on an experiential note. One measure of women's attainment in higher education, particularly for those moving into academic leadership positions where graduate degrees, conferences, and publications matter, is the opportunity for women to travel. I have accompanied several groups of Emirati, and other Arab Muslim, women to international conferences and guest lectures in the West. In all cases, we were accompanied by a husband, young brother, and/or nephew, sometimes by several male family members. Far from dominating women on these trips, the men act as supporters and take care of mundane travel chores, which allow the women to concentrate on finalising their presentation work, on networking, and on the important social and intellectual community, thus exercising their skills and knowledge in developing academic leadership roles. I have observed several families over five years become accustomed to what for them is a wholly new experience. In many families in the UAE and in the Gulf, the first family members to achieve higher education are women. Once they are assured that their wives and daughters are safe, that the experiences are constructive, and that they can retain important cultural and religious values while doing so, the families, particularly the fathers and older brothers have often become even more supportive of advanced academic achievement, as Al Rasbi (2012) also found in her research. The measure of foreigners is their degree of sensitivity to the need of traditional societies to evolve at a pace that does not have adverse effects on their culture, communities, and society. In many contexts they can provide the values, the formative experiences, and identity development that give women strength, empowerment, and constructive ways in leading their educational organisations.

Disclosure statement
No potential conflict of interest was reported by the author.

References
Abdalla, I. 1996. "Attitudes Towards Women in the Arabian Gulf Region." *Women in Management Review* 11 (1): 29–39.
AbouZeid, O. 2010. "Women's Empowerment Hammers Patriarchy: How Big is the Dent?" In *The Changing Middle East: A New Look at Regional Dynamics*, edited by B. Korany, 119–138. Cairo: American University in Cairo Press.
Al-Ali, J. 2008. "Emiratisation: Drawing UAE Nationals into their Surging Economy." *International Journal of Sociology and Social Policy* 28 (9/10): 365–379.
Al Farra, S. 2011. "Education in the UAE: A Vision for the Future." In *Education in the UAE: Current Status and Future Developments*, edited by Emirates Center for Strategic Studies and Research, 219–237. Abu Dhabi: ECSSR.
Alhaj, S., and C. Van Horne. 2013. "The Development of Arab Women Leaders: An Emirati Perspective." In *Culture and Gender in Leadership: Perspectives from the Middle East and Asia*, edited by J. Rajasekar and L.-S. Beh, 297–316. Basingstoke: Palgrave Macmillan.
Al Oraimi, S. 2011. "The Concept of Gender in Emirati Culture: An Analytical Study of the Role of the State in Redefining Gender and Social Roles." *Museum International* 63 (3–4): 78–92.
Al Rasbi, A. 2012. "Women's Challenges in Leadership and Factors that Affect Career Development for Women in the UAE: A Case Study from Dubai." Paper presented at the commonwealth conference for Educational Administration and Management, Cyprus, 2012.
Alsharekh, A., and R. Springborg, eds. 2008. *Popular Culture and Political Identity in the Arab Gulf States*. London: Saqi.
Alsumaiti, R. 2014. "Narratives of the Maps: Emirati Undergraduate Students' Stories of National Identity." EdD thesis, British University in Dubai, Dubai, United Arab Emirates.
Alvesson, M., and H. Willmott. 2002. "Identity Regulation as Organizational Control: Producing the Appropriate Individual." *Journal of Management Studies* 39 (5): 619–644.
Anderson, B. 1991. *Imagined Communities: Reflections on the Origin and Spread of Nationalism*. London: Verso.
An-Na'im, A. 2010. *Muslims and Global Justice*. Philadelphia, PA: University of Pennsylvania Press.
Atiyyah, H. 1996. "Expatriate Acculturation in Arab Gulf Countries." *Journal of Management Development* 15 (5): 37–47.
Augsburg, K., I. I. Claus, and K. Randeree. 2009. *Leadership and the Emirati Woman: Breaking the Glass Ceiling in the Arabian Gulf*. Berlin: Lit Verlag.
Badran, M. 2001. "Understanding Islam, Islamism and Islamic Feminism." *Journal of Women's History* 13 (1): 47–52.
Barlas, A. 2002. *Believing Women in Islam: Unreading Patriarchal Interpretations of the Qur'an*. Austin, TX: University of Texas Press.
Beech, N. 2008. "On the Nature of Dialogic Identity Work." *Organization* 15 (1): 51–74.
Bennett, C. 2010. *Muslim Women of Power: Gender, Politics and Culture in Islam*. London: Continnum.
Berman, M. 1981. *The Reenchantment of the World*. Ithaca, NY: Cornell University Press.
Bourdieu, P., and A. Sayad. 1964. *Le déracinement: La crise de l'agriculture traditionnelle en Algérie*. Paris: Minuit.
Bristol-Rhys, J. 2010. *Emirati Women: Generations of Change*. New York: Columbia University Press.
Burney, S. 2012. *Pedagogy of the Other: Edward Said, Post-colonial Theory and Strategies for Critique*. New York: Peter Lang.

Chatterjee, P. 1993. *The Nation and its Fragments: Colonial and Post-colonial Histories*. Princeton: Princeton University Press.

Chilisa, B. 2011. *Indigenous Research Methodologies*. Thousand Oaks: Sage.

Cole, J. 2009. *Engaging the Muslim world*. New York: Palgrave Macmillan.

Coleman, W. 2012. "Governance and Global Public Policy." In *The Oxford Handbook of Governance*, edited by D. Levi-Faur, 673–685. Oxford: Oxford University Press.

Creed, W., and M. Scully. 2000. "Songs of Ourselves: Employees' Deployment of Social Identity in Workplace Encounters." *Journal of Management Inquiry* 9 (4): 391–412.

Croft, S. 2012. *Securitizing Islam: Identity and the Search for Security*. Cambridge: Cambridge University Press.

Donn, G., and Y. Al Manthri. 2010. *Globalisation and Higher Education in the Arab Gulf States*. Oxford: Symposium Books.

Dubaifaqs.com. 2014. "United Arab Emirates (UAE) Population Statistics" Accessed September 10, 2014. http://www.dubaifaqs.com/population-of-uae.php.

Dubai Women Establishment. 2012. *Emirati Women Perspectives on Work and Political Participation: Social Media Poll Analysis Report 2012*. Abu Dhabi: Government of Dubai.

Engineer, A. 2004. *Rights of Women in Islam*. New Dehli: Sterling Publishers.

Esposito, J., and I. Kalin. 2011. *The Challenge of Pluralism in the 21st century: Islamophobia*. Oxford: Oxford University Press.

Fakhro, A. 2009. "Modernizing Education: Points of Departure, Conditions and Gateways." In *The Arabian Gulf: Between Conservatism and Change*, edited by Emirates Center for Strategic Studies and Research, 291–297. Abu Dhabi: ECSSR.

Findlow, S. 2000. *The United Arab Emirates: Nationalism and Arab-Islamic Identity, Occasional Paper*. Abu Dhabi: Emirates Center for Strategic Studies and Research.

Flood, C., S. Hutchins, G. Miazhevich, and H. Nickels. 2012. *Islam, Security and Television News*. Basingstoke: Palgrave Macmillan.

Fox, W. 2008. "The United Arab Emirates and Policy Priorities for Higher Education." In *Higher Education in the Gulf States: Shaping Economies, Politics and Culture*, edited by C. Davidson and P. M. Smith, 110–125. London: Saqi.

Fox, J., N. Mourtada-Sabbah, and M. Al-Mutawa. 2006. "The Arab Gulf Region: Traditionalism Globalized or Globalization Traditionalized?" In *Globalization and the Gulf*, edited by J. Fox, N. Mourtada-Sabbah and M. Al-Mutawa, 3–59. Abingdon: Routledge.

Gallant, M., and J. Pounder. 2008. "The Employment of Female Nationals in the United Arab Emirates (UAE): An Analysis of Opportunities and Barriers." *Education, Business and Society: Contemporary Middle Eastern Issues* 1 (1): 26–33.

Harold, B., and L. Stephenson. 2008. "Sustaining Social Development: Emerging Identity Development for Women in the UAE." Conference paper presented at the Australian Association for Research in Education, Brisbane, Australia, 2008.

Hasan, S. 2007. *Philanthropy and Social Justice in Islam: Principles, Prospects and Practices*. Kuala Lumpur: A. S. Nordeen.

Hashmi, H. 2002. "Islamic Ethics in International Society." In *Islamic Political Ethics: Civil Society, Pluralism and Conflict*, edited by J. Miles and H. Hashmi, 148–172. Princeton: Princeton University Press.

Heard-Bey, F. 2005. "The United Arab Emirates: Statehood and Nation-Building in a Traditional Society." *Middle East Journal* 59 (3): 357–375.

Held, D., and McGrew, A. 2002. *Globalization/Anti-globalization*. Cambridge: Polity Press.

Henry, C., and R. Springborg. 2001. *Globalization and the Politics of Development in the Middle East*. Cambridge: Cambridge University Press.

Hertz-Lazarowitz, R. 2005. "Muslim Women's Life Stories: Building Leadership." *Anthropology and Education Quarterly* 36 (2): 165–181.

Hirschkind, C. 2011. "What is Political Islam?" In *Political Islam: A Critical Reader*, edited by F. Volpi, 13–15. London: Routledge.

Hirst, P. 1997. "The Global Economy: Myths and Realities." *International Affairs* 73 (3): 409–425.

Hoogvelt, A. 2001. *Globalization and the Postcolonial World*. Basingstoke: Palgrave.

Ilias, M. 2011. "Dubai: The City and Sacredness." In *Society and Change in the Contemporary Gulf*, edited by A. Ramakrishnan and M. Ilias, 150–171. New Delhi: New Century Publications.

Jawad, H. 2002. *The Rights of Women in Islam: An Authentic Approach*. New York: Palgrave.

Kamali, M. 2002. *Freedom, Equality and Justice in Islam.* Cambridge: Islamic Texts Society.

Kazim, A. 2000. *The United Arab Emirates A. D. 600 to the Present: A Socio-discursive Transformation in the Arabian Gulf.* Dubai: Gulf Book Centre.

Lean, N. 2012. *The Islamophobia Industry.* London: Pluto Press.

Kovach, M. 2010. *Indigenous Methodologies: Characteristics, Conversations, and Contexts.* Toronto: University of Toronto Press.

Lootah, M. 2006. "United Arab Emirates Education: Modernization and the Challenges of Globalization." In *Globalization, Modernization and Education in Muslim Countries: In Education, Emerging Goals in the New Millennium*, edited by R. Zia, 237–247. New York: Nova Science.

Maestri, E. 2011. "Gulf Arab Women between Cultural Resistance and Knowledge Economy." In *Society and Change in the Contemporary Gulf*, edited by A. Ramakrishnan and M. Ilias, 74–91. New Delhi: New Century Publications.

Mandaville, P. 2011. "Reimagining the Ummah? Information Technology and the Changing Boundaries of Political Islam." In *Political Islam: A Critical Reader*, edited by F. Volpi, 331–354. London: Routledge.

Mannan, A. 2005. *Social Justice under Islam.* New Delhi: Ess Ess Publications.

March, A. 2009. *Islam and Liberal Citizenship: The Search for an Overlapping Consensus.* Oxford: Oxford University Press.

Marmenout, K., and P. Lirio. 2014. "Local Female Talent Retention in the Gulf: Emirati Women Bending with the Wind." *International Journal of Human Resource Management* 25 (2): 144–166.

Mashood, N., H. Verhoeven, and B. Chansakar. 2009. "Emiratisation, Omanisation and Saudisation – Common Causes: Common solutions?" Paper presented at the tenth international business research conference, Dubai, United Arab Emirates.

Mernissi, F. 1993. *Forgotten Queens of Islam.* Minneapolis, MN: University of Minnesota Press.

Metcalfe, B. 2006. "Exploring Cultural Dimensions of Gender and Management in the Middle East." *Thunderbird International Business Review* 48 (1): 93–107.

Moghadam, V. 1994. *Gender and National Identity: Women and Politics in Muslim Societies.* London: Palgrave Macmillan.

Moghadam, V. 2008. "Modernizing Women in the Middle East." In *A Companion to the History of the Middle East*, edited by Y. Choueiri, 425–443. Oxford: Basil Blackwell.

Moore-Gilbert, B. 2009. *Postcolonial Life-writing: Culture, Politics, and Self-representation.* London: Routledge.

Morgan, M. 2007. *Lost History: The Enduring Legacy of Muslim Scientists, Thinkers, and Artists.* Washington, DC: National Geographic.

Mostafa, M. 2005. "Attitudes towards Women Managers in the United Arab Emirates." *Journal of Managerial Psychology* 20 (6): 522–540.

Nader, L. 2013. *Culture and Dignity: Dialogues between the Middle East and the West.* Chichester: Wiley-Blackwell.

Olimat, M., ed. 2013. *Arab Spring and Arab Women: Challenges and Opportunities.* Abingdon: Routledge.

Omair, K. 2010. "Typology of Career Development for Arab Women Managers in the United Arab Emirates." *Career Development International* 15 (2): 121–143.

Omair, K. 2011. "Women in Management in the Middle East." In *Women, Management and Leadership – Naiset ja Johtajuus*, edited by L. Husu, J. Hearn, A.-M. Lämsä and S. Vanhala, 149–159. Helsinki: Hanken School of Economics.

O'Sullivan, E. 2008. *The New Gulf: How Modern Arabia is Changing the World for the Good.* Dubai: Motivate.

Peterson, J. 1989. "The political status of women in the Arab Gulf states." *Middle East Journal* 43 (1): 34–50.

Raghavan, C., and J. Levine, eds. 2012. *Self-determination and Women's Rights in Muslim Societies.* Waltham, MA: Brandeis University Press.

Ramakrishnan, A., and M. Ilias. 2011. "Introduction." In *Society and Change in the Contemporary Gulf*, edited by A. Ramakrishnan and M. Ilias, 1–9. New Delhi: New Century Publications.

Reagan, T. 2005. *Non-western Educational Traditions: Indigenous Approaches to Educational Thought and Practice*. Hillsdale, NJ: Lawrence Erlbaum.

Rosen, L. 1989. *The Anthropology of Justice: Law as Culture in Islamic Society*. Cambridge: Cambridge University Press.

Rosen, L. 2000. *The Justice of Islam: Comparative Perspectives on Islamic Law and Society*. Oxford: Oxford University Press.

Rugh, A. 2007. *The Political Culture of Leadership in the United Arab Emirates*. New York: Palgrave Macmillan.

Said, E. 1993. *Culture and Imperialism*. New York: Vintage.

Said, E. 2003. *Orientalism*. London: Penguin.

Saliba, G. 2011. *Islamic Science and the Making of the European Renaissance*. Cambridge, MA: MIT Press.

Schvaneveldt, P., J. Kerpelman, and J. Schvaneveldt. 2005. "Generational and Cultural Changes in Family Life in the United Arab Emirates: A Comparison of Mothers and Daughters." *Journal of Comparative Family Studies* 36 (1): 77–91.

Shaheed, F. 1999. "Constructing Identities: Culture, Women's Agency and the Muslim World." *International Social Science Journal* 51 (159): 61–73.

Sharabi, H. 1988. *Neopatriarchy: A Theory of Distorted Change in Arab Society*. Oxford: Oxford University Press.

Silverstein, P., and J. Goodman. 2009. "Introduction: Bourdieu in Algeria." In *Bourdieu in Algeria: Colonial Politics, Ethnographic Practices, Theoretical Developments*, edited by J. Goodman and P. Silverstein, 1–62. Lincoln: University of Nebraska Press.

Smith, L. T. 2012. *Decolonizing Methodologies: Research and Indigenous Peoples*. Winnipeg: Zed Books.

Soffan, L. 1980. *The Women of the United Arab Emirates*. London: Croom Helm.

Sonbol, A. 2006. "Women, Islam and Education." In *Globalization, Modernization and Education in Muslim Countries*, edited by R. Zia, 47–61. New York: Nova Science.

Stiglitz, J. 2003. *Globalization and its Discontents*. New York: Penguin.

Sveningsson, S., and M. Alvesson. 2003. "Managing Managerial Identities: Organizational Fragmentation, Discourse and Identity Struggle." *Human Relations* 56 (10): 1163–1193.

Syeed, N., and R. Zafar, eds. 2014. *Arab Women Rising*. Philadelphia: Knowledge@Wharton.

Teeple, G. 1995. *Globalization and the Decline of Social Reform*. Toronto: Garamond Press.

The National. 2013. "Emirati Women Beat the Odds to Become Leaders in Higher Education." March 8. Accessed January 2, 2015. http://www.thenational.ae/news/uae-news/education/emirati-women-beat-the-odds-to-become-leaders-in-higher-education.

The National. 2014. "Higher Education Minister Reiterates UAE Leadership Keen Interest in Women's Empowerment." April 3. Accessed January 2, 2015. http://www.wam.ae/en/news/general-emirates/1395242937572.html.

Volpi, F. 2011. "Introduction." In *Political Islam: A Critical Reader*, edited by F. Volpi, 1–7. London: Routledge.

Walter, M., and C. Andersen. 2013. *Indigenous Statistics: A Quantitative Research Methodology*. Walnut Creek, CA: Left Coast Press.

Williams, A., J. Wallis, and P. Williams. 2013. "Emirati Women and Public Sector Employment: The Implicit Patriarchal Bargain." *International Journal of Public Administration* 36 (2): 137–149.

World Economic Forum. 2014. "Social Progress Index." Accessed January 3, 2015. http://www.socialprogressimperative.org/data/spi.

Yaseen, Z. 2010. "Leadership Styles of Men and Women in the Arab world." *Education, Business and Society: Contemporary Middle Eastern Issues* 3 (1): 63–70.

Zempi, I., and N. Chakraborti. 2014. *Islamophobia, Victimization and the Veil*. Basingstoke: Palgrave Macmillan.

Leadership characteristics and training needs of women and men in charge of Spanish universities

Marita Sánchez-Moreno, Julián López-Yáñez and Mariana Altopiedi

Teaching and School Organisation, Universidad de Sevilla, Seville, Spain

This article discusses the results obtained by two consecutive enquiries into the leadership styles and training needs of women and men leading higher education organisations. It compares the findings of the first stage of two studies, based on ad hoc questionnaires responded to by 136 women and 129 men. Results showed only subtle differences between the leadership styles deployed by the two groups. Both groups viewed organisations as social constructions; they preferred characteristics such as *responsibility*, *ability to get on well with people*, *motivation capacity*, *communication and empathy*, *capacity to tackle difficult situations*, and *ethical issues*. Consistent with this both groups identified similar training needs, which included the acquisition of abilities to deal with interpersonal conflicts and the construction of personal criteria to select the best strategy to face every situation. As no significant differences between male and female leaders were found, it is suggested that research into higher education organisations and their management training needs from a gender perspective should focus on the way both men and women managers tackle problems and situations.

1. Introduction

Since the first reform in 1983 of the higher education system after Franco's dictatorship, the government system of Spanish universities has been characterised by a representative democracy, which in practice means the participation of the university community in both the decision-making process at different levels and the election of a number of the management positions. Although a governing body composed by the chancellor and vice-chancellors makes the executive decisions, an important role is assigned to the University Claustro in both the strategic decisions and the control of the executive positions and bodies. The Claustro is a university council composed of representatives of students, teaching staff, and administrative staff and is usually renewed every four years by means of the weighted voting of the three sectors.

In this system, some of the governing positions (such as chancellors, deans, or heads of department) are elected (directly or by means of representatives) by the academic community, while others (such as vice-chancellors, vice-deans, or secretaries of departments) are directly appointed by the chancellors, deans, or heads of department. This means that while some of the management responsibilities involve being in charge of professional managers who have no teaching or research role, others, usually the most senior in the hierarchy, are in charge of academics, although they have not usually received any specific preparation for such a role. They usually hold their management positions for renewable terms of four years. In sum, it is a non-professional model of governance with some traits of both the collegial and democratic model where the academic community takes over most of the decision-making responsibilities (Castro and Ion 2011). This system is reflected with slight variations in the public universities, which in the course 2010–2011 were responsible for 84.3% of the total number of graduate students in Spain. On the other hand, the organisational structures in private universities present more variation. Although some autonomy can be recognised in the functioning of higher education institutions, both public and private, they largely depend on the regional governments (autonomous communities), especially in terms of funding and personnel policy.

The participation of women in the governance of Spanish universities has been a relatively late phenomenon, mainly for sociocultural reasons. The first female student appeared in 1888 while Emilia Pardo Bazán, a well-known novelist, was the first female academic, entering the School of Humanities of the Central University of Madrid in 1906. However, with the extension of higher education in developed societies, there has been a progressive feminisation of the student body, particularly in the last two decades, almost reaching parity of the sexes. There has been an increase in the number of women in academia and they have been incorporated progressively into positions of management responsibility, although generally speaking this has been in smaller numbers and in lower positions than men. There is still a difference between the proportion of men and women academics and managers. The ways in which women and men enter university management positions is also different. While men tend to hold elected positions, more women tend to be in positions designed (by the elected male managers) rather than the elected ones. For example, in recent times there has been an increase in the number of women vice-chancellors (that is, in posts designed by the chancellors), according to a study of the Spanish Ministry of Education and Science (2007).

The aim of this article is to compare the characteristics of women and men academics holding management positions at universities. The results obtained by two funded research projects[1] carried out consecutively in 2002–2005 and 2006–2009 are discussed. The main issues brought up for discussion include leadership styles, training needs, and the power bases deployed by both women and men when performing their leadership roles.

2. Theoretical framework: gender and leadership in organisations

Despite leadership having been on the research agenda of many disciplines in the social sciences for decades, gender has rarely been taken into consideration in explaining leadership and organisational processes (Alimo-Metcalfe and Alban-Metcalfe 2005; Coleman 2003). This *invisibility* of gender is part of the assumption of the masculine vision of the world that is predominant in organisational analysis (Bensimon 1993; Coronel Llamas, Moreno, and Padilla 2002), and also of the predominance of theories about leadership that has to do with *heroic masculinity*. Implicit in such a vision is the claim to protect women while men's positional power is preserved (Kerfoot and Whitehead 1998, 451; White and Özkanlib 2011). For Blackmore and Sachs (2007, 77), while control and power in management, a traditionally masculine field, assume a positive symbolic capital, femininity assumes a negative one.

However, demographic changes in organisations have allowed an increase of females in management positions. In the case of university management positions, according to Breakwell and Tytherleigh (2008), this presence in Spanish universities has shifted from 9.5% in 1986 to 23% in 2006. The arrival of women in power positions in organisations is important as it gives them the opportunity to rethink organisations as workplaces from a gender perspective (Airini et al. 2011). Different organisational theories have advanced efforts to make gender more visible in the management field. According to Lavié (2009), we first find perspectives with a strong focus on *demanding equity* between men and women in the access to leadership positions. These perspectives concern the removal of the institutional barriers that make access difficult, but they do not problematise the difficulties that women have in achieving a level of performance comparable to that of their male colleagues.

On the other hand, there are perspectives that point out that management is an alien field for most women. They suggest that women have a particular contribution to make to the field and, accordingly, that their own forms of seeing, knowing, organising, and leading should be considered (Shakeshaft 1989; Tong 1998). These perspectives that consider the difference usually establish two clearly defined leadership styles. Although recognising that any style can be adopted by both men and women, it is suggested that men usually present a style based on *instrumental qualities* (including assertiveness, control, ambition, competitiveness, independence, and confidence), while women deploy a style based on *emotional qualities* (such as listening and supporting people), which are concerned with the well-being of others and oriented towards resolving interpersonal conflicts (Eagly and Johannesen-Schmidt 2001; Eagly, Wood, and Diekman 2000). According to this perspective, men who hold managerial positions tend to develop a more task-focused, transactional, and authority-based style, whereas women tend to develop a more transformational, relationship-focused, interpersonal, and democratic style.

Another set of traits characterising women's leadership styles in the literature includes team orientation, responsibility, and a preference for ethical over efficiency criteria in decision-making (Bensimon 1993), an intuitive approach to problem solving that leads towards creative forms of resolving conflicts (López-Yáñez and Sánchez-Moreno 2008); and continuity with regard to the duration and stability of social ties (Marshall 1990). Similarly, Coronel Llamas, Moreno, and Padilla (2002) pointed out that the extensive use of social skills and resources is characteristic, in particular: (a) listening, *perception of others, and empathy*; (b) the capacity to *express feelings* and to use them in decision-making and group management; (c) *familiarity and authenticity*, as well as the use of feedback in establishing personal relationships; and (d) recognition of *one's own emotional impact* on others.

In parallel with the above-mentioned approaches concerning gender in organisations, an increasingly important trend suggests that even though gender represents a constitutive dimension in organisations this should not be linked to closed and homogeneous categorisations about masculine and feminine traits, that is, reduced to essentialist understandings of gender and leadership practices. Key studies, such as those by Alvesson and Billing (1992), have suggested that the leadership styles deployed by both men and women are too diverse and contradictory in practice to reduce them simply to a bipolar model. These authors considered that the labelling of leadership as *masculine* or *feminine* is not supported empirically and they discouraged the adoption of these behaviour traits to describe both groups. The adoption of these traits would not help break down the gender stereotypes in this field (Billing and Alvesson 2000).

Court (2005) has also questioned the reduction of the gender-leadership phenomenon to masculine and feminine models. Along with Alvesson and Billing (1997) and other authors who are sceptical about the *feminine leadership* construct, Court suggested that the gender dimension needs to be related to other dimensions that influence the behaviour of leaders, such as social class or beliefs and culture. However, although the overgeneralisation of the differences between masculine and feminine approaches to leadership should be avoided, Madden (2005, 6) has claimed that such differences have to be taken into account when analysing the practice of leadership.

Other authors consider that leadership abilities have more to do with situational and contextual variables than with those linked to gender (Ball 2007; Bolden, Petrov, and Gosling 2009; Frenkel and Stretchman 2006; White and Özkanlib 2011). Sensitivity to context, according to Mills (2002, 300), means that 'to understand the gendered subjectivities of the actors involved we need to understand the discourses in which they were located and the relationships in which they were involved'. In a similar sense, Blackmore (2010) has pointed out that gender in organisations has to be analysed together with other personal and cultural factors with which it interacts.

Studies about gender in organisations are moving beyond the initial approaches of the last two decades, which focused on differentiating the styles and characteristics attributed to men and women. Recent studies have utilised the contributions of a variety of disciplines, and taken into consideration not only social, cultural, and political conditions influencing leadership (Blackmore 2005; White and Özkanlib 2011), but also institutional history, organisational structure, and culture (Mills 2002).

Of relevance here is the literature on the characteristics of leadership in university organisations. The abilities demanded of university leaders are so varied that it makes it difficult to simply import the models from the business literature (Spendlove 2007). In an attempt to understand the complexity of being a leader at a university, some authors have identified the tensions that are inherent in leadership in higher education, such as the need for both individualism and collaboration, or for organisational stability and the promotion of change (Blackmore and Blackwell 2006; Frenkel and Stretchman 2006; Scott and Webber 2008). Others have adopted a model based on the identification of the core dimensions of leadership in university organisations. For example, the research conducted by Scott and Webber (2008) identified eight dimensions that need to be taken into account when planning for the development of leaders. They are:

- Career stage, which is related to motivations and priorities
- Career aspirations, in relation to trajectory and interest in achieving promotion
- Visionary capacity, which is related to philosophical principles and the ability to translate these into orientations to action
- Boundary-breaking entrepreneurialism, which allows leaders to find new solutions to new challenges
- Professional skills, which facilitate positive social interactions
- Instructional design and assessment literacy
- Crisis management
- Multidimensional approaches to leadership development, which are relevant when considering the diversity of tasks and responsibilities the leader must face.

Another interesting development in the research literature concerns the patterns that make leadership in university organisations a widely distributed phenomenon (Bolden, Petrov, and Gosling 2009). Van Ameijde et al. (2009) suggested that distributed leadership provides university managers with a means of overcoming the problems derived from the increase in performance measurement, the seeking of effectiveness, and the bureaucratic devices for control and accountability. They described the conditions required for it to take place as being at two levels (the organisation and the team) and with two kinds of processes (internal and external). The conditions included autonomy, clearly defined goals, and shared support for goals. Important to the external processes were key agents, the provision of feedback about progress, and support from the community. The coordination of activities, the sharing of information, and mutual performance monitoring were seen as important to the internal processes.

Kezar and Lester (2009) identified some leadership orientations and skills that are needed to promote distributed leadership at the University: the ability to install a vision for continuous improvement; the willingness to sacrifice personal goals for the sake of organisational interests; the ability to be persuasive; the ability to network; political skills to navigate possible resistance; and the capacity to attract external support. The specific literature related to the professional development of university managers shows that these skills can and should be promoted through appropriate training programmes (Aasen and Stensaker 2007; Calabrese et al. 2008; Scott and Webber 2008).

In sum, following Blackmore (2005), the search for dialogic and people-centred leadership is particularly needed in university organisations, where diverse forms of management have been shown to be inefficient in the creation of innovative and creative cultures that encourage the sustainable development of both teaching and research.

3.   Methodology

The discussion is based on the results obtained from two enquiries: (1) *Woman in the headship and management of universities: Problems, leadership styles, and contribution to institutional development* (Spanish Ministry of Work and Social Affairs); and (2) *Management and government in universities: Training for good practice* (Spanish Ministry of Science and Innovation). Both research projects were carried out in two stages. In this paper we will focus on the first stages of the two projects, both of which used a quantitative/descriptive methodology.

3.1. *Instrument*

In the first project the survey *Opinion Questionnaire for Women who hold Managerial Posts in the University* (COMECADU in its Spanish initials) was used. This was designed specifically to collect data about the personal and professional profiles of the participants in the study and included four parts or dimensions: Professional and biographical information; Conditions of their access to both the university and management positions; Opinions and experiences about their management roles; and Institutional and workplace conditions. On the basis of such dimensions, secondary data about the managers' roles, their styles of leadership, and perceived problems and training requirements were elaborated by the research team.

For the second project, focusing on men, the questionnaire was linguistically adapted for male participants. The results showed the questionnaire items to have face validity; all participants understood the questions and the definitions of work-based situations on which they were based.

3.2. *Participants*

In the enquiry addressed to women managers the level of reliability was 99.99%, the error was 0.06, the alpha was 0.001, and there were 435 subjects in the sample. The criteria used for this selection ensured the variety of the sample in terms of autonomous community; type of university (public/private); and the department's field of knowledge (Humanities and Communication, Social and Legal Sciences, Biological and Health Sciences, Scientific Area, Technical Area). Systematic random sampling was used to select the subjects in respect of the first of the criteria and stratified random sampling was used for the rest. The questionnaire was completed and returned by 136 women managers, that is 31.26% of the initial sample. This shows that the information gathered was highly representative and suggests that the research aroused special interest among women participants.

Due to the large number of men in management positions in Spanish universities, only 20 institutions were selected in the research designed for male managers using the criteria of size, public/private typology, age, and location. A stratified proportional procedure was used to select the sample, starting by defining the four strata into which the population were grouped ($N = 1666$ managers in the 20 universities selected):

- Rector or vice-rector (144)
- Head of department and departmental secretary or area director (690)
- Dean or vice-dean (533)
- Head or co-head of a university school (299).

Using an error of 5% and a reliability level of 95.5%, the size of the sample was established as 323. These were classified across the four strata, obtaining 28 participants in the first stratum, 134 in the second, 103 in the third, and 58 in the fourth.

Finally, every manager in the population was assigned a number in order to enable the components of the sample to be randomly selected by means of the R programme. The questionnaire was sent to them and, after many reminders, 129 male managers finally answered the questionnaire.

3.3. *Analysis procedure*

Results obtained in both groups were processed using the statistical package SPSS 11.0. Descriptive analysis and other analyses were carried out to establish the relations between multiple variables. The specific way in which every dimension was analysed will be addressed in the corresponding results sections below. These analyses were the basis for depicting the personal and professional profiles of men and women in charge of university organisations who answered the questionnaire. In addition, these analyses were useful for defining a number of management styles.

4. Results and discussion

4.1. *Leadership styles*

In order to understand the leadership styles of the women managers, a scale was constructed of nine items grouped into three factors in the *COMECADU* questionnaire. The three factors were: (1) time and task management; (2) external vs. internal orientation of the management; and (3) priority given to formal vs. informal aspects of the organisation. The items had a bipolar structure, with a range of responses scored from 1 to 6, where 1 and 6 represented, respectively, the greatest preference for one of the poles (see Figures 1–3). This allowed leadership styles to be placed along a collegial – managerial continuum, which seems to be distinctive of leadership in higher education (Aasen and Stensaker 2007).

With respect to the management of time and tasks, our results confirmed the idea of a clear predominance of a polychronic conception over the monochronic, characterised by carrying out multiple tasks simultaneously. In their answers to questions the women managers in the study affirmed that they kept open several fronts of action simultaneously and often dealt with various matters at the same time (see Figure 1).

However, the data revealed that men also do more than one task at the same time and they are not concerned about being involved simultaneously in several courses of action. Therefore, the results obtained contradict the premise that men prefer a monochronic approach to time management, as Hargreaves (1994) suggested. With respect to factor 2 (external/internal orientation), both men and women managers appeared very much more oriented towards the internal aspects of the organisation than the external. As can be seen in Figure 2 both women and men practically disregarded the external image in order to give full priority to internal functioning (item 4), and they attached relatively little importance to relations with other organisations in dedicating themselves to their own affairs (item 8).

However, men and women participants differed in response to item 5, which dealt with the balance between the alternatives of attending to the well-being of members, on the one hand, and the completion of tasks and the fulfilment of agreements made previously, on the other. While female managers gave similar importance to both issues, male managers were polarised towards giving priority to the completion of tasks (53.1%), as their preference was for the fourth choice in this direction on the range of 1–6 (35.9%). As social abilities like providing support and empathy are frequently recognised as valued leadership characteristics (Bryman 2007; Kezar and Lester

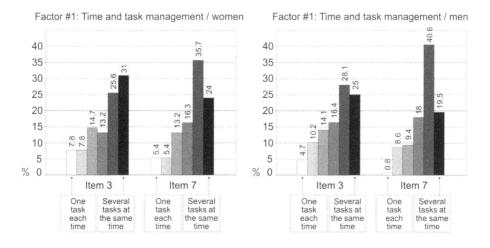

Figure 1.   Leadership style. Factor 1: time and task management.

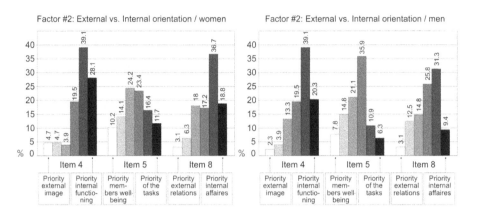

Figure 2.   Leadership style. Factor 2: external vs. internal orientation.

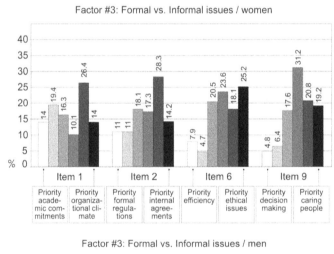

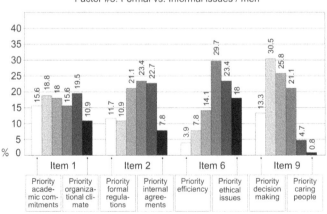

Figure 3.   Leadership style. Factor 3: formal vs. informal issues.

2009; Scott and Webber 2008; Spendlove 2007), this feminine preference could contribute to explaining the attribution of effectiveness to female leaders.

With regard to factor 3 (formal vs. informal aspects), women managers repeatedly chose the options that gave priority to informal aspects over formal ones. The most meaningful finding in this sense is found in responses to item 9 where men and women gave opposing answers. Female managers gave low priority (i.e. a score of 1–3 on a range of 1–6) to decision-making (28.8%), while male managers attached stronger importance to this option (69.6%). By contrast, female managers gave full priority to attention to people (71.2%) in comparison with male managers (26.6%). In item 1, women showed a significant balance between the two poles (formal/informal), something that did not happen with the other items of this factor. In item 1 there was virtual parity between the three options relating to the priority of academic commitments and the three options relating to the priority of the organisational environment (49.7% and 50.5%, respectively, see Figure 3). Although answers are distributed, male managers mainly gave priority to academic commitments (52.4%) and the organisational environment (46%).

Both men and women managers gave priority to internal agreements over formal regulations (item 2). Nevertheless, subtle differences can be observed in the items regarding the priority given to ethical issues/efficiency (item 6). Although both groups gave priority to ethical aspects over efficiency, the results show that men were slightly more inclined to the former.

In synthesis, regarding the use of time, both men and women present a clear predominance of the polychronic conception over the monochronic. They also seem to address their management efforts towards the internal and informal issues of their organisations, preferring these over the external and the formal regulations.

However, men tend more than women to task accomplishment and give greater importance to decision-making. On the other hand, women concede the highest priority to the group well-being, the workplace climate, and attention to people.

4.2. *Power basis on which men and women managers run their organisations*

From our point of view, the notion of *leadership* is delimited by the wider phenomenon of power in organisations. It is not only the managers who have power in an organisation. Many agents may have it or construct it, and to do so there are a wide variety of sources or bases (explicit or implicit, legitimate or not) on the basis of which both competitive and collaborative relationships will be established with certain agents. This idea assumes the dynamic character of power, which is in permanent construction, as opposed to the reification espoused by the traditional theory of leadership.

Our intention was to investigate the power bases used by women managers in the university. Contrary to our expectations that women would give priority to certain bases of power over others, the participants in our study used all of the power bases available, and they chose between them according to the problem or task we set them. To be precise, for each situation we offered a range of choices whose underlying structure reflected five tendencies or leadership styles based on Mintzberg (1983). These are: *authoritarian*, where the managers act in a personalistic fashion according to their own criteria or depending on the assigned post; *meritocratic*, resorting to an expert or the professional knowledge of someone to back their decisions; *bureaucratic*, where actions are legitimised by respect for rules and regulations; *ideological*, calling on shared values in order to justify their positions; and *political*, where alliances are established with colleagues, generally on a personal level. The statements that give rise to the responses to each item can be seen in Table 1.

On the basis of the results obtained (see Figure 4), the following conclusions were reached:

Item 1. Managing antagonistic positions. The managers consulted in this study preferred the strategies with a political component when dealing with matters involving antagonistic positions between participants. Specifically, 44.4% of women and 58.6% of men selected the option of 'persuading and negotiating a favourable solution with the other parties'. It is also very significant that in both groups only a low percentage chose option B, in which the bureaucratic component predominates.

Item 2. Response to confrontations between members of the group. The most significant aspects of this item were the low percentage that chose the strategy with a meritocratic component (1.5% women, 5.4% men), which consists of 'requesting the participation of a qualified mediator, making professional criteria count'. The number of choices for the other options was fairly evenly distributed, although the ideological option predominated (35.6% women, 31% men). This option consists of asking those involved to conform to the principles and values that the managers believed it was necessary to maintain.

Item 3. Attitude towards criticism received. In contrast to the responses to Item 2, for item 3 the most chosen option was the one with a meritocratic component, which consists of 'putting forward technical or professional arguments, related to efficiency in fulfilling objectives', chosen by 46.5% of women and 54.3% of men. The second most popular (for both women and men) was the strategy with an ideological component: 'organise meetings in which the people involved take part, and put forward ideological arguments which clarify their vision of the organisation', chosen by 37% of women and 25.6% of men. The majority of respondents chose one of these two options (83.5% women, 79.9% men).

Item 4. Decision-making. When it comes to taking important decisions, the majority of the women and men respondents preferred political strategies (53.4% and 55%, respectively), specifically those which consist of 'trying to negotiate previously and find the necessary support'. Some way behind this was the choice of a meritocratic component (21.4% and 22.5%, respectively) and a bureaucratic component (16% and 15.5%, respectively); while for women the choice of options for autocratic and ideological components were practically minimal (both with 4.6%) and for men the option of an ideological component was almost nonexistent.

Table 1. Items on the power basis scale.

Item 1. You have to deal with matters involving antagonist positions between participants …	Item 5. The first thing you do when new members arrive at the group/organisation is …
Item 2. In a meeting you coordinate, a confrontation between two participants arises …	Item 6. If you have to tackle an apathetic and unmotivated group …
Item 3. When you receive criticism …	Item 7. Before a predictably tense meeting …
Item 4. When you have to make important decisions …	Item 8. With respect to interpersonal relationships within the organisation, you are of the opinion that …

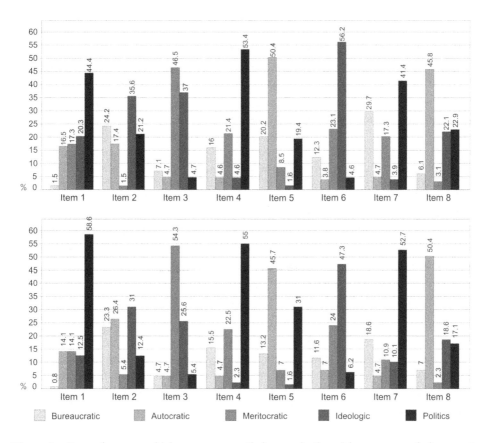

Figure 4.   Power bases on which managers run their organisations (above women, below men).

Item 5. Attitude towards the incorporation of new members. This is one of the few items (only two of the eight which make up this part of the questionnaire) where the authority component predominated in the choices of the participants. With the arrival of new members to the organisation, 50.4% of women and 45.7% of men preferred 'to orientate them personally with regard to the aims, objectives and activities of the group'. What seems clear enough through this type of strategy is the preference of women managers for direct social relations and their inclination to get personally involved with orientating the new member. In the case of women, it was followed in importance with similar percentages for two options with quite different components: the bureaucratic option (20.2%) and the political option (19.4%). In the case of men, these options were inverted: the most chosen option was the political one (31%) followed by the bureaucratic component (13.2%).

Item 6. Managing an unmotivated or apathetic group. Faced with the apathetic group, both the women and men respondents were inclined to choose an approach, more noticeably in the case of women, where the ideological strategy has precedence (56.2% and 47.3%, respectively), which consists of getting the members of the group involved through dialogue and establishing the need to work as part of a team. In this strategy, a predilection for managing social relations can again be appreciated, rather than rules and regulations (the bureaucratic option had 12.3% and 11.6%, respectively), reference to authority (the autocratic option had 3.8% and 7%, respectively), or the political option with a competitive nuance (4.6% and 6.2%, respectively).

Item 7. Strategy for dealing with conflict. Faced with a conflict (in this case, a predictably tense meeting) both women and men managers preferred to take the option with a political component, just as it was when dealing with contradictory positions (item 1) and when it was a matter of taking important decisions (item 4). The option consisting of 'holding prior meetings with the key agents' obtained a result of 41.4% for women and 52.7% for men. Nevertheless, it was followed in importance by another option of a quite different tendency, that is, a bureaucratic component which consists of 'getting the necessary legal information and preparing the strategy, conforming at all times to what is laid down by the regulations' (chosen by a notable 29.7% of women and 18.6% of men). The women and men surveyed rarely exerted their authority (4.7% in both groups) or preferred to resort to ideological arguments (3.9% women, 10.1% men).

Item 8. Attitude towards interpersonal relationships within the organisation. As with item 5, the predominance of the authoritarian option in this item (45.8% women, 50.4% men) implies a preference for personal and direct involvement in managing social relations and a preference for informal relations over formal ones. The way this option is stated seems to show this: 'I will personally take charge of this matter, acting as mediator and conciliator through informal contacts.' Significant percentages of respondents also selected options with ideological (22.1% women, 18.6% men) and political (22.9% women, 17.1% men) components.

In sum, it becomes evident that the tendency of the participant male and female managers was to adopt a *flexible* style instead of a fixed one, adapting themselves to the context and situation when carrying out managerial functions. It can be observed in Table 2 the prevailing trends of women and men regarding the underlying leadership styles.

Table 2.   Situational characteristics in the use of different power bases by women and men leaders.

Leadership: prevailing trend towards ...	Women	Men
Political style	In handling antagonistic positions As a way of decision-making In conflict management	In handling antagonistic positions As a way of decision-making In conflict management
Ideological style	In cases of confrontation among members In motivating the group	In cases of confrontation among members In motivating the group
Meritocratic style	In response to criticism	In response to criticism
Authoritarian style	In managing the arrival of newcomers In handling interpersonal relationships within the organisation	In managing the arrival of newcomers In handling interpersonal relationships within the organisation
Bureaucratic style	In cases of confrontation among members In managing the arrival of newcomers In conflict management	In conflict management

4.3. *Characteristics and training needs of women and men managers in the university*

We also analysed the training needs of women and men managers according to their responses to a list of valued/used characteristics of leadership. They were asked to assess to what extent (a) a certain characteristic was valued for managing university organisations, and (b) if they used it. As can be seen in Table 3, women and men managers shared the most valued characteristics: *responsibility, capacity to tackle difficult situations, conflict mediation, planning and organising,* and *ethical sense.* However, men added to that list: *diplomacy, leadership capacity, ability for decision-making,* and especially *communication and empathy.*

The D columns represent the difference between the quite/much valued and used characteristics for both women and men managers. The purpose of this is to analyse the gap between the use/possession of relevant characteristics and their attributed importance. Therefore, a highly positive score in the corresponding D column points to a potential training need for the participants. In the case of women, the highest differentials (>25) between quite/much valued and used characteristics are found in *leadership capacity* (+39.7), *authority* (+33.0), *ability to achieve resources* (+32.4), *motivation capacity* (+32.4), *resilience* (+30.2), and *capacity to tackle difficult situations* (+26.5). As can be seen, such characteristics are much more valued than used by female managers. In the case of men, the highest differentials (>25) are related to *authority* (+35.6), *diplomacy* (+26.5), and *motivation capacity* (+26.3). In general terms, the gaps in both the D columns are lower for male managers than for female managers. Two possible conclusions are that women either *have* more training needs than men or *recognise* more training needs than men.

One of the main findings from the comparison between the data gathered from men and women is related to the *ability to achieve resources.* It is quite/much used by 72% of male managers, compared to 49.2% of females – a huge difference of 22.8 points. In addition, such characteristics are more valued by women (81.6%) than by men (76%). This explains the maximum gap between the different scores for this characteristic (32.4% women against 4.0% men) or, in other words, it is the clearest training need in the case of women managers. Female managers' responses to this point are close to those obtained by Wolverton, Ackerman, and Holt (2005) from department chairs in Canada. Both our participants and those in the Canadian study recognised their lack of training in budgetary issues and the need to be more effective in the use of resources.

Also noteworthy are the responses about *leadership capacity.* It is quite/much used by 69.5% of men managers compared with 47.8% of women – a difference of 21.7 points. This characteristic is also more highly valued (5.9 points) by male managers.

Another remarkable difference between male and female managers is with regard to the *resilience* characteristic. It is reported to be quite/much used by 68.6% and valued by 89.3% of male managers, while it is quite/much used by 54.4% and valued by 84.6% of female managers. Although the gap between the quite/much valued and the quite/much used responses is high in both cases, it is much higher in the case of women (+30.2 points for men, +20.7 points for women).

Authority is a less used characteristic by both men (47.1%) and women (42.7%). However, it is slightly more valued by men than women (7 points difference). Actually, this is the least valued characteristic by women (75.7%), while *ability to achieve resources* is least valued by men (76.0%).

Table 3. Characteristics and training needs of women and men managers.

| | Valued/used women | | | | | Valued/used men | | | | |
| | Little/some | | Quite/much | | | Little/some | | Quite/much | | |
Characteristic	Valued	Used	Valued	Used	D	Valued	Used	Valued	Used	D
Responsibility	0.7	0.7	**97.1**	**95.6**	+1.5	1.7	3.3	98.3	95.9	+3.2
Ability to get on well with people	8.8	22.1	89.0	74.2	+14.8	11.6	28.9	88.4	69.4	+19.0
Diplomacy	8.1	30.2	89.7	65.4	+24.3	6.6	31.5	93.4	66.9	+26.5
Authority	22.1	52.9	75.7	42.7	+33.0	17.3	52.1	82.7	47.1	+35.6
Sensitivity	18.4	9.5	78.7	86.7	−8.1	14.1	8.2	85.1	90.1	−5.0
Cleverness	10.3	12.5	86.8	82.3	+4.5	10.8	16.5	89.2	81.8	+7.4
Leadership capacity	10.3	48.4	87.5	47.8	+39.7	5.8	28.9	93.4	69.5	+23.9
Motivation capacity	7.4	38.2	90.5	58.1	+32.4	10.8	37.2	88.3	62.0	+26.3
Ability for decision-making	6.6	27.2	91.2	68.4	+22.0	6.6	18.2	93.4	81.0	+12.4
Communication and empathy	3.6	13.2	91.9	81.6	+10.3	1.7	15.7	**98.3**	**83.5**	+14.8
Capacity to tackle difficult situations	2.2	24.3	**93.4**	**66.9**	+26.5	5.8	24.0	**94.2**	**75.2**	+17.0
Conflict mediation	3.7	20.6	**92.6**	**74.3**	+18.3	5.8	23.1	**94.2**	76.1	+18.1
Planning and organising	1.4	12.5	**94.1**	**81.6**	+12.5	4.1	13.2	**94.2**	85.1	+9.1
Ability to achieve resources	14.7	45.5	81.6	49.2	+32.4	23.9	37.5	76.0	72.0	+4.0
Resilience	11.8	40.0	84.6	54.4	+30.2	10.8	29.7	89.3	68.6	+20.7
Ethical sense	3.7	1.5	**92.6**	**92.6**	0	6.7	2.5	**94.2**	**95.9**	−1.7

Note: Figures considered relevant and commented in bold characters.

The highest level of agreement between men and women is found in both their valuation and use of *responsibility* and *ethical sense*. Also remarkable is that the only two characteristics reported to be possessed by women to a higher degree than men are the *ability to get on well with people* (74.2% and 69.4%, respectively) and *cleverness* (82.3% and 81.8%). Importantly, the first of these has been pointed out as one of the most valued leadership features in modern organisations (Bryman 2007; Kezar and Lester 2009; Scott and Webber 2008; Spendlove 2007; Wolverton, Ackerman, and Holt 2005).

Finally, 78.7% of women managers declared valuing quite/much the characteristic of *sensitivity* and 86.7% quite/much to using it, while the parallel scores for men were 85.1% and 90.1%, respectively. It should be noted that the difference between the quite/much valuation and use in both groups is the only negative score obtained, which means this characteristic is used more than it is valued, by both male and female managers.

In sum, women participants identified more training needs than did men participants. *Ability to achieve resources* and *leadership capacity* are the characteristics on which they reported need for training to a higher degree than did men. On the other hand, they rated mastering the *ability to get on well with people* and *intelligence* to a higher degree than did men. *Resilience* stands out in the women participant group as the characteristic with the highest differential between reported degrees of use/possession and importance. On the other hand, *authority* is the least used characteristic and both *responsibility* and *ethical sense* are those in which the highest levels of both use and importance have been found in the two groups.

5. Conclusions

This study suggests that women managers in university organisations do not deploy radically different leadership styles from men. Nevertheless, we found distinctive differences between women and men managers. Women managers in the study prioritised attention to people, the well-being of the group, and the informal aspects of managing to a higher degree than did men. Men managers tended to prioritise decision-making processes and formal task fulfilment to a higher degree than did women. In the women this apparent prioritisation of the collegial/social role over the managerial/technical role could support the notion of a feminine style of leadership that contrasts with a masculine style. In the same way, the *ability to get on well with people,* more used by women, seems to define the predominant leadership profile of female managers as being people not resource centred. By contrast, the more used characteristics of *ability to achieve resources* and *ability for decision-making,* and the little priority paid to *attention to people* by male managers define their predominant technical predilection. Although the capacity to obtain external support and resources – an outstanding characteristic of male managers – should not be undervalued as a component of effective leadership, it was not identified as being one of the most needed characteristics in university organisations. This could explain the decline of the *masculine* forms of leadership in dynamic and complex organisations such as those in the higher education field.

As already concluded in an earlier study (Sánchez-Moreno and López-Yáñez 2008), these differential characteristics do not allow us to suggest a fixed 'feminine' style of leadership as both men and women utilised a range of approaches depending on context. However, some specific traits can be related to the performance of women managers relative to their male colleagues. One of the most outstanding traits evident among the women participants was their orientation towards social relations, as confirmed in the literature. Bensimon (1993) explained this orientation by suggesting that women do not perceive the world so much as about managing the physical, but rather they see it embodied in people and expressed in a psychological and social manner. She suggests that this is consistent with running the world in ways that are more consistent with needs that are felt, than by means of rational control, and thus a significantly different orientation overall to leadership.

Both women and men managers in our study used a wide range of power resources when managing diverse problematic situations, adapting themselves to such situations rather than adopting a stable style. Furthermore, the idea of organisations as social constructions (Alvesson and Deetz 1996; Chia 2003; Willmott 2003) seems to be assumed by both groups in their use of characteristics such as *responsibility*, *ability to get on well with people*, *diplomacy*, *motivation capacity*, *communication and empathy*, *capacity to tackle difficult situations*, *conflict mediation*, and *ethical issues* to a significantly higher degree than *authority* and the *ability to achieve resources* (in the case of women). While women managers in the literature are considered to have a more multitasking orientation or polychronic conception of time in contrast with the men's orientation towards serial worker or monochronic conception (Hargreaves 1994), our enquiry clearly showed a polychronic conception in both groups in relation to managing time and tasks.

Finally, a notable difference was found between women and men managers with regard to the interest and sensitivity shown to our research. Not only was the number of questionnaires received from women remarkably higher – both in relative and absolute terms – but so were their level of motivation and the complexity of their answers. Men managers did not answer the questionnaire or they left the task unfinished more often than women. In sum, although organisational or leadership behaviour cannot be depicted under rigid gendered categories, we can identify some different tendencies evident in men and women managers with regard to how they perceive their leadership role and also the training needs to develop better preparation programmes. Undoubtedly, management practice requires adopting adequate behaviours according to multiple contextual and situational demands. In consequence, any attempt to prepare male and female academics for management positions should attend to a wide spectrum of abilities and skills, including reflection on their own dispositions towards relational or shared approaches to leadership (Scott and Weber 2008; Wolverton, Ackerman, and Holt 2005).

Disclosure statement
No potential conflict of interest was reported by the authors.

Note
1. Sánchez-Moreno, M., Head of the Research Project, 2003–2005, Women in the headship and management of universities: Problems, leadership styles and contributions to organizational development, National Planning of Scientific Research, Development and Technological Innovation, Spanish Ministry of Work and Social Affairs, Women's Institute. Sánchez-Moreno, M., Head of the Research Project, 2006–2010, Management and government of universities: training for good practice, National Planning of Scientific Research, Development and Technological Innovation, Spanish Ministry of Science and Innovation. Project code: SEJ2006-07147/EDUC.

References

Aasen, P., and B. Stensaker. 2007. "Balancing Trust and Technocracy? Leadership Training in Higher Education." *International Journal of Educational Management* 21 (5): 371–383.

Airini, Collings S., L. Conner, K. Mcpherson, E. Midson, and C. Wilson. 2011. "Learning to Be Leaders in Higher Education: What Helps or Hinders Women's Advancement as Leaders in Universities." *Educational Management Administration and Leadership* 39 (1): 44–62.

Alimo-Metcalfe, B., and J. Alban-Metcalfe. 2005. "Leadership: Time for a New Direction?" *Leadership* 1: 51–71.

Alvesson, M., and Y. Billing. 1992. "Gender and Organisation: Towards a Differentiated Understanding." *Organisation Studies* 13 (12): 73–103.

Alvesson, M., and Y. Billing. 1997. *Understanding Gender and Organisations*. London: Sage.

Alvesson, M., and S. Deetz. 1996. "Critical Theory and Postmodernism Approaches to Organisational Studies." In *Handbook of Organisational Studies*, edited by S. T. Clegg, C. Hardi, and W. R. Nord, 191–217. London: Sage.

Ball, S. 2007. "Leadership of Academics in Research." *Educational Management, Administration and Leadership* 35 (4): 449–477.

Bensimon, E. M. 1993. "A Feminist Reinterpretation of President's Definition of Leadership." In *Women in Higher Education: A Feminist Perspective*, edited by J. Glazer, E. M. Bensimon, and B. K. Townsend, 465–474. Nedham Heights, MA: Ginn Press.

Billing, Y. D., and M. Alvesson. 2000. "Questioning the Notion of Feminine Leadership: A Critical Perspective on the Gender Labelling of Leadership." *Gender, Work and Organisation* 7 (3): 144–157.

Blackmore, J. 2005. "'The Emperor Has No Clothes': Professionalism, Performativity and Educational Leadership in High-Risk Postmodern Times." In *Leadership, Gender and Culture in Education: Male and Female Perspectives*, edited by J. Collard and C. Reynolds, 173–194. Maidenhead, UK: Open University Press and McGraw Hill.

Blackmore, J. 2010. "Disrupting Notions of Leadership from Feminist Post-colonial Positions." *International Journal of Leadership in Education* 13 (1): 1–6.

Blackmore, P., and R. Blackwell. 2006. "Strategic Leadership and Academic Development." *Studies in Higher Education* 31 (3): 373–387.

Blackmore, J., and J. Sachs. 2007. *Performing and Reforming Leaders*. New York: SUNY Press.

Bolden, R., G. Petrov, and J. Gosling. 2009. "Distributed Leadership in Higher Education: Rhetoric and Reality." *Educational Management Administration and Leadership* 37 (2): 257–277.

Breakwell, G. M., and M. Tytherleigh. 2008. "UK University Leaders at the Turn of the 21st Century: Changing Patterns in Their Socio-demographic Characteristics." *Higher Education* 56: 109–127.

Bryman, A. 2007. "Effective Leadership in Higher Education: A Literature Review." *Studies in Higher Education* 32 (6): 693–710.

Calabrese, R. L., B. E. Roberts, S. McLeod, R. Niles, K. Christopherson, P. Singh, and M. Berry. 2008. "Emerging Technologies in Global Communication: Using Appreciative Inquiry to Improve the Preparation of School Administrators." *International Journal of Educational Management* 22 (7): 696–709.

Castro, D., and G. Ion. 2011. "Dilemas en el gobierno de las universidades españolas: Autonomía, estructura, participación y desconcentración." *Revista de Educación* 355: 161–183.

Chia, R. 2003. "Organisation Theory as a Postmodern Science." In *The Oxford Handbook of Organisation Theory*, edited by H. Tsoukas and C. Knudsen, 113–140. Oxford: Oxford University Press.

Coleman, M. 2003. "Gender and the Orthodoxies of Leadership." *School Leadership and Management* 23 (3): 325–339.

Coronel Llamas, J. M., E. Moreno, and M. T. Padilla. 2002. "La gestión y el liderazgo como procesos organisativos: Contribuciones y retos planteados desde una óptica de género." *Revista de Educación* 327: 157–168.

Court, M. 2005. "Negotiating and Reconstructing Gendered Leadership Discourses." In *Leadership, Gender and Culture in Education: Male and Female Perspectives*, edited by

J. Collard and C. Reynolds, 3–17. Maidenhead, UK: Open University Hill and McGraw Hill.

Eagly, A. H., and M. C. Johannesen-Schmidt. 2001. "The Leadership Styles of Women and Men." *Journal of Social Issues* 57 (4): 781–797.

Eagly, A. H., W. Wood, and A. B. Diekman. 2000. "Social Role Theory of Sex Differences and Similarities: A Current Appraisal." In *The Developmental Social Psychology of Gender*, edited by T. Eckes and H. M. Trautner, 123–174. Mahwah: Erlbaum.

Frenkel, M., and J. Stretchman. 2006. "Too Much of a Good Thing? Values in Leadership for Educational Organisations." *International Journal of Educational Management* 20 (7): 520–528.

Hargreaves, A. 1994. *Changing Teachers, Changing Times: Teachers Work and Culture in the Postmodern Age*. New York: Teachers College Press.

Kerfoot, D., and S. Whitehead. 1998. "'Boys Own' Stuff: Masculinity and the Management of Further Education." *The Sociological Review* 46: 436–457.

Kezar, A., and J. Lester. 2009. "Supporting Faculty Grassroots Leadership." *Research on Higher Education* 50: 715–740.

Lavié, J. M. 2009. "El liderazgo a debate: nuevas perspectivas sobre un viejo conocido." In *Mujeres dirigentes en la universidad: Las texturas del liderazgo*, edited by M. Sánchez Moreno, 59–79. Zaragoza: Sagardiana.

López-Yáñez, J., and M. Sánchez-Moreno. 2008. "Women Leaders as Agents of Change in Higher Education Organizations." *Gender in Management: An International Journal* 23 (2): 86–102.

Madden, M. 2005. "2004 Division 35 Presidential Address: Gender and Leadership in Higher Education." *Psychology of Women Quarterly* 29 (1): 3–14.

Marshall, J. 1990. *Women Managers: Travellers in a Male World*. Chichester: John Wiley.

Mills, A. 2002. "Studying the Gendering of Organisational Culture over Time: Concerns, Issues and Strategies." *Gender, Work and Organisation* 9 (3): 286–307.

Ministry of Education and Science, Spanish Government. 2007. "Académicas en cifras." http://www.uned.es/rectoras/2007-academicas-en-cifras.pdf.

Mintzberg, H. 1983. *Power In and Around the Organisation*. Upper Saddle River, NJ: Prentice Hall.

Sánchez-Moreno, M., and J. López-Yáñez. 2008. "Poder y liderazgo de mujeres responsables de Instituciones Universitarias." *Revista Española de Pedagogía* 240: 345–363.

Scott, S., and C. F. Webber. 2008. "Evidence-Based Leadership Development: The 4L Framework." *Journal of Educational Administration* 46 (6): 762–776.

Shakeshaft, S. 1989. *Women in Educational Administration*. London: Sage.

Spendlove, M. 2007. "Competencies for Effective Leadership in Higher Education." *International Journal of Educational Management* 21 (5): 407–417.

Tong, R. 1998. *Feminist Thought: A Comprehensive Introduction*. 2nd ed. Boulder, CO: Westview.

Van Ameijde, D. J., P. C. Nelson, J. Billsberry, and N. van Meurs. 2009. "Improving Leadership in Higher Education Institutions: A Distributed Perspective." *Higher Education* 58: 763–779.

White, K., and Ö. Özkanlib. 2011. "A Comparative Study of Perceptions of Gender and Leadership in Australian and Turkish Universities." *Journal of Higher Education Policy and Management* 33 (1): 3–16.

Willmott, H. 2003. "Organisational Theory as a Critical Science? Forms of Analysis and 'New Organisational Forms'." In *The Oxford Handbook of Organisation Theory*, edited by H. Tsoukas and C. Knudsen, 88–112. Oxford: Oxford University Press.

Wolverton, M., R. Ackerman, and S. Holt. 2005. "Preparing for Leadership: What Academic Department Chairs Need to Know." *Journal of Higher Education Policy and Management* 27 (2): 227–238.

Complexities of Vietnamese femininities: a resource for rethinking women's university leadership practices

Van Hanh Thi Do[a] and Marie Brennan[b]

[a]School of Education, University of South Australia, Magill, Australia; [b]College of Education, Victoria University, Melbourne, Australia

This paper develops a dialogical encounter between northern-inspired theorisations of gender and Vietnam's historical and cultural differentiation identified through the presence of matriarchy in ancient societies and its popularity in folklore and contemporary politics. The article draws on interviews with 12 senior women from 8 universities in Northern and Southern Vietnam. Three main themes are explored: (1) the Vietnamese woman as 'general of the interior'; (2) the 'woman behind the throne'; and (3) 'behind a woman is another woman'. These themes illustrate the distinctiveness of a historically produced Vietnamese gender order as reflected in current university women's experience. By providing insights into the complex dynamics of Vietnamese women's 'informal power', as evident in both spheres of home and university, the paper presents a discussion of forms of Vietnamese femininity that contributes to re-theorising Connell's concepts of 'hegemonic masculinity and emphasized femininity'.

Challenges in analysing gender in Vietnam

There are challenges in discussing gender, femininities or masculinities in Vietnam. For a start, there is no term for gender or feminism in the language, and only a relatively small history of feminist-inspired analyses. However, many international loans and grants require official policy changes around gender, largely based on analyses that have emerged from countries in the global North. We do not work from a neat binary between North and South: the term 'Global North' is used to refer to rich countries, while 'Global South' also 'references an entire history of colonialism, neo-imperialism, and differential economic and social change through which large inequalities in living standards, life expectancy, and access to resources are maintained' (Dados and Connell 2012, 13). In *Southern Theory*, Connell (2007) contends that the dominant genres of Northern theories that 'picture the world as it is seen … from the rich capital – exporting countries' obviously does 'matter' (vii). She asserts that we can have social theory that

> … does not claim universality for a metropolitan point of view, does not read from only one direction, does not exclude the experience and social thought of most of humanity, and is not constructed on *terra nullius*. (2007, 47)

She also argues that 'the alternative to "northern theory" is not a unified doctrine from the global South'; rather 'a genuinely global sociology must, at the level of theory as well as empirical research and practical application, be more like a conversation among many voices' (Connell 2006, 262). These views provoked us to explore local conceptualisations of women that might contribute to a wider and more diversified global conversation about gender and higher education leadership. In this paper, we explore a dialogical encounter between Northern theorisation of gender and Vietnam's historical and cultural differentiation of femininities, identified (1) through the presence of matriarchy in ancient societies and the continued popularity of women leaders in folklore and popular culture; and (2) from political uses of women in anti-colonial and modernisation struggles. The insights drawn from this conversation are believed quite helpful in considering the place of women in Vietnamese universities, where there is a difficulty in raising issues of gender equality in public debates about the university.

The data for this article are part of a (the first author's) doctoral thesis, drawn from life-story interviews with 12 senior women from 8 universities in Northern and Southern Vietnam about their experience in work and life. There was no specific criterion for choosing informants except that they were or currently are leaders/managers in Vietnamese universities. Each interview was analysed to identify key themes or patterns of Vietnamese femininity. The project was given ethical clearance by the Ethics Committee of the University of South Australia. To maintain anonymity, position titles are not mentioned since the representation of senior women in university educational leadership is modest. Consistent with Vietnamese naming protocols, first name pseudonyms are used throughout.

After this brief introduction, there are three major sections to this paper. First, folklore is used to discuss the interplay between Vietnamese historical matriarchy and Confucianism in constructing distinctive Vietnamese femininities. The next section is a dialogical encounter between Connell's theorisation of gender, particularly masculinities and femininities, and Vietnamese folklore literature: treated as a cultural source for the distinctiveness of Vietnamese women. The third section provides insights into the complex dynamics of women's 'informal power' in settings of family and university, to foreground arguments on (1) the differentiation of Vietnamese femininities and (2) the under-theorisation of the interrelation nexus between 'informal power' and 'formal power' in gender and educational leadership research. The paper argues that the complexity of Vietnamese femininity emerges from the dynamics of Vietnamese women's 'informal power' evident in both spheres, home and university. This complexity helps to construct certain forms of Vietnamese femininity, which are not adequately accounted for in Connell's (1987, 2009) theorisation of gender order and 'hegemonic masculinity and emphasized femininity'. By using the term 'complexity', we refer to the diversity, contradiction and overlap of Vietnamese femininities manifested in the gender politics of families and universities. The article ends with questions to open up analysis, debate and action in terms of theorising femininities and masculinities in universities in one country with implications for gender debates locally and globally.

Historical matriarchy, Confucianism and Vietnamese women

The literature on Vietnamese folklore plays a crucial role in supporting the argument that 'Vietnam had a matriarchal society' (Drummond and Rystrom 2004, 1) or that 'Vietnam was originally a matriarchy' (Chiricosta 2010, 125). The presence of

Vietnamese matriarchy forms a historico-cultural foundation as well as a nationalistic aspiration for Vietnamese womanhood.

According to Vietnamese folk literature, a unique Vietnamese femininity originates from the legend of Lạc Long Quân and ÂuCơ who are believed to be the Father and Mother of the Vietnamese People's ancestors known as the Hùng Kings, the 18th of whom died in 258 BCE. In spite of the numerous ways such folklore has been orally transmitted and subject to possible distortions, the story of ÂuCơ 'testifies to the presence of an original "matriarchy" in North Vietnam', as well as 'the uniquely high status' of Vietnamese women' which is believed to be 'an emblem of national distinctiveness' (Chiricosta 2010, 125). One of the most distinctive characteristics of Vietnamese women is that they 'feature prominently as warriors and defenders', emerging as 'key icons of heroism in the fight against Chinese cultural and political domination', patriarchy and discrimination against women (Chiricosta 2010, 125). Examples include: The Trung Sisters (14–43 CE) who led a rebellion to drive out the Chinese in around 40 CE; Lady Triệu Thị Trinh (226–248 CE) who led a revolt against the Wu of China (AD 222–280); Queen Regent Ỷ Lan who successfully ruled the country; and the historical figure of Liễu Hạnh later recognised as an incarnation of the Mother Goddess. LêThịNhâmTuyết (1987) contends that historical documents about those female figures such as 'social anthropological documents recorded scattered in old files during the first millennium ... affirm that until the tenth century the role and social status of Vietnamese women remained remarkable' (95).

This tradition lived on: the spirit of such honoured characters was called upon during the wars against France and America, aiming to mobilise women to the national revolutionary cause, and then again in the post-war period for the national development cause and most recently for modernisation of the country. With strong 'masculine' attributes (bravery, heroic, resilience, indomitability and patriotism) constantly encouraged through Vietnamese women's movements launched by the Vietnamese Women Union,[1] Vietnamese women appear as 'a metaphor for the entire nation's struggle for Vietnamese independence' (Chiricosta 2010, 125). Working in the fields at night and fighting during the daytime, Vietnamese women were 'not simply replacing men, but more importantly, strengthening the nation/family by directing their feminine virtues' to the cause of national liberation and protection (Pettus 2003, 46). This strong image of Vietnamese women is respectfully described in 'eight golden Vietnamese words' (or four golden phrases) awarded by President HồChí Minh in March 1965: 'Heroic, Indomitable, Faithful and Responsible', and women's invaluable contributions were acknowledged by a number of prestigious awards, of which the highest is the 'Heroic Vietnamese Mother'.

The existence of matriarchal culture, with a 'double kinship system' in Vietnam, 'combined matrilineal and patrilineal patterns of family structure and assigned equal importance to both lines' – which continued until the eleventh century (Lý Dynasty) when Confucianism officially became the state philosophical ideology (Chiricosta 2010, 125). More than a religion, Confucianism was considered as a 'mandate for an entire way of life' (Bergman 1975, 20), promoting a social hierarchy based on the leading principle: 'namtônnữti' – man respectable, woman despicable (BùiTrânPhượng 2011, 2–9). However, it needs to be noted that, in spite of the strong influence of Confucianism and the harsh and strict rules of feudalism, 'virtually every dynasty produced at least one woman who took part in politics and state affairs, served as a military leader, or distinguished herself nationally in public office' (Duong 2001, 255). The clashes of Confucianism, feudalism, colonialism, socialism and historical matriarchy resulted in an ambivalent and contradictory set of Vietnamese femininities.

Dialogical encounters between Connell's theorisation of gender and Vietnamese folklore literature

Gender relations occur everywhere, from formal institutions such as schools or state offices to informal milieux such as markets and streets. Any institution is always 'structured in terms of gender and can be characterized by their gender regimes' in which 'the state of play in gender relations' occurs (Connell 1987, 120). We are not free to make gender entirely in the way we like; instead, 'our gender practice is powerfully shaped by the gender order in which we find ourselves' (Connell 2009, 74). Connell's theorisation of gender order/regime has been widely acknowledged as 'a preliminary taxonomy of gender relations', which not only demonstrates 'important nodes for analysis but guides for practice' because of 'Connell's emphasis on the dynamics of practice in the context of multiplicity and contradiction' (Hollway 1994, 247–248; see also Kojima 2001 and Alsop, Fitzsimons, and Lennon 2002). Connell's concept of a 'gender order' is particularly relevant to our research as it is neither essentialist nor universalist, allowing for production and reproduction of power relations while focussing on the specific practices by which this occurs in diverse cultural settings, including in Vietnam. The concept is also analytically helpful to unpack the practices which are specific to the institution and how they link to wider practices in the society.

Breaking the concept of a gender order into four main distinguishable but inseparable dimensions, Connell (2009) develops a four-dimensional framework to provide a broad map for thinking about 'gender relations of contemporary industrial, post-industrial and global society' (76): (1) power relations; (2) division of labour; (3) emotional relations (Cathexis); and (4) symbolism, culture and discourse. These point to ways to 'identify and map the structures involved' in a gender order as gender relations are 'internally complex … involving multiple structures' (Connell 2009, 75).

According to Connell (1987), power relations are embodied in social hierarchies from the state to families, and through every facet of life, where 'the main axis of the power structure of gender is the general connection of authority with masculinity' (109). Bureaucracies, or university leadership in this case, function as sites for 'the mobilization of masculine bias', which is exercised through such processes as selection and promotion of staff (Burton 1992). Another site is the domestic sphere (Franzway 1997), where gender relationships are 'so extended in time, so intensive in contact, so dense in their interweaving of economic, emotion, power and resistance' (Connell 1987, 121) that the domestic sphere is central to the production of gender relations.

To provide more insight into the dynamics of power relations, Connell (1987, 1995) develops the concept of 'hegemonic masculinity', which has been influential in analysing gender, especially masculinities (Demetriou 2001; Hearn and Morrell 2012; Wedgwood 2009). For Connell, hegemonic masculinity is a pattern of gender practices which guarantees and supports men's domination over women and over other marginalised men; however, it is not 'a self-reproducing system' but 'a historical process' (Connell and Messerschmidt 2005, 844). Hegemonic masculinity is 'always constructed in relation to various subordinated masculinities as well as in relation to women' as 'the interplay between forms of masculinity is an important part of how a patriarchal social order works' (Connell 1987, 183). Although favoured in social power relations, men do not evenly enjoy privileges in their labour segregation; other social regulations based on class, 'race', and qualities of masculinities divide them into different groups with different levels of privileges. Connell (1995) proposes four major forms of masculinities, including: (1) hegemony (heterosexual); (2) subordination (homosexual); (3) complicity (referring to those who are not actually meeting the normative standards of masculinity); and (4) marginalisation (always relative to *authorisation* of the hegemonic masculinity of the dominant group) (76–81, italics original). These forms are 'historical mobile' and 'subject to change', she contends.

Despite acknowledging that 'actual femininities in our society are more diverse than actual masculinities' (187), Connell (1987) has not yet theorised multiple forms of femininities. Instead, she argues:

> At the level of mass social relations ... forms of femininity are defined clearly enough. It is the global subordination of women to men that provides an essential basis for differentiation. One form is defined around compliance with this subordination and is oriented to accommodating the interests and desires of men ... Others are defined centrally by strategies of resistance or forms of non-compliance. Others again are defined by complex strategic combinations of compliance, resistance and co-operation. (183–184)

She asserts 'there is no femininity that is hegemonic in the sense that dominant form of masculinity is hegemonic among men' (183). However, in reflecting on such theorisations in the Vietnamese context, there appear some critical differentiations that need to be accounted for.

First of all, it is important to note that the overall picture of power relations in the Vietnamese context is not much different from Connell's argument above. The main patterns of power relations remain those of male dominance and patriarchy as comprehensively captured in one of the famous poems *BánhTrôiNước* (the floating cake):

The Floating Cake[2]
My body is white; my fate, softly rounded,
Rising and sinking like mountains in streams.
Whatever way hands may shape me,
At centre my heart is red and true.

Using the metaphor of floating cakes, the famous feminist poet Hồ Xuân Hương demonstrates the 'fate' of Vietnamese women. Each step in the cake-making process illustrates a stage of a Vietnamese woman's life, from childhood to adulthood. The poem pictures a woman with her whole life dependent on men's hands. They not only 'knead' women's lives to whatever size and shape they want, but also require women to be submissive and subordinated with a heart that is 'red and true'.

Yet, along with such a major pattern of power relations, there remains another pattern emerging that may not be as strong but is not subtle either: women's power over men in the domestic sphere, both symbolic and practical. Such a distinctive form of the power of women in the family economy historically constructs a form of power in which the voice of women is more powerful than that of their men in the domestic sphere. This special role is praised through the title, *NộiTướng*, general of the interior, who 'lock[s] the key and open[s] the drawer of treasury' (Duong 2001, 227) and/or who has the highest responsibility to control and manage internal affairs including finance.

This pattern of power is also found in gender symbolism that is transmitted in Vietnamese language by the word *cái* (female) in a compound noun. *Cái* is used to refer to *fertilising ability* or *reproductive capacity*. Interestingly, when *cái* comes after a noun to form a compound noun, it not only expresses the sense of *fertilise* but also refers to something very large and very important. For example, *sôngcái* (a big river), *trôngcái* (the largest drum in a drum kit) or *đườngcái* (highway or inter-communal/-district roads). There is no equivalent term for *masculine* or *male* in such usages. This seems to predicate a consistency between this form of language and the power and high status of women in folklore stories about historical matriarchy.

The role of 'general of interior' is also captured in the poem 'Love for my wife' written by TúXương in the nineteenth century, in which he expresses gratitude to his wife who replaces him as a family breadwinner by 'trading at the riverbank all the year round to nurture five children and one husband' (Tran 2008, 3). Women as household heads were common during the French and American wars when almost all men were mobilised for the front. They were recognised as 'the arbiters quasi-exclusively' (O'Harrow 1995, 164) in the national economy by running small businesses as active and successful merchants (see also Drummond and Rydstrom 2004). This practice did not change much after the colonial wars because thousands of men never returned and many men returned home injured. This role of women is still relevant in the contemporary context of Vietnam (see Hoang and Yeoh 2011).

It is not difficult to find proverbs and folk songs and stories about men who are bullied at home or who are not able to act as 'king'. Nor is it difficult to find stories about women who replace men and occupy the elite and powerful position in the domestic sphere, such as: *Nhấtvợ, nhìtrời* (Wife first, God after). This form of feminine power is also evident in the relationship between a stepmother and her husband's children, where the husband's voice is often ignored or unheard in this triangular relationship.

The contested dynamics of power relations between different forms of femininities is profoundly evident in the relationship between daughter-in-law and her husband's mother, in which the husband's mother uses her power to 'mistreat' or 'maltreat' the daughter-in-law (Phạm 1999). As Werner (2004) observes:

> [m]other and daughter-in-law relations are marked by parent/child terms of address. Mother is the 'parent', not a lateral relative as implied in the English 'in-law' terminology. This gives Mother higher status and seniority, while conferring a junior status on the new addition to the family. (28)

This higher status of the husband's mother is reinforced when she plays both roles of being a carrier and a maintainer of Confucianism. By using Confucian teachings to exert her power in the domestic sphere, she is often known as 'King's Mother' in terms of her harsh and strict supervision of her daughter-in-law who is required to meet the traditional standard of a self-sacrificing mother, devoted daughter-in-law and dedicated wife (NgôThịNgânBình 2004). The status of the son/husband is ambiguous between these two women (Werner 2004), seen in the dilemma of deciding which is most important: love (his wife) or filial piety (his mother). Often, the Confucian filial piety code does not permit the husband to act against his mother by expressing his commitment to his wife.

According to Connell (1987), 'no pressure is set up to negate or subordinate other forms of femininity in the way hegemonic masculinity must negate other masculinities' (187). Nevertheless, the overlapping authority of women in the Vietnamese domestic sphere discussed here illustrates the complexity in power relations both between and within genders, which provides a necessary basis for differentiation between the Vietnamese context and the contexts about which Connell writes. The domination and oppression by the husband's mother of her daughter-in-law and the step-mother of her husband's children is recognised at the level of mass social relations as a harsh practice which is no less contested than the power relations of men on women. This kind of mother's/wife's power amongst Vietnamese women constructs specific forms of femininity and masculinity which are different from those in Connell's (1987) theory of 'hegemonic masculinity and emphasized femininity'. Additionally, with the growth of a monetary economy, women's capacity to maintain the family economy as head of the household through retail business has reinforced their power in the domestic sphere and created more complexity in the dynamics of power relations.

In examining how such a form of gender relations affects gender practices in Vietnamese universities, we are able to see something of the distinctiveness of the historically produced Vietnamese gender order as played out in the gender regime of universities.

Dynamics of Vietnamese femininity as evident in women's university leadership

This section explores the dynamics of women's 'informal power' in the settings of family and university, and argues for the differentiation of Vietnamese femininity as well as the under-theorisation of the interrelation nexus between 'informal power' and 'formal power' in gender and educational leadership research. This section is organised under three sub-headings: (1) Vietnamese women and the 'general of the interior'; (2) the 'woman behind the throne'; and (3) 'behind a woman is another woman'.

Vietnamese women as 'generals of the interior'

The military title 'General' provides a descriptor of Vietnamese women's power and position in the domestic space. However, the real power of the 'general of the interior' is often confined to the interior and hidden in external relations to 'save face for the husband' for the sake of keeping family harmony. What follows are two narratives from Đào and Vy that provide insights into how Vietnamese senior women engage as the 'general of the interior'.

The first story from Đào describes her mother as the most powerful person in orienting and deciding her higher education and career. Đào's mother, in her words, is a woman who is 'very smart, nimble, responsible, and decisive'. In her family, her mother is the person who has 'full responsibility' to 'decide all domestic decisions despite my father being the breadwinner'. She recalled her childhood here:

> Honestly, I was a good looking girl and had abilities in the arts. I was crazy with the dream of making art. I loved singing and dancing so I participated in every artistic activity held by the schools. It may be the reason why I was not an excellent student at secondary and high school. My mother yielded to me a lot. Even my grandmother said to my mother 'I do not care what you will do, if she still keeps thinking of taking up that 'outcast' (xướng ca vô loài) career, do not blame me [for what I may cause if you fail]' (nếu nó cứ vương vấn trong đầu đi làm cái nghề xướng ca vô loài thì mày đừng có trách tao). So my mother wiped my mind of any thinking about that career. She told me 'do not think about arts, study only'. As I was good at literature,

> I really wanted to enroll in Tổng hợp văn (Faculty of Literature) to study journalism. I liked travelling. I thought, if I could not do art, I would become a journalist to travel … However, my mother did not agree. She did not allow me to pursue journalism as she thought I was too romantic and often spoke about things that were not practical and suitable for a girl, a woman in this society. Instead, she advised me to choose this profession [her current area]. In the first year of the university program, I had a literature subject; my teachers often said to me that I was sitting in the wrong class because my score was always far higher than my classmates. They said my seat should have been in the literature faculty. I said I also thought so and I wished to be in the literature faculty, but my mother did not permit so I had to accept [it].

The first point underscored here is the role and power of women in the family through the presence of Đào's grandmother. In one sentence, Đào describes the ascendancy of the mother in the family through the relationship between the husband's mother (her grandmother) and the daughter-in-law (her mother). The phrase 'do not blame me' is not simply a warning but also invokes the power of the husband's mother to evaluate the responsibilities of the daughter-in-law.

The second point to note is the mother's domination over her children's education. In reshaping the children's desires in a direction she thinks is best, she is a policy-maker for the family, regulating 'have-to-dos' and 'not-to-dos'. Đào's mother, in Đào's words, is 'extremely dominant in making decisions' about her study regarding what is suitable and what is not in her preparation for a 'good' future. Obeying the mother's decisions is seen as a moral duty for children, and satisfying a mother's expectations and respecting her wishes is one of the child's duties so as to fulfil the requirements of filial piety.

Importantly, the continuity of a mother's interference in her children's life reveals the strength and vitality of a mother's power. More nuances in this theme can be found in another story that Đào recalled about the first steps of her career. She said:

> In spite of graduating at the university with excellent results, I was refused the opportunity to stay and work at the university because they did not want to receive a female. At that time, a university in […] offered me a lecturer position. After the war, [that university] were seriously lacking teaching staff in my area. However, my mother did not agree to let me go. She said I could not go so far away because I was a girl. I had to find a job somewhere that was near home. Taking the home as the centre, the radius from my home to the workplace could not be farther than a few kilometres. Later I finally found a job in an institution which was not far from my house.

Making sense of this mother's interference cannot rely on the explanation of the child 'lacking experience' as Đào assumes. In constructing gender identity, Đào's mother uses her authority as a mother, her knowledge and experience to decide and judge what is and is not suitable for a girl (Đào). As a consequence, Đào was not given any space either to develop her hobbies and capacities or to pursue the study area she wished. Even finishing university in her 20s was not considered a milestone for Đào to access the right to make independent decisions about her life. The authority of her mother remained even after society recognised her as a mature person who could access her civil and political rights, such as the right to vote.

Not only influencing her teenage years, her mother continues to influence Đào's life after marriage. After Đào's husband passed away, her mother was diagnosed with cancer and whilst the mother was in the hospital for treatment, she advised Đào to change her job:

> Before passing away, my mother advised me to shift my career into teaching. In her opinion, teaching would lighten me up as it was a joyful job. I followed my mother's advice and became a lecturer in the university where my mother had worked.

What would have happened if Đào's mother had not influenced her? What would her life have been now? It is impossible to predict; however, she would not have become a senior manager in a leadership position in university education. Her mother's authority did shape her options to take up her current position in leadership.

A final point here is the absence of Đào's father in family issues. The father's silence illustrates Đào's comment about the domination of her mother in the domestic sphere. As Đào says, her mother 'makes decisions from A to Z' related to domestic issues, but 'when moving out of the domestic sphere … my mother always steps back and stands behind my father to let him perform as the household head'. In her words, this behaviour is very 'tactful and delicate', which 'is only recognized by the family members'. The hidden power of the mother as a 'general of the interior' and the dependence of men on women in maintaining their hegemonic masculinity and patriarchy in both social and domestic spheres is again revealed.

On the same theme, another senior woman, Vy, asserts that 'actually, women are family organizers'. She gives an example to clarify her comment that 'my family's dining time is very flexible. It depends on my working schedule'. According to Vy, her husband and children do not feel uncomfortable with her arrangements nor her working schedule. 'They never make any complaints. They often sit quietly [lặnglặng] to wait for dinner'. Their compliance tells a story of a pattern of dependence of men on women taking care of their personal and daily needs. Vy's husband retired since they got married, so she became the family pillar in terms of economy and her children's education. Simply put, she was not only the key decision-maker in her university, but in her family as well. Vy's story reinforces the presence of the 'general of the interior' in normal Vietnamese family life.

To sum up, Đào's and Vy's stories have provided insights into how matriarchy influences power relations in the domestic sphere and its interdependent relationship with patriarchy. Being the prop and stay of the home on which men rely to maintain their wellbeing and daily needs, and making decisions on almost all domestic affairs from physical labour to emotional labour, women appear much more decisive and powerful than men. However, this practice is still undervalued by men and/or sometimes ignored by women in the shadow of cultural beliefs 'Xấuchàng, hổai' (the husband's disgrace is the wife's shame). Therefore, although women are often decision-makers for internal affairs 'from A to Z', they 'step back and stand behind' men and let them 'perform as the household head' (Đào's story). This practice reflects conflicts and clashes in the paradox of power between women and men that need more attention in Connell's 'hegemonic masculinity and emphasized femininity'. The notion of the 'general of the interior' is not the only practice which requires further theoretical work. The next discussion – women behind the throne – is further evidence for depicting a distinctiveness of Vietnamese femininity as well as the need for such theoretical work.

Women behind the throne

Analysing the stories of senior women reveals a strong theme of the power of the woman who stands behind her husband's leadership to help and/or control his authority: the 'women behind the throne'. This theme is drawn from stories narrated by two informants from the same university. Whilst one informant retells her own story as a victim, the other talks about it as evidence for the intrusion of personal relationships in university leadership regarding selection and promotion of senior managers.

In order to maintain confidentiality of the informants, the two informants whose stories are presented in this discussion are not mentioned even by their pseudonyms. Instead, they are presented with another code based on the time order they participated in the interviews. Cutting off cross-referencing between sections or other papers eliminates the possibility of identification.

The theme 'women behind the throne' is first mentioned as a critical incident for SW02. She was a potential dean at her university. The incident occurred when her new university president recruited deputies for his presidential management board. A recommended list of prospective candidates was announced and a survey poll was held. SW02's name was on that list. When the result of the poll was disclosed, she was shortlisted as the highest voted candidate. She also gained the highest credibility in comparison with other female counterparts. In spite of 'having the highest number of confidential votes and satisfying all the necessary and sufficient conditions in terms of age, experience, expertise, and achievements', SW02 was not the person selected for the position of deputy president, refused without any specific reasons given. However, through her networks and other information channels, SW02 understood that she was not selected for a very particular reason. She smiled and said:

> A manager of the human resource department tells me that 'the boss chooses you, but the boss lady does not agree'. The president is a person who understands other people as well as himself (biếtngườibiết ta). He understands very clearly what I am: responsible, capable, credible, faithful, and serious minded. He knows my validity but he does not use me. He listened to his wife as he may reckon that it would be too risky if he let me sit side by side with him on the university management board. He nominated a very normal woman in terms of experience, capacities, and achievements. She has nothing to excel or to highlight BUT she is his wife's friend.

SW02's story was also repeated in SW04's narrative. The consistency between the two different interviews about one 'boss lady' or 'first lady' (Sếpbà) reinforces the significance of SW02's story and signifies another difference of Vietnamese femininity. According to SW04:

> Since he became the university president, it could be said that his wife was his counsellor or his right hand woman who helped him in organizing human resources for his leadership cabinet and stabilizing the university situation. For example, she phoned twice and each call lasted over an hour to discuss what the president intended to do to reform my department as a result of criticism of my male boss' weak points and incapacities.

> Almost all of the recruitment for deputies of the presidential management board occurred as she planned. For example, without her lobby, I think nobody voted for the current female deputy as nobody thought of her when the president commenced staff selections for his presidential cabinet. The reason was she had nothing special in terms of capacities, qualifications, and achievements. However, she was still nominated because she was the boss lady's friend, and she was not beautiful (smile).

> No wife wants another woman who is more active and intelligent than her husband to become his assistant. In addition, nobody wants to have a beautiful woman working beside her husband. Consequently, this woman (SW02) was pushed far away.

There are three consistent points in their stories. The first is the interference of the 'first lady' in her husband's leadership. The second is the unexpected nomination of the current female deputy in terms of her capacity and achievements. The last is the woman (SW02) who is 'pushed far away' from the chair of deputy. These three points reveal the power of a woman behind the scenes, who has no apparent formal authority, but great influence over her husband. This kind of power is described by an old Vietnamese proverb: 'His command is not as powerful as her gong'. The assured authority of the wife is exercised in the shadow of her husband's power. Behind the university leader, the 'boss lady' does have a hand in arranging and organising her husband's cabinet as she wants. Her invisible authority is apparent through her lobbying for a woman who has 'nothing special' to be selected as a deputy. It is obvious that the dominance of the 'boss lady' has institutionalised the structure of leadership practice of the university as her husband's shadow. In this way, 'unofficial power' is actually translated into 'official power' and possibly shapes a significant part of the gender regime of universities. This kind of 'power outside the symbols of power' (Roces 2009) is inconsistent with Connell's (1987) argument, in which she proposes that 'the concentration of social power in the hands of men leaves limited scope for women to construct institutionalized power relationships over other women' (187). This form of Vietnamese femininity reveals an absence in Connell's theory of femininity, where she claims that 'all forms of femininity in this society are constructed in the context of the overall subordination of women to men' (186–187). This absence is reinforced by a third theme about the distinctiveness of Vietnamese women – Behind a woman is another woman – which is the focus of the next discussion.

Behind a woman is another woman

This title is extracted from another senior woman, Xuân's response about how professional women balance their work and family life. 'Behind a woman is another woman' refers to physical and mental support from female kinship, as well as female paid assistance. Female paid assistance emerges as the normal way to balance senior women's commitments to both family and university. Out of 12 informants:

- Four had full-time home help (live-in servants);
- One employed a full-time home help during a two-year pursuit of extra evening classes;
- Three others hired part-time or seasonal home help;
- The other four managed their domestic burdens by themselves; of these one was a single woman, one was a widow, one was a divorced woman and one had only one child.

Having a domestic servant was seen as slavery in feudal times due to the division of class and class discrimination. This type of job declined during the period when Vietnam shifted to social collectivism. However, this kind of labour has returned because of work demands, but under a new name 'ngườigiúpviệcgiađình' (home help). A home help is still supposed to cover all of the housework that a domestic servant did previously.

According to Thu, if women want to advance in their professional careers 'they need to have a home help'. For Thu, having a home help is crucial to ameliorating the high demands for commitment to both university and family. As she says 'I am very lucky to have a trusty home help, so I almost do not have to think at all about shopping and cooking. I think it is one of my advantages in advancing my career'. Similarly, Hà confirms that she would not have advanced as far as she did in leadership had she not employed a home help because 'the university workload was so heavy that I hardly ever got home before 9 p.m. I was always the last person who turned off the lights and left the office'. She describes this devotion to university work as requiring her to sacrifice some of her family responsibility.

However, it is undeniable that the labour purchase of paid home help involves unequal power between employers (intellectual women) and employees (poor and/or country women and country girls who have not finished their schooling). In such a relationship, the woman 'behind' takes up a subordinate and/or compliant femininity and the woman 'at the front' is more dominant. Connell's theory on this point does not account for the two forms of femininity evident in 'behind a woman is another woman'. Why is a woman 'behind' another senior woman not as powerful as a woman 'behind' a senior man (the throne)? The differentiations between these forms of femininities as well as the different notions of being 'behind' have not yet been accounted for in either the theory of femininities specifically or theories of gender in general.

Questions to open up analysis, debate and action beyond universities

Emerging from the discussion of the three themes, we can begin to see how the distinctiveness of a historically produced Vietnamese gender order is reflected in the gender politics of Vietnamese universities, as well as how it has been translated into the construction of the university gender regime. The complex dynamics of women's 'informal power' has constructed a certain 'order' of Vietnamese femininity and masculinity which is differentiated from or has not yet been theorised in Connell's theory of 'hegemonic masculinity and emphasized femininity'.

As Schippers (2007) comments, the notions of multiple masculinities and hegemonic masculinity proposed by Connell 'have been taken up as central constructs in the sociology of gender' (85). Connell and Messerschmidt (2005) also agree that 'the resulting six pages in Gender and Power ... on "hegemonic masculinity and emphasized femininity" became the most cited source for the concept of hegemonic masculinity' (830–831). However, they also admit that

> The concept of hegemonic masculinity was originally formulated in tandem with a concept of hegemonic femininity – soon renamed 'emphasized femininity' to acknowledge the asymmetrical position of masculinities and femininities in a patriarchal gender order. In the development of research on men and masculinities, this relationship has dropped out of focus. (848)

Femininity is still 'under-theorised' and 'a compelling and empirically useful conceptualization of hegemonic femininity and multiple, hierarchical femininities *as central to male dominant gender relations has not yet been developed*' (Schippers 2007, 85, italics original) in spite of many important attempts to theorise female masculinities and male femininities (Francis 2010) or 'gender monoglossia', 'gender heteroglossia' (Francis 2012; Fuller 2014).

The selection of data analysed here, only enough to illustrate key points of debate about senior women, poses important challenges to explaining the place of women in Vietnamese universities. It is clear that diverse femininities are resourced from multiple sources with historical traces in the local culture and those universities, whilst still strongly patriarchal, are not necessarily fixed in a rigid gender order but are open to the construction of different gendered relations. This is not to deny the significant struggles that lie ahead for both men and women if more equal relations of power are to emerge. The history of Vietnam, with long periods of colonisation and anti-colonisation struggles, has local cultural resources which can interplay with new developments across the globe. Yet the histories of Confucianism intertwined with interaction with modernist forms of patriarchy still play out, needing resources from socialist, warrior women and historical folk literature as well as global networks to continue the struggle. Being a 'general of the interior', a 'woman behind the throne' or relying on unequal relations with other women are not significant enough roles to challenge continued patriarchal domination. They do not result in shifts that recognise that leadership practices need to change more broadly, not merely in the practices of the current incumbents.

However, this article's exploration of the complexity of Vietnamese femininities can be considered as providing new sources for theorising multiple forms of femininities. The distinctiveness of Vietnamese femininity is formed by historical matriarchy, rooted in ancient histories, maintained in Vietnamese folklore literature, promoted in national revolutions and embedded in contemporary gender practices. Emerging from this analysis is an image of Vietnamese women as strong, active, capable, independent, heroic and powerful in both public and domestic spheres. These can result in shifts from the accounts given in this paper of aspects of women's power that remain hidden, constrained and oppressed even when they are holding senior positions. Such complex and shifting forms of femininity appear not to have been accounted for yet in Connell's definition of the forms of femininity. Nor does the form of femininity in which the disharmonious relationship between husband's mother and daughter-in-law is noted as an always-critical-and-unavoidable problem. These forms are, evidently, constructing some kind of hegemony over other forms of femininity as well as masculinity. The question is: Is there any possibility that patterns of femininity are socially defined not in contradistinction but in parallel, symmetry, compensation or correlation to those of masculinity? And, is there any possibility it is shaped not only in the form of opposition and conflict but also in the form of consistency and compensation, as in the theory of yin-yang?

Finally, power relations and their dynamics in gender politics need to be questioned. Power, as a dimension of gender, is often connected with patriarchy and formal or legislative authority in political systems, often demonstrated as the embodiment of masculinity. However, on the evidence of this study, the idea of 'power outside the symbols of power' (Roces 2009) has become important. The intervention of 'informal/unofficial power' into 'formal/official power' signifies a sense of institutions in which 'formal power' that is recognised does involve 'informal power', and domestic authority does not only embody male patriarchy. The interrelation nexus between 'informal power' and 'formal power' regarding the formation of gender relations is still undertheorised in gender and educational leadership research.

Disclosure statement

No potential conflict of interest was reported by the author.

Notes

1. Some of the most famous women's movements are 'Five Goods' in 1961, 'Three Responsibilities' in 1965, and 'Good at national affairs, responsible for family affairs' in 1989.
2. Translated by John Balaban cited in Trần Văn Dinh (2001).

References

Alsop, Rachel, Fitzsimons, Annette, and Lennon, Kathleen. 2002. *Theorizing Gender*. Malden, MA: Polity Press.

Bergman, Arlene Eisen. 1975. *Women of Vietnam*. San Francisco: People Press.

BùiTrânPhượng. 2011. "PhụnữvàgiớitrongtruyềnthốngViệtnam [Women and gender in Vietnamese tradition]." *Newsletters of Gender and Society Research Centre of HoaSen University* 3: 1–32.

Burton, Clare. 1992. "Merit and Gender: Organisations and the Mobilization of Masculine Bias." In *Gendering Organisational Analysis*, edited by Albert J. Mills and Peta Tancred, 185–196. London: SAGE.

Chiricosta, Alessandra. 2010. "Following the Trail of the Fairy-Bird: The Search for a Uniquely Vietnamese Women's Movement." In *Women's Movements in Asia: Feminisms and Transnational Activism*, edited by Mina Roces and Louise Edwards, 124–143. London: Routledge: Taylor & Francis Group.

Connell, Raewyn. 1987. *Gender and Power*. Sydney: Allen & Unwin.

Connell, Raewyn. 1995. *Masculinities*. Crows Nest, N.S.W: Allen & Unwin.

Connell, Raewyn. 2006. "Northern Theory: The Political Geography of General Social Theory." *Theory and Society* 35 (2): 237–264.

Connell, Raewyn. 2007. *Southern Theory*. Cambridge: Polity Press.

Connell, Raewyn. 2009. *Gender in World Perspective*. 2nd ed. Cambridge: Polity Press.

Connell, Raewyn, and James W. Messerschmidt. 2005. "Hegemonic Masculinity: Rethinking the Concept." *Gender and Society* 19 (6): 829–859.

Dados, Nour, and Raewyn Connell. 2012. "The Global South." *Contexts* 11 (1): 12–13. http://contexts.sagepub.com.

Demetriou, Demetrakis Z. 2001. "Connell's Concept of Hegemonic Masculinity: A Critique." *Theory and Society* 30 (3): 337–361.

Drummond, Lisa, and Helle Rystrom. 2004. *Gender Practices in Contemporary Vietnam*. Singapore: Singapore University Press.

Duong, Wendy N. 2001. "Gender Equality and Women's Issues in Vietnam: The Vietnamese Women – Warrior and Poet." *Pacific Rim Law & Policy Journal* 10 (2): 191–326.

Francis, Becky. 2010. "Re/theorising Gender: Female Masculinity and Male Femininity in the Classroom." *Gender and Education* 22 (5): 477–490.

Francis, Becky. 2012. "Gender Monoglossia, Gender Heteroglossia: The Potential of Bakhtin's Work for Re-Conceptualising Gender." *Journal of Gender Studies* 21 (1): 1–15.

Franzway, Suzanne. 1997. "Making Feminist Politics: Gender and Power in the Trade Union Movement." PhD diss., Flinders University of South Australia.

Fuller, Kay. 2014. "Gender Educational Leadership Beneath the MonoglossicFaçade." *Gender and Education* 26 (4): 321–337.

Hearn, Jeff, and Robert Morrell. 2012. "Reviewing Hegemonic Masculinities and Men in Sweden and South Africa." *Men and Masculinities* 15 (3): 3–10.

Hoang, LanAnh, and Brenda S. A. Yeoh. 2011. "Breadwinning Wives and 'Left-Behind' Husbands: Men and Masculinities in the Vietnamese Transnational Family." *Gender & Society* 25 (6): 717–739.

Hollway, Wendy. 1994. "Separation, Integration and Difference: Contradictions in a Gender Regime." In *Power/Gender: Social Relations in Theory and Practice*, edited by H. L. Radtke and H. J. Stam, 247–269. London: SAGE.

Kojima, Yu. 2001. "In the Business of Cultural Reproduction: Theoretical Implications of the Mail-order Bride Phenomenon." *Women's Studies International Forum* 24 (2): 199–210.

LêThịNhâmTuyết. 1987. "Đặcthùgiới ở Việt Nam vàbảnsắcdântộc – Nhìntừgócđộnhânhọcxãhội [Vietnamese gender features and ethnic identity from the perspective of social anthropology]." In *LịchsửphongtràophụnữViệtnam* [The history of Vietnamese women's movements], edited by LêThịNhâmTuyết, 94–101. Hanoi: NhàxuấtbảnPhụnữ [Women Publisher].

NgôThịNgânBình. 2004. "The Confucian Four Feminine Virtues (Tứđức): The Old versus the New – Thừakế versus Pháthuy." In *Gender Practices in Contemporary Vietnam*, edited by Lisa Drummond and Helle Rydstrom, 47–73. Singapore: Singapore University Press.

O'Harrow, Stephen. 1995. "Vietnamese Women and Confucianism: Creating Spaces from Patriarchy." In *'Male' and 'Female' in Developing Southeast Asia*, edited by Wazir Jahan Karim, 161–180. Oxford: Berg.

Pettus, Ashley. 2003. *Between Sacrifice and Desire: National Identity and the Governing of Femininity in Vietnam.* New York: Routledge.

Phạm, VănBích. 1999. *The Vietnamese Family in Change: The Case of the Red River Delta.* London: Curzon Press.

Roces, Mina. 2009. "Power Outside the Symbols of Power." In *Women in Asia*, edited by Louise Adwards and Mina Roces, 20–45. London: Routledge.

Schippers, Mimi. 2007. "Recovering the Feminine Other: Masculinity, Femininity, and Gender Hegemony." *Theory and Society* 36 (1): 85–102.

Tran, Phi Phuong. 2008. "Balancing Work and Family Roles: Perspectives of Vietnamese Professional Women." PhD thesis, University of South Australia.

Trần Văn Dinh. 2001. "The Cleansing Power of Poetry." *War, Literature, and the Arts* 13 (1–2): 328–334.

Wedgwood, Nikki. 2009. "Connell's Theory of Masculinities – Its Origins and Influences on the Study of Gender." *Journal of Gender Studies* 18 (4): 329–339.

Werner, Jayne. 2004. "Managing Womanhoods in the Family: Gendered Subjectivities and the State in the Red River Delta in Vietnam." In *Gender Practices in Contemporary Vietnam*, edited by Lisa Drummond and Helle Rydstrom, 26–46. Singapore: Singapore University Press.

Diverse experiences of women leading in higher education: locating networks and agency for leadership within a university context in Papua New Guinea

Rachel McNae[a] and Kerren Vali[b]

[a]Te Whiringa, School of Educational Leadership and Policy, University of Waikato, Hamilton, New Zealand; [b]Uniting Worlds Organisation, Suva, Fiji

The ways in which women deliberately press back against practices of oppression and demonstrate agency in higher education institutions are highly contextual and culturally bound. The formal and informal networks that women develop and maintain are important elements of generating agency and enhancing women's access to and opportunities for leadership. This article presents a case study from research that explored women's leadership experiences in a higher education context in the Pacific Islands – Papua New Guinea. Situated within a feminist poststructural methodology, the research examined women's experiences of leadership and considered aspects that influenced women's access to formal leadership roles. The findings illustrated that the women faced numerous barriers to formal leadership opportunities. A range of culturally and contextually located approaches supported women to demonstrate agency with regard to their own leadership development and practice. This research highlighted the importance of considering the relationship between networks and agency and the impact of associated cultural and contextual practices within organisations, providing insights into the culturally located complexities of women's leadership in higher education contexts.

Introduction: contextualising women's leadership in higher education

The burgeoning literature on women and educational leadership has continued to direct scholarly attention to women's overrepresentation in the teaching population, and their under-representation in educational leadership positions (Grogan and Shakeshaft 2009). Much of this literature serves the purpose of reminding us of the ever-present barriers, contradictions and achievements associated with women leading in education. The emergent literature on women and educational leadership in global contexts demonstrates the significance of sociocultural, historical, economic and political context with regard to women's leadership. Historically, leadership in higher education has been organised in hierarchical structures that have continued to be reinforced by social formations of bureaucracies informed by liberal political theories premised upon individual merit (Blackmore 2005; Fletcher 2007). These structures have frequently favoured male academics in senior educational leadership positions (Shakeshaft et al. 2007), for example, as Faculty and Academic Deans, Pro-vice

Chancellors, Departmental Chairpersons, and in positions chairing university-wide committees. Historic debates around gender focus on the numerical figures of women's representation in formal leadership roles and the differing rates of female academics' promotion compared to their male colleagues.

But leadership is situational (Fitzgerald 2006) and contextual (Strachan et al. 2010). Morley (2012, 121) argues that we need to 'unmask the "rules of the game" that lurk beneath the surface rationality of academic meritocracy'. Some argue that further investigation is required to consider how women as a group understand what enhances or hinders their access to leadership positions (Airini et al. 2010). Again, Blackmore (1999) argues that the popularisation of discourses that relate to women's ways of leading often fails to take into account the differences based on race, class and belief systems. These discourses treat women as a homogeneous group, marginalising many women from different racial, religious and class backgrounds. Much of the research is western-centric (for some exceptions see Akao 2008; McNae and Strachan 2010; Vali 2010; Warsal 2009), informed by a mainstream epistemology about women in educational leadership roles that has been constructed, classified and theorised from a white hegemonic perspective (with some exceptions, see Oplatka 2006). Fitzgerald (2006) notes that Western values and leadership practices homogenise, marginalise and silence women educational leaders from developing countries, arguing 'there is a need to formulate Indigenous and non-western theories of educational leadership that are grounded in research that account for and explain Indigenous women's ways of knowing and leading' (6–7). Furthermore, with increasing attention being paid to the role of context in influencing leadership practice and experiences, Blackmore (2009, 80) states, 'research is needed to further explore the significance of the relations between context and leadership practice in order to comprehend how context shapes the practice of leadership' and how women leaders actively negotiate their positioning within specific contexts.

More diverse perspectives from developing countries and the Pacific Islands thus contribute to the growing debate about women's representation in senior leadership positions in higher education. A key focus of this research in a higher education institution in Papua New Guinea (PNG) was to explore indigenous women's experiences of leadership and the cultural and contextual meanings associated with these. Examining the situated meanings and understandings of the practice and learning and development of leadership illuminated the ways in which women demonstrate agency and deliberately and strategically align with or resist organisational discourses that generate systems and practices of oppression within their institution. The experiences of women leaders in this university were explored through three focus questions: What were the leadership experiences of women in a higher institution in PNG and what had influenced these? What influences women's access to leadership positions within higher education and their career advancement within the formal university leadership structure? In what ways did women find and demonstrate agency with regard to their leadership development and practice?

Research approach

The project undertook feminist qualitative research that made women's voices and experiences central in order to uncover and remove the blinders that obscure knowledge and observations concerning human experiences and behaviours that have traditionally been silenced by mainstream research (Ardovini-Brooker 2001). According to Reinharz (1992), a key characteristic that identifies feminist research is that it is research carried out by women who identify themselves as feminists and draws directly from the experiences of women who are central to the research process, as is the case of the researchers in this project. The two authors were located in two different cultural locations – McNae, a New Zealand European, worked in the higher education sector in New Zealand and Vali, a Papua New Guinean worked in the higher education sector in PNG. In both of our respective institutions, we had observed instances where women had been marginalised in their leadership endeavours and sought to understand the nature of this marginalisation and how these women made sense of these experiences. Lather (1988, 571) states that to do feminist research is to ' … put the social construction of gender at the centre of one's inquiry'. This investigation therefore sought to understand how internal organisational patterns and broader cultural and political influences impacted the gendered experiences of the women leaders of higher education.

The analysis was framed through the theoretical work of Bulbeck (1998) in *Re-orienting Western feminisms* which insists on shifting away from the dominant Western epistemological lens. In her critical analysis of political and social practices surrounding the social relations of gender, Bulbeck purports that cultural context is critical to understanding particular issues in terms of how its shapes and generates new questions around how we interpret the world and especially the role of women, highlighting tensions between the similarities and differences of women's experiences. Bulbeck (1998, 2) argues that in these analytical practices we can 'use the image of the other to make our familiar faces look strange, to offer new interpretations'. In so doing, there is an opportunity to disrupt the historical Western cultural discourses upon which many understandings of feminism and women's experiences are founded thus 'challenging the imaginative spaces "we" occupy in our own minds' (Bulbeck 1998, 2). A critical analysis of the political and social practices that shape how we as researchers interpret the world offers new ways of understanding the experiences of women leaders in universities.

Bulbeck's 're-orienting' lens works in tandem with feminist poststructuralist positions that engage with the social construction of gendered subjectivities. Feminist poststructuralism recognises that both individual subjectivity and the collective culture of an organisation are socially and historically constructed and co-constructed. Furthermore, power relations (and therefore gender relations) are embedded in those constructions, which continue to exist and change over time through discourse and the formation of institutional structures (Weedon, 1992). Like Bulbeck's work, feminist poststructuralism provides 'a way of understanding the world through a rich plurality of voices and perspectives, which may lead to a greater recognition and connection between people of competing viewpoints' and potentially will 'prompt social and educational transformation' (Baxter 2002, 5).

Methodologically, the issue for white feminist researchers is also how to represent the diverse responses generated among women in academic contexts in the analysis? Charlesworth (1999) suggests first, researchers must be aware of the limits of their experience, and be cautious about constructing realities based on their own lives. Second, asking questions and challenging the assumptions of women's leadership in higher education settings might be seen as more valuable than attempting to reconcile core meanings and generate homogeneous and overarching theories of how women experience leadership, oppression and agency within their own contexts. Third, rather than invoking a conception of universal patriarchy, researchers must engage in the interrogation and appreciation of the different forms that oppression can take from a multitude of cultural positions and how the women themselves interpret these instances in both their personal lives and their roles as leaders in higher education.

This approach might reveal ways in which dominant discourses positioned women and their experiences through traditional meaning and ways of being (Davies 1990). Weedon (1992) argues that the relationship between experience, social power and resistance must be central to this theorising, and that women's lived realities are subjective realities, influenced by discursive practices within a specific context. This perspective calls for an understanding that, rather than existing as a unique, individual, fundamental or essential self, meaning is given to experiences through language and 'we speak ourselves into existence within the terms of available discourses' (Davies 2000, 55). These lived realities are diverse, changing and located within and drawn from hierarchical networks and structures, underscoring the importance of being attuned to issues of power, subjectivity, discourse and language (Grogan 1996).

Studies of discourse can seek to examine how institutions and organisations function as systems of control over individuals and how cultural and political nuances materialise as embodied experiences of women (Sawicki 1991). Key to feminist poststructuralism are these embodied experiences which can provide insight into women's perceptions of how they exercise agency with regard to negotiating power relations and interests that are historically and culturally embedded within their organisation. Munro's (1998) definition of agency was foundational for this research where she defined agency as ' ... an individual's multiple and conflicted negotiations of power relations in a specific context' (224). The notion of agency itself is not without its complexities. Munro (1998) defines agency as 'effective action by women against patriarchal oppression' (133), thus requiring women to be 'active citizens against [their] own subordination' (132). However, she also highlights that understandings about this subordination can be very different, subjective and culturally located. This engenders the need for a shared understanding of agency between the two authors where agency was considered to be a multifaceted and complex process in which both individual and collective consciousness interacted with the organisational structures and cultural milieu of the university. It was therefore important in this research to carefully examine the women's experiences *within* their own contexts. Situating this research within a feminist poststructuralist theoretical framework enabled exploration into how the women from different cultural and class backgrounds sought agency with regards to accessing formal leadership positions within the discursive fields of power within a university setting.

The research process

The research involved 13 Papua New Guinean women who were employed in one higher education institution. Invitations were sent to all academic university staff at the institution inviting women who held formal leadership positions to be involved in the research. The women came from diverse disciplines/strands within different schools of their institution and held senior leadership positions (e.g. Department Chairperson, Head of Committees, Associate Dean and Programme Leader). As a precaution of ethical means, pseudonyms will be used to protect their identities. Also, due to the small number of women represented in leadership positions, the location of the women's specific roles or schools will not be reported in order to minimise the likelihood of the women being identified. The investigation was purposefully designed to elicit an in-depth account of the individual women's leadership experiences within their specific context in order 'to open up an appreciation of the diversity and richness of […] competing perspectives' (Baxter 2002, 17). Data were generated through semi-structured interviews of approximately 60 minutes in duration that were digitally recorded, transcribed by the researchers and shared with the individual women to ensure accuracy and affirm meaning. Through a process of thematic analysis (Braun and Clarke 2013), emerging groups of data and observations of differences, absences and similarities of content and meanings were explored.

Women's journey for empowerment in PNG

PNG is a Melanesian country situated on the eastern half of the island of New Guinea in the South Pacific Ocean. PNG shares international borders with Solomon Islands on the southeast and Australia to the south and was once an Australian protectorate until 16 September 1975, when it gained independence. Considered a developing country, PNG is the most highly populated nation in the Pacific Islands and has an estimated population of seven million people. It is ranked 153 out of 187 countries worldwide for gender equality. This inequality is evidenced in education, employment, health, safety and political representation (Wilson 2012). The PNG government subscribes to a multitude of documents spanning decades including the United Nations Declaration of Human Rights (1962), The United Nations Convention on the Rights of the Child (1989), Education for All (United Nations Declaration 1990), the Beijing Declaration on Gender Issues (1995), CEDAW (1995), the National Gender Equity Policy (2003), Gender Equity Strategic Plan (2009–2014), Equal Employment Opportunity Policy (2009), and more recently, the National Policy for Women and Gender Equality (2011–2015), indicating the country's commitment towards establishing equality for women. However, that has not been the case and in the context of this research higher education leadership opportunities have not been fully extended to women academics. In PNG, women academics represent a small proportion of those who contribute to the economic and social development of the country through higher education. Across the six PNG universities, there are 430 male academics compared to 128 female academics (Office of Higher Education 2011). The Office of Higher Education was unable to further segregate these statistics with employment data and leadership positions.

The influence of the sociocultural context on PNG women's leadership experiences

The findings revealed that the ways in which PNG women perceived, experienced and practiced leadership were influenced significantly by the sociocultural context. Power manifested itself within both family and workplace contexts and was evidenced through traditional leadership practices, cultural ideals and expectations.

Traditional leadership practices

Traditional leadership practices shaped opportunities for women in leadership roles both within the university and in the community. 'Big Man Leadership' (putting men first as leaders) is a common term and practice in PNG and signifies the conflation of men with leadership. Described by Nanau (2011) as an acknowledged stance in Melanesian interpersonal relationships, rather than official title, many women identified how this practice excluded women from formal leadership roles and responsibilities.

For example, Jill identified the uneven distribution of leadership within her culture because of this cultural practice and commented:

> From the cultural perspective, looking back into our traditional ways – men were always being the leader. Men were always being the provider and the fighter (tribal wars). So women were only to bear and cook … women's place was at the kitchen and at the garden, bearing and rearing children. That is still part of our culture so men come to work with that mentality.

Understandings of masculinity in PNG culture may have corresponding dualities in their identities as men too become socialised and shift their historical roles from being the hunter/gatherer provider for the family and the fighter in the community (roles of high status) to being the wage earner and assuming positions of power in PNG's postcolonial society. Masculinity in PNG is in a process of hybridity as male identity is constructed through a negotiation of traditional, postcolonial and modern values. The association between leadership with masculinity is generated from, and substantiated by, multiple perspectives. Isaacs (2002) makes the case, however, that although men can be socialised and aspects of hybridity are evidenced, they are 'socialized in ways that promote, rather than hinder their abilities to act in the world' through processes of modernisation (142), and this contributes to the 'patriarchal conditions that subordinate women' (143). Hall (1995) cited in Bulbeck (1998) muses that in discussions of hybridity 'Power always tends to gravitate back to the binary … and that binaries do not go away because hybridity is around, or because we make a theoretical critique of them. So you have to keep asking why the binaries reappear' (54).

These binaries are played out in the professional lives of the women interviewed where many commented that some men, who seek or wish to retain for themselves positions of power and authority, actively undermined women leaders. Examples included instances where men were deliberately uncooperative and unproductive so that leadership became difficult, or poor performance of a department was deemed to reflect upon the woman who was in a leadership role. In one example, Jolly referred to a male colleague who chose to work in isolation when she was appointed the head of division, 'Because of who and what he is [from a PNG region where traditional big man leadership was still persistent]'. Many of the women associated holding a leadership position with holding power over others. Comments such as Jolly's above provide insight into the informal source of power where although men may not be in a formal leadership role, they still were in positions of significant influence within the institution and were continually holders of power informally as individuals and as men.

Many of the participants felt that the culmination of enduring traditional gender roles and stereotyping even within new postcolonial influences positioned them as subordinates in PNG society. Most of the women expressed how traditional principles of kinship predicated domestic life, and women's roles were prescribed accordingly as caregivers, child bearers and having the role of preparing food for their families and village events. Some women spoke of how these culturally ascribed roles for women impacted on how they were viewed as leaders in their employment as these views held by men were then transferred into their higher education institution. For example, Betty commented, 'Some of the Papua New Guineans [male] have this thing about women; a woman may be qualified but men still think that you are a woman [so] your place is at home in the kitchen.' Jill made similar comments explaining that it was difficult for women to 'shake off' the gendered cultural assumptions associated with being a woman in PNG society commenting that 'men think because they have power over women in the home that they can have authority over women even in professional circles'. Their comments indicate the transferability of values around gender identity from the social or personal to the organisational and professional, and how this impacts on women's experiences of institutional leadership. Furthermore, the construction of PNG masculinity works at a collective level thus reproducing existing power structures and cultures of leadership. Consequently, many of the participants believed that this left most women congregated at the lower level of the institution's leadership hierarchy. Monica explained:

> Many of the positions such as acting deans, deans and chairpersons are headed by males even though they (male) know we are capable of doing that. I see that men are greedy because they do not want women to overtake them.

Furthermore, in PNG many of the women perceived men as gatekeepers in leadership, appointment processes and academic promotion. As men held the majority of senior leadership positions, they dominated appointment committee panels within the institution and on the highest authority body that endorsed overall appointments. Many women spoke of how they not only experienced limited career progress due to male gatekeepers but were also recipients of intensive surveillance after being appointed. In one example, a participant shared how she had difficulties in her re-appointment despite having the necessary credentials for the position. After challenging this appointment process and eventually being reappointed to her original contract, she was then closely monitored by a number of men and felt intimidated, as they did not use this practice with any other male staff members. In a further example, one woman stated, ' … male colleagues keep challenging our work as if they are trying to see faults and not genuinely challenging with good intentions. They [males] look for every single loophole to target us'. Actions like this suggest that gatekeeping was a sustained and enduring practice within the institution.

 With few leadership opportunities available for women, the women themselves also acted in ways that could be considered gatekeeping. It would appear that in some cases women internalised and misused power within the hierarchical structures of the university in order to safeguard their own leadership positions. They created barriers to ensure that other women did not advance in their careers, especially if they were junior academics. As Geno explained, 'The senior female would not want to see a junior female rising up; it's not really rising up but they wouldn't want to see you taking the lead'. Similarly, Jill explained:

> They do not think big in terms of supporting women to advance to leadership positions once they are already there. We are jealous of other women and do not want them to excel because otherwise they will replace us.

Others found that tokenistic leadership positions were offered to project an image that women were represented in leadership positions. Instead, the women felt that their appointments to leadership positions should be based on their merits as an individual, for example, the case of Vavi who stated, 'I always oppose the idea of people suggesting "we are going to nominate a woman" I don't like that! I want to be nominated because of my merit that I can be a leader and they see quality in me … And not because I am just a mere woman!'

These discourses of individualism and individual merit butt up against the principles of the PNG's kinship system, the wontok system which also plays a significant role in women's opportunities for leadership, securing positions and academic promotion. According to Nanau (2011), the wantok system 'is an important concept associated with networks of distinct tribal, ethnic, linguistic, and geographic groupings in Melanesia' (32). This concept is founded on a cultural system based on kinship principles where people from similar tribes, families or ethnic groups showed favour to each other. This cultural practice is perceived by many as

> an unwritten social contract, between those that speak the same language, to assist each other in times of need. This ranges from little things such as assistance in school fees to favours that border corruption, such as offering a job or contract to a person or persons because they are a wantok. (The Solomon Island Press 2008)

The women from PNG perceived this system as a mechanism which both hindered and enhanced their access to formal leadership positions. For example, this cultural practice of favouring a wontok member had a significant influence on the appointment and promotion processes within the university and was a concern for many of the women. Jill claimed, ' … if they were to choose between me and them [wantoks], it's the wantoks over me'. The negative attributes of the wantok system highlight the likelihood of how supporting a fellow wantok in times of need can also be perceived by others as corruption and nepotism (Nanau 2011). However, for some women the wantok system was an important network that provided support and opportunity (discussed further in the following section).

Navigating cultural discourses that influence opportunities for leadership was an important part of how the women went on to challenge existing practices of both men and women. An internalisation of individualism was also evidenced where many of the women felt personally responsible to respond to the insurmountable quest of changing cultural discourses, and some found this perceived responsibility overwhelming. Interestingly, many of the women showed high levels of strategy and planning, and even aligned with some of these cultural practices to *assist* them in their career. The women interviewed negotiated through the various contradictions and alignments involved in the meeting of cultural values of community and kin, and ideologies of individualism and merit. Bulbeck (1998, 93) writes that 'western discourses are much more uneasy in their attempt to hold these apparently opposing aspects in view at once. Individual rights-claims are a powerful and popular currency'. However, as the following discussion demonstrates, the PNG interviewees draw on many discourses in their demonstrations of agency.

Women's networks in PNG: aligning and engaging existing cultural practices

Evidence of agentic actions performed by the women was seen in the ways they interacted with and formed various networks to disrupt gendered leadership practices. One deliberate strategy employed by many of the PNG women involved engaging with the wantok system to best serve their own needs. By aligning themselves alongside relatives in positions of leadership, women were able to employ this system and gain leadership positions and academic promotions. One example of this was Rigo who, at the completion of her Master of Education, was handpicked by a relative for a position during an organisational restructuring process. However, although this supported her progression into a leadership position within the institution, as she had not formally applied for the position she received significant backlash from her colleagues due to the lack of transparency. For many of the women the wantok system was also a key feature that assisted them to successfully manage a busy academic career and family life. Many of the women (especially those with children) mentioned the importance of involving relatives in caring for children and assisting with the day-to-day running of the household so that they could work full time. For example, Monica described how her relatives had shown sacrifice and loyalty and supported her in her decision to work and pursue her academic career:

> I always had my family or wantoks assisting me to babysit although it was difficult at times when playing the role of a mother ... trying to meet the demands of your job especially a teaching job that requires you longer hours at work and then you carry work back home to continue there.

Kinship networks were critical to women accessing leadership.

Legitimising leadership practice: the power of formal and informal networks for learning

Power was also evidenced on a more global scale where the women used education as a commodified form of social capital. Many of the women believed their influence within the organisation could be enhanced with the gaining of further qualifications. All of the women believed that higher qualifications (e.g. Masters of Education, Educational Administration or Ph.Ds) were essential in order to counteract discrimination and were vital for holding formal leadership roles within the institution. A number of participants believed the qualifications served to legitimize and validate women as leaders while others expressed they felt it gave them more authority within the organisation. As Vavi stated, 'That is why women need educational merit (qualifications) to substantiate their leadership positions so they are not looked down on but instead treated with respect they deserve'. Eleven of the women had travelled abroad (e.g., to New Zealand or Australia) to gain higher qualifications, such as Masters or Ph.D. degrees. However, although many of the women were positive about this experience and the benefits which sometimes eventuated (e.g. more respect from colleagues, higher wages and in some cases promotions), some commented on the sacrifices they made in order for this to happen (e.g. including having to leave secure employment, the breakdown of personal relationships and being faced with professional jealousy from both men and women upon their return).

Other than the formal qualification pathways mentioned above, there were few formal leadership learning opportunities and much of the women's learning about leadership came informally from outside of the university, for example, through their involvement in their church and through planning and leading events in the villages. Many of the women voiced concerns that there were few female role models in the university and that those women in senior positions were incredibly busy, leaving minimal time or inclination for them to mentor other women. Monica commented 'there is no networking amongst women'. Similarly, Jill observed:

> There is no such thing as women leaders coming down to young aspiring women leaders, encouraging them to bring each other up ... Women are in isolation ... You don't find a

network of women coming together to work in achieving common goal or common interest for the betterment of women.

Some senior women admitted that they saw aspiring women leaders as a threat to their leadership roles and therefore they were reluctant to support and mentor them. To illustrate, one participant mentioned how a particular senior female academic undermined her leadership efforts by continually challenging her views and ideas, and opposing her involvement in professional learning. This led her to believe some women did not recognise the significance or the value of professional informal networking as a means of accessing leadership positions. However, many of the women engaged in activities and actions which generated networking opportunities and what could be recognised as a form of sisterhood in places within the community, for example, in the church they attended, the sports groups they belonged to and the interactions with others within their own village social activities. It was acknowledged that these networks outside of their institution provided emotional support when times were challenging, and support of physical means such as childcare and informal mentoring. It would appear that although the women understood the value of this sisterhood and solidarity in their personal lives, they did not see this extending to their place of employment.

In summary, the women identified numerous aspects that influenced their access to leadership positions within their university context. In the upper echelons of PNG universities there are many formal and informal, local and global ways for women to progress and substantiate their positions in leadership. The use of networks through kinship and extra-organisational connections were key features in assisting women in leadership positions. However, these networks were not without their tensions as women strived to balance the sometimes volatile and fragile relationships of home and work life. Similarly, being educated in a postgraduate degree in an international university is a double-edged sword: bringing benefits of social capital, but also the potential losses of ongoing connection with community and family.

Discussion

Despite the advances women have made in many areas of public life in the past two decades, in the area of leadership in higher education they are still a long way from participating on the same footing as men (Lumby and Coleman 2007). This is not only a feature of higher education systems reported in much of the literature on women and educational leadership in developed countries but also in developing countries such as PNG. The context of this research was significantly different with regard to culture in terms of Western culture, and women perceived a number of different cultural practices that created barriers and challenges to women practicing leadership.

The findings illustrated that the women faced a range of barriers in their context that impacted on their experiences of leadership. Although the women used similar words to label these barriers, the descriptions and associated meanings were highly contextual, located in broader political discourses with differences within the context and even within individual responses. The notion of agency (choice), as Bulbeck points out (1998, 96) is revealed 'within structural constraints and social meanings', and understanding it in this way 'expands our understanding of decision made in both the east and the west'. The findings demonstrated the ways in which the women actively sought agency within their institution to address these barriers, although largely at an individual rather than collective level. Underpinning these findings were the key features of networks (both formal and informal), and the male-dominant centralised location of power within the workplace. In Melanesia, the views, perceptions and values about what constitutes leadership and who should be a leader are based on enduring and strongly embedded societal discourses, cultural practices, beliefs and values systems which are based on older patriarchal systems of leadership in PNG (Akao 2008; Strachan 2009; Warsal 2009). Based on the traditional social construction of masculinity, leadership has become the 'technology of [the] masculine' (Theobald 1996, 174). According to Strachan et al. (2010, 73), ' ... big man leadership is normalised and sets a superior and privileged standard', which positions men as the most suitable candidates for leadership roles (Kilavanwa 2004). This ingrained cultural practice was enacted in both private and public spheres, and as Warsal (2009) found investigating women's leadership in Vanuatu, fundamental and significant inequalities were generated between men and women with regard to access to leadership opportunities. Eagly and Johannesen (2001) highlight that 'gender roles spill over to influence leadership behaviour in organisations' (787), and as found in this research, gender socialisation can influence what could be the respective roles and behaviours for men and women leaders. Gender regimes in Western organisations are also not fixed and are ' ... part of the wider gender order of society' (Grogan 2014, 8).

Many women found that the cultural practices from outside of the university were so embedded that it was difficult to change or shift existing university structures and processes (e.g. committee representation and appointment processes), and there was little senior political will to do so. Furthermore, in PNG a number of the women felt they were not necessarily well-positioned or prepared to challenge and change the system that created the barriers for them. In fact to challenge these existing cultural practices may be very dangerous with high levels of violence against women commonplace in PNG society. Critically reflecting on cultural and social discourses can expose unfair practices that marginalise women. But it is important to realise that not all discourses are perceived by all women as oppressive. Some are cultural practices that the women participate in and accommodate. However, what is clear is that the notion of power and masculinity is firmly entrenched within cultural discourses. Uncovering and critiquing cultural practices in ways that also allow women to remain safe, both personally and professionally, were important future actions identified by these women.

In the context of this higher education setting, networks were central to the women's leadership. Whether the networks are crafted from circumstance such as cultural practices or whether they were developed through deliberate planning and strategic encounters, the important role of networks to assist women to be agentic cannot be overlooked. The nature of networks within the context highlighted the locations of power, especially in decision-making roles. The culturally embedded nature of the wantok system was a key example of this. Findings supported the work of Tivinarlik and Wanat (2006) who also found that the wantok system created instances of nepotism in the selection and appointment process in education settings, and lesser qualified relatives were preferred over more suitable applicants, many of them women. Instead, some of the women in this study chose to embrace the system and use it to progress in their professional position. This finding is not restricted to PNG. Warsal's (2009) study in Vanuatu also indicated that although the wantok system restricted women's access to leadership opportunities, it also provided some women with a 'gateway to occupying leadership roles' (116) and supportive networks. The issue raised in this paper is whether individual women see their leadership position as being used to facilitate other women moving up.

With regard to appointment processes and promotion, the practice of gatekeeping continued to impede women accessing leadership positions, mirroring key themes in Western literature (e.g. Acker 1994; Bagilhole and White 2008; Blackmore 1999; Blackmore, Thomson, and Barty 2006; Coleman 2007, 2009) and similarly, literature from non-Western sources such as Uganda (Sperandio and Kagoda 2008), China (Coleman, Haiyan, and Yanping 1998), Nigeria (Uwazurike 1991) and Vanuatu (Strachan and Saunders 2007). In PNG, self-preservation led to a number of women acting as gatekeepers. This finding is similar to Cooper and Strachan's (2006) study that examined the experiences of women academics in three countries: USA, New Zealand and Romania. They found that in one case in New Zealand, a department woman chairperson attempted to sabotage another woman's tenure application in order to protect her own positioning with the university. The woman applicant confronted the woman and also filed a personal grievance to her faculty union. This is one of the few studies that mentioned such an action within educational settings.

Mavin (2008) acknowledges the concept of 'Queen Bees', a phrase coined by Staines, Tavris, and Jayaratne (1974) and used to describe a general phenomenon where women who had been individually successful in male-dominated contexts were less likely to support other women to gain similar experiences. However, rather than blaming women for this behaviour, she emphasises the importance of examining the underpinning gender systems 'embedded in organizations [which] socially construct and impact upon women's behaviour towards women … ' (83). Certainly, the assumption that all women will support other women in their careers was challenged. However, irrespective of gender, the importance of confronting such behaviour and exposing unjust practices was clearly an important action. This highlights the need to critically examine the broader contexts in which women practice their leadership and are modelled leadership (Walker and Dimmock 2002), and not just the inter-relationships between women within their institution.

Research has shown that the gendered nature of universities has enforced a gendered research economy (Morley 2014) where 'research performance is implicitly associated with the prestige economy in Higher Education, and is a pathway to academic seniority and an indicator for promotion' (116). Blackmore (1999) identified ways in which power relations are reproduced and maintained within educational settings. She concluded that it was these power dynamics that created assumptions with regard to the normative role and the position of male leaders within the institution. These dynamics also reinforced causal hegemonic links between masculinity, hierarchy and leadership.

With many women located in lower ranked positions that were teaching-intensive, women are influenced into a position described by Cubillo and Brown (2003, 278) as 'the sticky floor'. This culture has also positioned women to occupy the lower level of the institutional hierarchy and compete in a hostile environment and one that is difficult for them to have impact on the masculine organisational cultures and hierarchal structures (Bagilhole and White 2005; Court 1998; Weyer 2007). The phrase 'chilly climate' coined by Sandler and Hall (1986) refers to women's experiences within many Western university cultures (Cooper and Strachan 2006). This research indicates that a similar climate was experienced by most women in PNG. Unless challenged, this climate will continue to reproduce structures that continue to exclude and/or marginalise women leaders.

The relational aspects of women's leadership in higher education settings purported in Western literature were not as extensive nor as evident in the PNG context. The work of Newcombe (2014) highlights the value of relationships formed between academic women in Western universities arguing that these relationships can assist with identity construction, developing research agendas and research strategies, and addressing feelings of being isolated in their professional work. In PNG, the interviewees did not intensively engage in these formal professional networks. Instead, informal networks from outside of the university provide opportunities for women to learn about leadership, even though the skills they learnt in these environments did not transfer as valuable for the university organisation. Harris, Ravenswood, and Myers (2013, 232) state that informal networks within organisations are just as 'important for mentoring, information, decision making on appointments and research collaborations'. According to Grogan (2002), 'mentoring leads to networking' (125), and arguably the lack of networking within the professional sphere contributes to a sense of academic isolation for the women in PNG. It would appear that developing and sustaining both formal and informal opportunities for women to network, within and outside of the university, are important aspects for supporting and enhancing women's leadership within the academy.

Concluding remarks

According to Yoder (2001, 815), we must never lose sight of the fact that the leaders we are discussing are women, 'that doing leadership may differ for women and men and that leadership does not take place in a genderless vacuum.' Coming to understand women's experiences of leadership within and across diverse contexts is crucial in exposing gendered discourses that marginalise women within higher education. Bulbeck highlights that 'women of the world are connected *both* through shared language and ideas *and* in structures of unequal power' (1998, 6). However, how these are expressed, felt, acted upon and valued can often be very different. This research has illustrated that there are some significant differences in the ways women develop their understandings about leadership and perceive their leadership practice and although similar phrases and words may have been used to describe these, the lived experiences themselves were in fact very diverse.

This research has illustrated how women are simultaneously constrained by and resist normative, dominant culture. The culture of the university posed many challenges for the women educational leaders in PNG. Evidence of discrimination within the structures of the university, unclear appointment processes, gatekeeping and in some cases the lack of support systems (e.g. mentoring, professional learning about leadership and networking among women) were identified as key areas that influenced women's representation in leadership. Although these barriers to leadership are not exclusive to the context of PNG, the pervasive and culturally embedded nature makes addressing change within the systems of the academy very difficult. The findings also highlighted aspects of university culture, which had a positive influence on the women and their leadership. Interestingly, many of the aspects that supported, inhibited and out rightly prevented women from gaining positions of leadership in higher education were similar in name to those reported in Western literature. However, the cultural complexities provided significant differences in the ways women identified these. This research highlighted the importance of considering cultural and contextual practices with regard to leadership practice and development for women leaders in higher education. It makes an important contribution to extending the knowledge associated with women's educational leadership in the Pacific and identifies ways in which women sought and demonstrate agency with regard to their leadership within their university.

Acknowledgements

We would like to acknowledge the contributions of the women leaders involved in the research who generously gave their time and comments, enabling this research to happen. We would also like to acknowledge the detailed supportive feedback on the draft manuscript from colleagues and reviewers as conceptual and theoretical understandings for this paper were developed and crafted.

Disclosure statement

No potential conflict of interest was reported by the authors.

References

Acker, S. 1994. *Gendered Education: Sociological Reflections on Women, Teaching, and Feminism*. Buckingham: Open University Press.

Airini, S. Collins, L. Conner, B. Midson, K. McPherson, and C. Wilson. 2010. "Learning to be Leaders in Higher Education: What Helps or Hinders Women's Advancement as Leaders in Universities." *Educational Management Administration and Leadership* 39 (1): 44–62.

Akao, M. S. 2008. "Seen but not heard: Women's experiences of educational leadership in Solomon Islands secondary schools." Unpublished master's thesis. Hamilton, New Zealand: University of Waikato.

Ardovini-Brooker, J. 2001. "The Debate Surrounding Feminist Research and Its Distinction from Traditional Research." *Advancing Women in Leadership*. http://advancingwomen. com/awl/.

Bagilhole, B., and K. White. 2005. "Benign Burden: Gender and Senior Management in UK and Australia." Paper presented to the 4th European conference on gender equality in higher education, Oxford, August 31–September 3.

Bagilhole, B., and K. White. 2008. "Towards a Gendered Skills Analysis of Senior Management Positions in UK and Australian Universities." *Tertiary Education and Management* 14 (1): 1–12.

Baxter, J. 2002. "A Juggling Act: A Feminist Post-structural Analysis of Girls and Boys Talk in the Secondary Classroom." *Gender and Education* 14 (1): 5–19.

Blackmore, J. 1999. *Troubling Women: Feminism, Leadership and Educational Change*. Buckingham: Open University Press.

Blackmore, J. 2005. "The Emperor Has No Clothes: Professionalism, Performativity and Educational Leadership in High-risk Modern Times." In *Leadership, Gender and Culture in Education: Male and Female Perspectives*, edited by J. Collard and C. Reynolds, 173–194. Maidenhead: Open University Press.

Blackmore, J. 2009. "Re/positioning Women in Educational Leadership: The Changing Social Relations and Politics of Gender in Australia." In *Women Leading Education across the Continents: Sharing the Spirit, Fanning the Flame*, edited by H. C. Sobehart, 73–83. Lanham, MD: Rowman & Littlefield Education.

Blackmore, J., P. Thomson, and K. Barty. 2006. "Principal Selection: Homosociobility, the Search for Security and the Production of Normalized Principal Identities." *Educational Management Administration & Leadership* 34 (3): 297–317.

Braun, V., and V. Clarke. 2013. *Successful Qualitative Research: A Practical Guide for Beginners*. London: Sage.

Bulbeck, C. 1998. *Re-orienting Western Feminisms: Women's Diversity in a Postcolonial World*. London: Cambridge University Press.

Charlesworth, H. 1999. "Feminist Methods in International Law." *The American Journal of International Law* 93 (2): 379–394.

Coleman, M. 2007. "Gender and Educational Leadership in England: A Comparison of Secondary Headteachers' Views over Time." *School Leadership and Management* 27 (14): 383–399.

Coleman, M. 2009. "Women in Educational Leadership in England." In *Women Leading Education across The Continents: Sharing the Spirit, Fanning the Flame*, edited by H. C. Sobehart, 13–20. Lanham, MD: Rowman & Littlefield Education.

Coleman, M., Q. Haiyan, and L. Yanping. 1998. "Women in Educational Management in China: Experience in Shaanxi Province, Compare." *A Journal of Comparative and International Education* 28 (2): 141–154.

Cooper, J., and J. Strachan. 2006. "Welcome Ground for Women Faculty in Academe: An International Perspective." *Advancing Women in Leadership* 21: 1–13.

Court, M. 1998. "Women Challenging Managerialism: Devolution Dilemmas in The Establishment of Co-principalship in Primary School in Aotearoa/New Zealand." *School Leadership and Management* 18 (1): 35–57.

Cubillo, L., and M. Brown. 2003. "Women into Educational Leadership and Management: International Differences?" *Journal of Educational Administration* 41 (3): 278–291.

Davies, B. 1990. "The Problem of Desire." *Social Problems* 37 (4): 501–516.

Davies, B. 2000. *A Body of Writing*. Oxford: Rowan & Littlefield.

Eagly, A., and M. C. Johannesen-Schmidt. 2001. "The Leadership Styles of Women and Men." *Journal of Social Issues* 57 (4): 781–797.

Fitzgerald, T. 2006. "Walking Between Two Worlds: Indigenous Women and Educational Leadership." *Educational Management Administration & Leadership* 34 (2): 201–213.

Fletcher, C. 2007. "Passing the Buck: Gender and Management of Research Production in UK Higher Education." *Equal Opportunities International* 26 (4): 269–286.

Grogan, M. 1996. *Voices of Women Aspiring to the Superintendency*. New York: State University of New York Press.

Grogan, G. 2002. "Influences of the Discourses of Globalization on Mentoring for Gender Equity and Social Justice in Educational Leadership." *Leading and Managing* 8 (2): 123–134.

Grogan, M. 2014. "Re(considering) Gender Scholarship in Educational Leadership." In *Women Interrupting, Disrupting and Revolutionizing Educational Policy and Practice*, edited by W. Newcombe and K. Mansfield, 3–20. Charlotte, NC: Information Age Publishing.

Grogan, G., and C. Shakeshaft. 2009. "Conscious Leadership in Political World." In *Women Leading Education across The Continents: Sharing the Spirit, Fanning the Flame*, edited by H. C. Sobehart, 21–28. Lanham, MD: Rowman & Littlefield Education.

Harris, C., K. Ravenswood, and B. Myers. 2013. "Glass Slippers, Holy Grails and Ivory Towers: Gender and Advancement in Academia." *Labour & Industry: A Journal of The Social and Economic Relations of Work* 23 (3): 231–244.

Isaacs, T. 2002. "Feminism and Agency." *Canadian Journal of Philosophy* 32 (1 Suppl): 129–154.

Kilavanwa, B. 2004. "Women Leaders in Schools in Papua New Guinea: Why Do Women Leaders Labour in the Shadows?" Unpublished master's thesis. Hamilton, New Zealand: University of Waikato.

Lather, P. 1988. "Feminist Perspectives on Empowering Research Methodologies." *Women's Studies International Forum* 11 (6): 569–581.

Lumby, J., and M. Coleman. 2007. *Leadership and Diversity: Challenging Theory and Practice in Education*. London: Sage.

Mavin, S. 2008. "Queen Bees, Wannabees and Afraid of Bees: No more 'Best Enemies' for Women in Management?" *British Journal of Management* 19: S75–S84.

McNae, R., and J. Strachan. 2010. "Researching in Cross-cultural Contexts: A Socially Just Process." *Waikato Journal of Education* 15 (2): 41–54.

Morley, L. 2012. "The Rules of the Game: Women and the Leaderist Turn in Higher Education." *Gender and Education* 25 (1): 116–131.

Morley, L. 2014. "Lost Leaders: Women in the Global Academy." *Higher Education Research and Development* 33 (1): 114–128.

Munro, P. 1998. *Subjects to Fiction*. Philadelphia, PA: Open University Press.

Nanau, G. L. 2011. "The Wantok System as a Socio-economic and Political Network in Melanesia." *The Journal of Multicultural Society* 2 (1): 31–55.

Newcombe, W. 2014. "Collaborative Feminism at Work." In *Women Interrupting, Disrupting and Revolutionizing Educational Policy and Practice*, edited by W. Newcombe and K. Mansfield, 193–209. Charlotte, NC: Information Age Publishing.

Office of Higher Education. 2011. Papua New Guinea Office of Higher Education. Accessed December 13. http://www.ohe.gov.pg/index.php/downloads.

Oplatka, I. 2006. "Women in Educational Administration within Developing Countries." *Journal of Educational Administration* 44 (16): 604–624.

Reinharz, S. 1992. *Feminist Methods in Social Research*. New York, NY: Oxford University Press.

Sandler, B., and R. Hall. 1986. *The Campus Climate Revisited: Chilly for Women Faculty, Administrators, and Graduate Students*. Washington, DC: Association of American Colleges.

Sawicki, J. 1991. *Disciplining Foucault: Feminism, Power and the Body*. New York: Routledge.

Shakeshaft, C., G. Brown, B. J. Irby, M. Grogan, and J. Ballenger. 2007. "Increasing Gender Equity in Educational Leadership." In *Handbook of Gender Equity in Schools*, edited by S. Klein, 103–129. Mahwah, NJ: Laurence Erlbaum Associates.

The Solomon Island Press. 2008. "The Cost of the 'Wantok System.'" Online publication of the Solomon Island Press, 16 February 2008. Accessed from: http://www.solomontimes.com/news/the-cost-of-the-wantok-system/1368.

Sperandio, J., and A. Kagoda. 2008. "Advancing Women into Educational Leadership in Developing Countries: The Case of Uganda." *Advancing Women in Leadership Journal* 18 (27): 1–13.

Staines, G., C. Tavris and T. E. Jayaratne. 1974. "The Queen Bee Syndrome." *Psychology Today* 7: 55–60.

Strachan, J. 2009. "Women and Educational Leadership in New Zealand and Melanesia." In *Women Leading Education across the Continents: Sharing the Spirit, Fanning the Flame*, edited by H. C. Sobehart, 100–109. Lanham, MD: Rowman & Littlefield Education.

Strachan, J., S. Akao, B. Kilavanwa, and D. Warsal. 2010. "You Have to Be a Servant of all: Melanesian Women's Educational Leadership Experiences." *School Leadership & Management* 30 (1): 65–76.

Strachan, J. M. B., and R. Saunders. 2007. "Ni Vanuatu Women and Educational Leadership Development." *New Zealand Journal of Educational Leadership* 22 (2): 37–48.

Theobald, M. 1996. *Knowing Women: Origins of Women's Education in Nineteenth Century Australia*. Melbourne: Cambridge University Press.

Tivinarlik, A., and C. L. Wanat. 2006. "Leadership Styles of New Ireland High School Administrators: A Papua New Guinea Study." *Anthropology and Education Quarterly* 37 (1): 1–20.

Uwazurike, C. N. 1991. "Theories of Educational Leadership: Implications for Nigerian Educational Leaders." *Educational Management and Administration and Leadership* 19 (4): 259–263.

Vali, K. 2010. "Women Leading in Silence in Papua New Guinea Higher Education." Unpublished master's thesis. University of Waikato, Hamilton, New Zealand.

Walker, A., and C. Dimmock. 2002. "Educational Leadership: Taking Account of Complex Global and Cultural Contexts." In *School Leadership and Administration: Adopting a Cultural Perspective*, edited by A. Walker and C. Dimmock, 33–44. New York: Routledge Falmer.

Warsal, D. 2009. "The Impact of Culture on Women's Leadership in Vanuatu Secondary Schools." Unpublished masters' thesis. University of Waikato, Hamilton, New Zealand. http://researchcommons.waikato.ac.nz/handle/10289/2776.

Weedon, C. 1992. *Feminist Practice and Poststructural Theory*. Cambridge, MA: Blackwell Publishers.

Weyer, B. 2007. "Twenty Years Later: Explaining the Persistent of the Glass Ceiling for Women Leaders." *Women in Management Review* 22 (6): 482–496.

Wilson, C. 2012. "Women Demand Equality in Papua New Guinea." Inter Press Service. http://www.ipsnews.net/2012/12/women-demand-equality-in-papua-new-guinea.

Yoder, J. D. 2001. "Making Leadership Work More Effectively for Women." *Journal of Social Issues* 57 (4): 815–828.

Good jobs – but places for women?

Pat O'Connor

Department of Sociology, Faculty of AHSS, University of Limerick, Limerick, Ireland

This article is concerned with men and women's experience of elite positions and with the extent to which such positions are seen as places for women, so as to provide an insight into their commitment to continuing in them. Senior management in universities are elite positions in terms of income; those who occupy them are relatively powerful internally, although relatively powerless in relation to the state and the market. Drawing on a purposive study of those at the top three levels (i.e. presidential, vice-presidential, and dean) in public universities, it finds little difference between men and women's perceptions of the advantages/disadvantages of these positions. However, in a context where roughly four-fifths of those in university senior management are men [O'Connor, P. 2014. *Management and Gender in Higher Education*. Manchester: Manchester University Press.], at the level of organisational narratives and at the interactional level, gender differences persist. These differences are reflected in variation in commitment to continuing in senior management positions.

Introduction

Universities internationally are under pressure from neo-liberalism and other global processes and are undergoing considerable change. The centralisation of power internally, which is a feature of managerialism, is associated with greater external pressure and accountability. However, senior managers, at least potentially, have power within their own organisations, and have a considerable impact on the lives of the staff they employ and the students who attend them. The position of senior managers can be regarded as an elite one, with many attractive characteristics, not least in terms of salary. Relatively little attention has been paid to senior managers' experience of these elite positions, a topic that seems particularly relevant in a context where they can be perceived as potentially occupying a contradictory position. Thus, as managers, they have power within their own organisations and are ultimately responsible for their shape and direction, while they 'are also subordinate to powerful corporate interest groups in the business and industrial sector' (Lynch 1999, 53). This article is concerned with the extent to which such elite positions are seen as places for women, so as to provide an insight into their commitment to continuing in them.

The majority of those holding senior management positions are men. Within most organisations, there are formal hierarchies of positional power predominantly occupied by men. Gender is thus typically highly conflated with organisational power, with universities being male-dominated organisations. In Ireland, roughly four-fifths of those in senior management positions in universities are men (O'Connor 2014). A good deal of attention (albeit outside the mainstream) has been paid to the underrepresentation of women in senior positions in universities, to the structural and cultural barriers they experience in trying to access these positions and the difficulties they experience as holders of such positions (Morley 2013; Bagilhole and White 2011; Coleman 2011; Shah and Shah 2012; Fitzgerald 2014). The situation of women in senior management positions has been seen as particularly fraught because of the construction of leadership as an appropriately masculine activity. The concept of organisational culture has been used to refer to a complicated fabric of management myths, values and practices that legitimise women's positions at the lower levels of the hierarchy and portray managerial jobs as primarily masculine (Bagilhole 2002; Benschop and Brouns 2003; Deem, Hilliard, and Reed 2008; Leathwood and Read 2009). Thus, 'management incorporates a male standard that positions women as out of place' (Wajcman 1998, 2). The reality of the gendered organisational culture in universities has been widely documented by academics and accepted by policy-making organisations (EU 2012; OECD 2012).

It has been suggested that 'Organisational culture is a function of leadership' (Parry 1998, 93). Thus, changing women's position in universities requires changes to a gendered culture where 'women's place' is defined by men and it is a subordinate one. Men, as Hearn (2001, 70) sees it, are 'a social category associated with hierarchy and power ... Management is a social activity that is also clearly based on hierarchy and power ... Academia is a social institution that is also intimately associated with hierarchy and power'. Thus, 'in simply going along with institutionalised features of the gender order, men perpetuate masculinism, a bias in favour of men' (Yancey Martin 2003, 360). Women choosing to enter male-dominated areas of employment 'may perform femininity or resist such a performance' (Mackenzie Davey 2008, 655), but their positioning is always relative to men, with a strong possibility that regardless of what they do, they will be seen as 'Other' (O'Connor and Goransson 2015). Thus, although the minority of women in senior management in universities occupy an elite position, which itself is contradictory, they experience a further contradiction in that, although they are members of an elite in terms of their occupational position, they are subordinate in terms of gender: 'They are insiders to the organisational bureaucracy ... On the basis of their gender they are outsiders to the masculinist culture ... ' (Fitzgerald 2014, 9).

The concept of 'organisational culture' has been variously defined, although there is a common core to such definitions (Tierney 1998). Drawing on Wicks and Bradshaw (2002, 137), in this article, it is defined as those 'attitudes, values and assumptions ... which become entrenched in the minds and practices of organisational participants' and which plays an important part in concealing and legitimating gendered inequalities. Smircich (1983) distinguishes between culture as something an organisation 'has'; and culture as something an organisation 'is', with the former definition implicitly suggesting that managers can change the organisational culture, while the latter focuses on day-to-day interactions which are less amenable to change by management. In problematising senior management as a place for women, attention is focused on organisational narratives and interactional perceptions (Risman 2004; Wharton 2012) and in particular, on how those occupying elite positions think they are perceived by colleagues, and the gender variation in this.

In summary, this article is concerned with men's and women's experience of elite positions, and particularly their perceptions of their advantages/disadvantages; with the organisational culture and its impact on commitment to continuing in such positions. It was undertaken as part of a wider cross-national study 'of women's representation in, experience of and influence on senior management' (Bagilhole and White 2011, 1). There is thus an opportunity to explore the similarities and differences between the experiences of men and women in the Irish context, compared to others in similar positions cross-nationally (Neale 2011; Riordan 2011).

Methodology

The public university system in Ireland consists of seven universities. Roughly four-fifths of those in senior management positions in Irish universities are men (O'Connor 2014). In ways the Irish public university system can be seen as a bounded, relatively undifferentiated system, although Trinity College Dublin is the most prestigious and most long-established university and the one whose structure contrasts most strongly with the rest. However, the small size and relatively low level of differentiation in the total pool enables them to be analysed collectively to a far greater extent than might be possible in a more structurally differentiated system.

The approach used is a critical realist one. Thus, although it is accepted that there is a real world that exists independently of our perceptions, our understanding of this world is inevitably related to our positioning (Maxwell 2012). Semi-structured qualitative interviews were used as the method of data collection. Such data can be regarded as constituting an edited story (Nilsen 2008), although unlike more typical narrative studies (Hyvarinen 2008), the priorities and interests of the researcher were reflected in the method of data collection. A semi-structured interview schedule was devised by the eight country Women in Higher Education Management (WHEM) Network (Bagilhole and White 2011). Ethical approval was sought and given in each national context.

Senior management was defined as those at dean level or above who had been in such a position in a public university within the previous five years. Such senior management teams varied in size and composition, although they all included a mix of academics and other professionals. The sample was a purposive one. A total of 40 people were identified, involving those at presidential, vice-presidential and dean levels; including academics and other professionals; men and women; and including a range of disciplines across all seven universities funded by the state. Of the 40 people (15 women and 25 men) contacted, interviews were completed with 34 (13 women and 21 men): an 85% response rate. All of the interviews took place in the interviewees' own office. All were tape-recorded. They varied in length from 40 minutes to one hour 30 minutes, with the majority being over an hour. The tone of the interviews was very positive and typically very open. It was clear that for many of the respondents, it was an enjoyable opportunity to reflect on their lives and the organisations they led. Detailed verbatim notes were made during the interview. Following the interviews, the tapes were replayed and transcribed.

The method of analysis was thematic, with themes being influenced both by the national and cross-national data, as well as by the literature in the area. Grounded theory (Glaser and Strauss 1967) was used in a context where, although the gendered nature of senior management positions has been extensively documented, particularly by gender theorists, less attention has been paid to the extent and nature of gender variation in the experiences of those in elite positions in gendered organisational contexts, and the differential impact of such experiences on men and women's commitment to continuing in them. It has been recognised that 'validity in interpretative social science is complicated by subjectivity' (Mabry 2008, 221). However, issues related to validity also arise in quantitative research, with Hammersley (2008, 51) noting that in assessing the validity of research findings, 'Judgement is always involved and this necessarily depends upon background knowledge and practical understanding.' In these terms, the author, at that time a member of a senior management team, brought credibility and 'insider knowledge' to the collection and interpretation of the data.

Because of the small size of Ireland in general (4.6 million) and of the university sector in particular, to ensure that individuals were not identifiable, the sample was not disaggregated by level. Pseudonyms are also used to conceal the identity of the participants, although reflecting the face-to-face character of Irish society, fictitious names are used, with manager-academics being differentiated from other professionals by the use of the designation professor.

Good jobs?

In assessing this, attention is focussed on senior managers' perceptions of the advantages/disadvantages of being in senior management. For the majority, the former far exceeded the latter. At the level of advantages, among these senior managers, the university as a source of meaning featured prominently. Thus, despite the fact that universities in Ireland are becoming increasingly managerialist, many of the senior managers referred to the university's 'noble purpose' (Professor Gerard Anderson); its 'national importance, institutional importance ... a chance to think of the greater good' (Tony Noonan). The importance of the university's engagement with the local community was also occasionally mentioned by respondents (Bargh, Scott, and Smith 2000), as was its role in relation to the economy: 'The higher education sector is vital to the national economy; life-long learning and all those issues; making a contribution to the country and the future well-being of the country' (Thomas Hennessy). The power to influence the overall direction and shape of the university and to make a difference was also widely valued by men and women in the cross-national study (Riordan 2011).

In the Irish study, male manager-academics were particularly likely to refer to shaping the institution as an advantage: 'it gives you the opportunity to shape things ... to shape the direction of an institution' (Professor Denis Tobin). There was no evidence to support Blackmore's (1999) suggestion that women were ambivalent about positional power: 'power, whether we like it or not, the capacity to make decisions and to effect change was a challenge, a challenge that I enjoyed' (Professor Geraldine Maguire). For her, 'power was always a useful thing to have' and like Kloot's (2004) respondents, it was not too much but too little of it that was frustrating: 'Things I wanted to do, I couldn't do.' Fitzgerald (2014, 113) also refers, albeit very briefly to the fact that in her study 'for some women, playing the game is intensely pleasurable'. In the present study, women manager-academics were particularly likely to focus on the possibility of using positional power to open up opportunities for other people, reflecting a gendered orientation to power (Baker-Miller 1986): 'you identify good people, relatively junior, who are buzzing with ideas, and find a niche and give them small incentives to implement those ideas' (Professor Cathy O'Riordan); 'the opportunity and the task to try to access resources, to allow the really good people around the system to make their mark' (Professor Sheila Furlong). This may reflect a construction of femininity in Ireland that is strongly relational (O'Connor 1998), with nurturing being important in legitimating women's occupancy of positions of power, thus reducing the tension between leadership and gender roles (Eagly and Sczesny 2009; Coleman 2011).

One of the well-recognised appealing characteristics of a university as a knowledge-based institution is the intellectual calibre of the people who work there (Lindholm 2004). This was very frequently noted as an advantage by men and women in the Irish study as well as in the wider cross-national one (Riordan 2011): 'The university is a fabulous community to work in terms of how much it enriches your intellectual life. There are so many different, very bright, people that you get to meet and deal with' (Professor Gerard Anderson).

The university as an institution has survived by alliances with other powerful institutional structures which have funded it. In an Irish context, the main source of such funding is still the state. However, the senior managers (as in the Australian and Portuguese studies: O'Connor, Carvalho, and White 2014) saw the difficulties of accessing sufficient resources for their own university as one of the main disadvantages of being in senior management: 'Attempting to manage on reduced resources … is difficult' (Professor Marie Walsh); 'Having lots of good ideas that I can't implement because of lack of resources' [is a disadvantage] (Professor Sean Murphy). Indeed, some referred to 'the huge lack of underfunding by the State' (Pauline Hanratty). The internal organisational structures were also seen as a disadvantage. Thus, they referred to the difficulties created by a bureaucracy that attempted to be consensual: 'We are forever looking for consensus and end up not making decisions' (Peter Delaney); and to 'an almost Japanese management concept, it takes a long time to reach a decision' (Gerard Donnelly). Such concerns about internal decision-making structures are not peculiar to Irish universities (O'Connor, Carvalho, and White 2014). Frustration was also expressed with what was seen as the increasingly managerialist micro-management by structures such as the Higher Educational Authority, which interface between the universities and central government.

Lindholm (2004) noted that the ability to structure time was one of the key attractions of academic work. However, much of this autonomy is lost when academics assume senior management roles and they themselves become part of a 'Panoptical surveillance system' (Foucault 1978, 201). That very system corrodes their control over their own time, and hence erodes their autonomy. Both men and women mentioned this loss of discretionary time: 'Now I have lost that, 95 per cent of it anyway' (Professor Joan Geraghty). Some noted that the higher you went, the less freedom in this sense you had, until 'you have no freedom at all … you are committed every minute. Your life is not your own, utterly and completely' (Professor Kieran Naughton).

There was a sense that a long-hours culture existed: '12 hours a day and in at weekends' (Professor Geraldine Maguire); 'you could just keep going' (Thomas Hennessy). Similar trends were identified in other countries, although it was recognised that ideas about 'appropriate' work–life balance varies between individuals and that imbalances are not inevitably negative (Riordan 2011). For the majority of both men and women in the Irish study, work/life imbalance was not seen as a problem, because of their life stage: 'if I was younger, a disadvantage would be that I would not see my family growing up. I would have missed out. But … my children have grown up' (Professor Kieran Naughton). As in Hewlett and Buck Luce's (2006) study, insofar as there was any reference to work–life balances, it was most likely to be made by the men. This contrasts with the picture emerging in Fitzgerald's (2014) study of women academic leaders in Australia and New Zealand. This is a major source of tension among academic senior managers in Australia (Bagilhole and White 2011; Fitzgerald 2014; O'Connor, Carvalho, and White 2014), a pattern that was interpreted as reflecting the greater presence of managerialism in such contexts. In the Irish study, women occasionally also referred to long hours, but located this in the context of a wider range of work-related pressures, or else saw it as an acceptable cost: 'those kinds of pressures are part of the deal you sign up to' (Jane Morrison); 'increasing pressure on academics to do everything, publish, administer, PhDs … and then on top of that juggling home responsibility' (Professor Eileen Greene). Stress was very rarely referred to by men or women. Some had adopted what they saw as effective strategies to limit the personal cost, including 'being disciplined' about it intruding on their home life; keeping time for things that were very personally important' and scheduling family time at week-ends. In the present study, both men and women prioritised management, albeit sometimes regretfully, over what they saw as their contribution to the key functions of the university (i.e. research and teaching). In the Irish study, it was simply seen as an inevitable part of senior management.

Yet, these women in senior management positions were more likely than their male counterparts to say that they were actually looking forward to a movement out of management in five years' time: 'hopefully I will return to being one of those privileged people who have quiet time for research, writing in my office or in the library somewhere' (Professor Eileen Greene). The women also had more positive attitudes to making what in Ireland is a compulsory transition to retirement at 65 years: 'I have done lots of things, happy to draw it to a close' (Professor Ann Joyce). In contrast, for the male manager-academics, the thought of retirement was very daunting: 'I am old and done now' (Professor Kieran Naughton). For those who would not be of retirement age in five years' time, as in Doherty and Manfredi's (2010) study, the possibility of remaining in senior management (after their current assignment) was more likely to be entertained by men than by women: 'I guess I might be still in senior management' (Professor Niall Phelan). Women had greater difficulty articulating such a possibility, although they did so very occasionally: 'that is quite difficult … There are two obvious routes: I look for the president post or I go back to my first love, in a corner somewhere, reading and writing', with the attraction of these options 'changing on a daily basis' (Professor Sheila Furlong). Thus, although female manager-academics accepted and even valued the opportunity to occupy such positions, they saw them as temporary assignments, arguably reflecting their uneasy cultural positioning in them (see next section). However, since the women were frequently at a lower level than their male counterparts, it is possible that such attitudes also reflect their level in the organisation.

At the organisational level, the majority of the women in senior management embodied positions of resistance as 'tempered radicals' (Meyerson and Scully 2011) in the sense that they were committed to the organisation, but highly critical of some aspects of its culture. Such a positioning has been seen as ambivalent, emotionally exhausting and involving considerable organisational pressure as regards co-option. However, it is also 'a unique source of vitality, learning and transformation' (Meyerson and Scully 2011, 200). There was evidence that although some of these women had paid a price for their attitudes (in terms of not being re-appointed or not moving further up the hierarchy), they valued the opportunities these positions offered, and enjoyed the authenticity and the challenges that stemmed from the complexity of their position, and the opportunities they offered as regards reducing the influence of stereotypes (Ridgeway 2011; O'Connor and Carvalho 2014; O'Connor and Goransson 2015).

In summary, university senior managers saw the perceived purpose of the university and the intellectual calibre of the people they worked with as important sources of meaning and pleasure. In terms of disadvantages, the most common references were to the difficulties of getting funding and the management structures. Overwhelmingly, both men and women prioritised management and saw its costs as acceptable, although women's commitment to these positions was time limited. Overall, however, other than in this area, there were few differences between men and women, implicitly suggesting the possibility of common ground which might be explored (Ridgeway and Correll 2004), potentially reducing gender barriers but reinforcing elite ones.

Places for women?

A wide range of academic work has concluded that the barriers women face in universities include those related to a 'chilly' organisational culture premised on male lifestyles and priorities and on a particular concept of the ideal academic, which Thornton (2013) calls 'Benchmark Man'. Thus, although the specific characteristics prescribed for 'Benchmark Man' may vary across time and space, the equation of the ideal academic with a stereotypical male construct does not change. In such contexts, women by definition do not fit. Such phenomena are not peculiar to Ireland (Bagilhole and White 2011; Neale 2011; OECD 2012; Shah and Shah 2012; O'Connor 2014). Here, attention is focused on two dimensions of this gendered organisational culture: organisational narratives and interactional perceptions.

Organisational narratives: valuing of gender

Typically, men are more likely to deny the existence of gender, reflecting wider patterns of the invisibility of privileges to those who are privileged (Connell 1987; Acker 2006). The practice of gender and the creation and maintenance of gender inequalities may be unintentional, with men mobilising 'masculinities without being conscious of doing so' (Yancey Martin 2006, 261). In any case, men were more likely to deny, and women more likely to identify gendered organisational cultures in academic environments as a systemic problem (Currie and Thiele 2001; Kloot 2004; Grummell, Lynch, and Devine 2009; Linehan, Buckley, and Koslowski 2009) with male professors in particular stressing that 'there is no sex discrimination in university or academic life' (Harris, Thiele, and Currie 1998, 259). Similar patterns emerged in the present study. Thus, for example, Paul Meaney says that he has 'never believed there is a glass ceiling ... because I have not come across it'. The invisibility of gender to their male counterparts was referred to by women in the current study: 'in relation to gender, I just wonder are they gender blind? They don't see it as an issue' (Professor Tina Mc Cleland); 'You think are we in the twenty-first century or in the eighteenth. There is chauvinism to the Irish psyche' (Professor Sheila Furlong). The majority of the women in the present study identified 'systematic biases' within their universities, characterising them as having 'an unsupportive culture for women to inhabit': 'Women are conscious that men are unconsciously misogynistic but men aren't conscious of this' (Pauline Hanratty). Naming a gendered organisational culture as such can be seen as a form of resistance (O'Connor 2001) and has similarities with contestation, that is, verbally challenging the existing rules and resources (Whitchurch 2008).

Men's relationships with other men are a key factor in creating/maintaining a culture of privilege and entitlement. For Hartmann (1981), men as men can hope to benefit, at least to some extent, from the status quo, so they have a vested interest in perpetuating male bonding as well as in the marginalisation or subordination of women. There have been references to 'the male "clubbiness" of the culture' (Kloot 2004; see also Deem, Hilliard, and Reed 2008; Coleman 2011; Fitzgerald 2014). Similar patterns emerged in the present study, where women depicted senior management as: 'a male club at the top level … very hard as a woman … It is a very male domain' (Professor Ann Joyce). Pro-male attitudes of varying degrees of intensity were perceived by women in senior management: 'the biggest thing really is that men are generally more comfortable working with men, communicating with men, being with men, understanding men' (Claire Hartigan):

> Most of the men that I work with, the bottom line is that they would be much more comfortable to be working with men. They vaguely put up with you, accept that you have a right to be there, but if it was up to themselves, they are more comfortable around men. This is not a generational thing. Those most uncomfortable are seriously younger. (Professor Tina Mc Cleland)

The differential value attached to activities undertaken predominantly by men/women has been seen as a core element in a gendered organisational culture (Ely and Meyerson 2000; Lynch, Grummell, and Devine 2012). The women in the present study were aware of these gendered processes:

> Women are given welfare and minding the student type roles, advisees and counselling. The dynamic, high profile, getting funding, creating buildings is seen as male and is given to the male so [they] build up their own profile … Women are left with the nice ones. They are critically important but are not valued … not THAT important really, not sexy, not going to get you ahead. (Jane Morrison)

As they saw it, 'women tend to be dumped with stuff that the men don't want to do … We are the ones who will tend to pick up stuff because the others are not doing it and because we know it needs to be done' (Pauline Hanratty). Similar trends emerged in other studies (Krefting 2003; Kloot 2004; Carvalho and Santiago 2010). For the most part, references to discrimination by the men only occurred in the context of positive discrimination, which was depicted as 'making allowances' 'the suspension of academic standards' (John Keane). Thus, the implicit suggestion was that no male privileging exists.

Currie and Thiele (2001) found that the proportion of men who denied gender inequality varied across countries. However, even within countries, individual men and women may, because of their own experiences or positioning, highlight their existence. In the present study, a small number of male manager-academics referred to particular aspects of the organisational culture (albeit not those related to management) as reflecting underlying attitudes that they saw as essentially unfair to women. Thus, for example, although Professor Gerard Anderson said that he did not see any evidence of discrimination in the sense that he 'heard no one saying we are not going to have another woman around or there or too many women around here', he had noticed that women were disproportionately involved with the administration of teaching: 'Teaching is the new housework'. Some men, particularly those who had formative experiences outside the Irish academic system saw the continued existence of a male-dominated organisational culture as legally and morally unacceptable or as an embarrassing anachronism. Thus, Professor Larry Mc Donald thought that having women in senior management in universities: 'is right because it is right'. For others, the importance was rhetorical: 'one can point to the fact that one has lots of women in senior management' (Professor Michael Mc Grath). Men who had worked outside the Irish academic system were much more aware of gender and more willing to name it. Other professional managers who had entered the university sector recently, and who had worked in mixed gender groups in the private sector, appeared to be benignly unreflective about gender but went on to ask refreshingly 'unthinkable' (Lukes 2005) questions, implicitly suggesting that they did not see women as having a 'negative symbolic coefficient' (Bourdieu 2001, 93). Thus, for example, Mark Noonan said that, although he remembered that he had read an article about 'glass ceilings', which said that women needed supports to avail of opportunities: 'I don't know what these supports are, maybe I should know'. Some of them went on to ask refreshingly 'unthinkable' (Lukes 2005) questions. Thus, for example, those who had come from the private sector and who retained a concern with profit noted: 'Where have you ever heard one of the universities come out and say the women's university as an angle on student recruitment?' (Timmy Collins). Thus, in this case, managerialism led to the endorsement of a perspective that ignored the greater value typically attached to men's activities/arenas.

In summary, gender inequalities in the organisational culture were visible to the majority of women senior managers. Men who had worked in higher educational institutions outside Ireland, or in the private sector, were more aware of the existence of gender inequalities than those who had not had such experiences.

Interactional perceptions: valuing of gender

Where individuals have multiple identities, the question arises as to which of these are activated in a particular context. Others' perceptions can be complicated by stereotypes: 'As individuals "do" and "accomplish" gender … they are assisted, directed and constrained by the ideology and practice of gendered institutions … that define forms of behaviour as gender appropriate or inappropriate' (Mihelich and Storrs 2003, 404; see also Deutsch 2007; Coleman 2011; Ridgeway 2011; Fitzgerald 2014). Whether gender as an ascriptive characteristic is visible and/or valued provides an indication of its differential significance in the interactional context of senior management.

The existence of a status hierarchy among men has been seen as characteristic of patriarchy (Hartmann 1981). Women, despite their senior position, have no place in that hierarchy because of their gender. In that context, women are positioned as 'supportive/submissive' or posing 'resistance and … disruptive of hegemonic masculinities' (Bird 2003, 367). Many of the female manager-academics in the present study thought that they were seen in problematic terms by their male counterparts because of their gender. Thus, Professor Geraldine Maguire reflected that she was seen by her male colleagues as 'too questioning; too challenging, asking uncomfortable questions' and describing her male colleagues as 'quite frightened of me, scared of me in some senses'. Others referred to male colleagues' perception of them as 'awkward … that irritating person down the hall' (Professor Eileen Greene); 'to my surprise, I was seen as quite formidable' (Professor Cathy O'Riordan); 'as one seriously intimidating individual who knows how to get her own way' (Katherine Mc Elligott). These comments indicate their perception by male colleagues as disruptive, confrontational, dissenting, and that, as such, these women frightened them. They have resonances with Kanter's (1993) description of the iron maiden archetype into which women in predominantly male organisations in the 1970s were thrust if they 'insisted on full rights in the group ... . Displayed competence in a forthright manner'. The word 'frightening' was also used by Husu's Finnish respondents (2001, 144). It is evocative of both women's perceived power and yet their unacceptability as equal players in what purport to be degendered organisations. Other studies have shown that when women do seek and gain leadership roles, and push aside the stereotypical gendered nurturing role, they are often perceived as being 'bossy' and domineering' (Coleman 2011). Thus, although a small number of women were included in university senior management, as the women perceived it, there was a certain discomfort with having them there. Yet, their presence reflected presidential support, and in an increasingly managerialist system, overwhelmingly relied on presidential nomination (O'Connor 2014). But their inclusion was on certain terms, and, there were limits to their acceptance because of their gender: 'One thing you can never be in this job is one of the boys ... [there is] a certain place that other male colleagues can go with regard to one another that you won't go' (Professor Joan Geraghty).

Those in senior management in Lynch, Grummell, and Devine's study (2012, 143, 144), also referred to not being accepted as 'one of the gang'; being 'positioned as 'other': the 'outsider who ... asks embarrassing questions' (Gherardi 1996, 194 and 196; see also Fitzgerald 2014) with some of the women seeing their male colleagues as having a rather paternalistic view of them (see also Krefting 2003). In the present study, there was also evidence of such patronising attitudes. Thus, Professor Sheila Furlong described her male colleagues' view of her as 'quite efficient, a little misguided. At times I'm told I give people too much air time' (i.e. she manages a couple of people by talking to them). Similarly, although Pauline Hanratty was very clear that: 'I am totally equal to them' (i.e. male colleagues), as she saw it, this was not the way that some of them perceived her. Very occasionally, women saw their male colleagues as perceiving them positively: 'in a positive light as a very able skilled ... person. I think I am seen as politically astute, being able to manage the political situation ... generally seen as supportive but also as challenging' (Clare Hartigan). The reference to political skills is interesting, and echoes an underlying perception of universities as highly political arenas, a perspective that many women see as problematic (O'Connor 2014).

The depiction of women's relationships with each other as uniformly negative can be seen as a key mechanism of patriarchal control (O'Connor 2002). However, there is evidence that high potential women are most likely to include women in their networks and to identify women as key sources of career-related information and strategies, with women-dominated support systems providing encouragement, instrumental help and facilitating women's career development (Ibarra 1997; Mavin and Bryans 2002; Fitzgerald 2014). On the other hand, Ely (1994) found that in organisations with few senior women, women were less likely to get support from other women. Thus, it appears that women's relationships with each other are affected by the gender profile of the organisation. In Ireland, despite the rapidity of cultural and social change (reflected in, for example, dramatic increases in women's attainment of higher education, their participation in paid employment in general and as academic staff in universities in particular), much of social life remains highly gender segregated, reflecting and reinforcing essentialist gender stereotypes. It was striking that overwhelmingly, the female senior managers in the present study saw other women's perception of them as positive 'as a leader, somebody who has managed to get into a senior position and has done it while raising a family, and doing other things, and hence fairly useful as a role model' (Professor Joan Geraghty).

> as ambitious, capable, fairly competent to get our point across at the big table if I have to; also seen as supportive of female colleagues' careers, and supportive of challenging a lot of the structures that have existed for years, and that women might not necessarily agree with. (Professor Eileen Greene)

Much more ambivalent, and in some cases hostile perceptions were perceived to exist between women in other countries in the cross-national study, including Sweden, New Zealand, and Turkey (Neale 2011). This difference may reflect the segregated nature and essentialist construction of femininity still persisting in Irish society: one in which the negative evaluation of women by public patriarchy is not fully accepted, and alternative evaluations are created and maintained by women in female-dominated contexts. Alternatively, it may be that these women grew to adulthood during the 1960s–1970s at a time when the second women's movement was at its height (O'Connor 1998; Connolly 2003). In any case, the majority of these female academic-managers were strongly identified with other women; were very comfortable in all women groups and stressed the understanding they felt in such all women groups where: 'people automatically and intrinsically understand your female issues. In a pre-dominantly male one, it depends on the man' (Jane Morrison).

It has been suggested that: 'It is only those who can take for granted their place in the world, those who are already privileged, who can leave themselves and their iden-tity out of the picture' (Yates 2009, 18). The men in this study had far more difficulty than the women in thinking about how they were perceived by their colleagues: 'I have not given that a lot of thought' (Tony Noonan); 'It's hard to know' (Professor Tommy Ryan). On reflection, however, they were able to identify such perceptions. For most of them, their gender was invisible to their colleagues. A small number referred to what could be regarded as masculine qualities (whether present or desired: drawing on an implicitly tough, aggressive stereotype of masculinity): 'I think they probably see me as quite tough when it comes to taking difficult decisions, particularly in relation to people' (Professor Denis Tobin). Nevertheless, their colleagues' perceived evaluations were typically seen as very positive. There were occasional rejections of other's percep-tions, reflecting resistance to what were depicted as simplistic criticisms: 'some think that I sold out on research … somebody has to manage the place. I believe I am seen as being very effective: I make things happen' (Professor Niall Phelan). Thus, even in these cases, they still saw others' evaluation as positive.

Overwhelmingly, the men thought that there was no difference in the way they were seen by men and women. However, a minority of men thought that women saw them more positively than their male counterparts: 'in this environment I am probably seen as a whinger rather than someone who gets things done. [My female colleagues] see me as someone who is trying to get things done, as someone who listens' (Timmy Collins). The language that is used ('whinger') is stereotypically associated with women, and in this case it seems to reflect a discomfort with the wider gendered organisational culture, one which is not seen as valuing stereotypically female qualities. As Professor Gerard Anderson saw it, his colleagues' perceptions of him either reflected an acceptance or a challenging of his position of power: and with female colleagues 'the combative piece is not so obviously there'. A minority of men saw the perceptions of their female colleagues as more accurate, less challenging and more positive than those of their male colleagues. These men were also those who indicated some degree of discomfort with all male groups: seeing them as having 'a slightly laddish feel' (Professor Gerard Anderson), implicitly suggesting a discomfort with the dominant male culture, where the stereotypical managerial style was seen as one involving aggression (O'Connor and Goransson 2015). Such men are potential allies in challenging dominant constructions of masculinity and hence in changing the organisational culture.

In summary, women overwhelmingly saw their male colleagues' perceptions of them as disruptive, frightening, and so on, thus underlining their suspect positioning in these senior management structures. The majority of the men saw both their male and female colleagues' perceptions of them as positive. A minority of men saw their female colleagues' perceptions as more positive than those of their male colleagues, reflecting a discomfort with a masculinist organisational culture.

Summary and conclusions

This article is concerned with men's and women's experience of elite positions and with the extent to which such positions are seen as places for women. It is concerned with exploring the existence of gender-differentiated patterns in both areas and ultimately with their impact on a commitment to continuing in senior management. These issues are explored in the context of a study of senior management in public universities in Ireland. More specifically, it is concerned with two aspects of the experience of university senior management: first, their perceptions of the advantages/disadvantages of being in senior management and gender variation in this; and second, with gender variation in the organisational narratives and interpersonal perspectives of men and women occupying these positions, and its impact on commitment to continuing in these positions.

It shows that there is surprisingly little gender difference in these respondents' experiences of the advantages and disadvantages of being in senior management. The levels of meaning and pleasure that these respondents identified as advantages of being in university senior management were striking, partly stemming from the perceived purpose of the university, and partly from the calibre of people working there. There was general consensus that limited resources for the university and the external and internal structures were disadvantages. The impact of senior management on academic activity and work–life balance was generally seen as an acceptable cost. Yet, the women were more likely than their male counterparts to say that they were actually looking forward to a movement out of management in five years' time.

In terms of organisational narratives, in this as in a range of other studies, men were more likely to deny the existence of gender while women were more likely to name it. At the interactional level, the majority of women saw their gender as visible to their male colleagues and for the most part not in a positive way. On the other hand, the majority of them saw themselves as viewed positively by their female colleagues, a trend which did not emerge in other countries (Neale 2011). Men had greater difficulty in thinking about how they were perceived, and overwhelmingly saw their gender as invisible (reflecting a well-recognised tendency for characteristics to be invisible to those in hegemonic positions). A minority of the men in this study thought that they were seen more positively by their female than their male colleagues. Such men can be seen as potential allies in challenging hegemonic male discourses and highlight the inadequacy of a binary construction of gender.

Women constitute roughly one-fifth of those in university senior management and the majority in this study are effectively contesting such gendered structures. In addition, not all men are supporting these structures. Pressure as regards gendered change is also supported by cross-national structures whose concern is with economic growth and who see the failure to address gender inequality as inhibiting that growth. Organisational narratives and interactional contexts involve possibilities and difficulties as regards 'undoing gender' (Deutsch 2007). Ely and Myerson's (2000) work has shown how organisations, under certain conditions, can do this. There is clear evidence of such transformations within private sector organisations (Huse 2013). However, it is not yet clear to what extent these patterns can be transferred to universities, where the identification of a compelling corporate goal (such as company profit) related to gender diversity is more difficult to identify. However, it is at least possible that they may be transferable, with appropriate leadership.

Pressures as regards gendered change are being supported by forces within the universities themselves as academic staff dissent from a neo-liberal and/or gendered agenda. The economic collapse and the increasing awareness of power and its partiality in Irish society may also facilitate change within Irish universities. Gendered processes and practices are supported, implicitly or explicitly, by the state structures that interface with universities. However, the gendering of higher education is being challenged by international structures such as the EU and the OECD. These are increasingly aware of the extent to which future economic growth is related to the ability to use the skills and talents of women, the best educated of its citizens. In conclusion, although being in senior management is attractive, it is a still a gendered place, with uneasy resonances for women.

Disclosure statement

No potential conflict of interest was reported by the author.

References

Acker, J. 2006. "Inequality Regimes Gender, Class, and Race in Organizations." *Gender and Society* 20 (4): 441–464.

Bagilhole, B. 2002. "Challenging Equal Opportunities: Changing and Adapting Male Hegemony in Academia." *British Journal of Sociology of Education* 23 (1): 19–33.

Bagilhole, B., and K. White, eds. 2011. *Gender, Power and Management. A Cross Cultural Analysis of Higher Education.* Basingstoke: Palgrave Macmillan.

Baker-Miller, J. 1986. *Towards a New Psychology of Women.* 2nd ed. Middlesex: Pelican.

Bargh, C. J. Bocock, P. Scott, and D. Smith. 2000. *University Leadership: The Role of the Chief Executive.* Buckingham: The Society for Research into Higher Education and Open University Press.

Benschop, Y., and M. Brouns. 2003. "Crumbling Ivory Towers: Academic Organising and Its Gender Effects." *Gender, Work and Organisation* 10 (2): 194–212.

Bird, S. 2003. "De-Gendering Practice/Practicing Gendering: Response to Yancey Martin." *Gender and Society* 17 (3): 367–369.

Blackmore, Jill. 1999. *Troubling Women: Feminism, Leadership and Educational Change.* Buckingham: Open University Press.

Bourdieu, P. 2001. *Masculine Domination.* Redwood City, CA: Stanford University Press.

Carvalho, T., and R. Santiago. 2010. "New Challenges for Women Seeking an Academic Career: The Hiring Process in Portuguese HEIs." *Journal of Higher Education Policy and Management* 32 (3): 239–249.

Coleman, M. 2011. *Women at the Top: Challenges, Choices and Change.* Basingstoke: Palgrave Macmillan.

Connell, R. 1987. *Gender and Power.* Oxford: Blackwell.

Connolly, L. 2003. *The Irish Women's Movement: From Revolution to Devolution.* London: Palgrave Macmillan.

Currie, J., and B. Thiele. 2001. "Globalisation and Gendered Work Cultures in Universities." In *Gender and the Restructured University*, edited by A. Brooks and A. Mackinnon, 90–116. Buckingham: SRHE and Open University.

Deem, R., S. Hilliard, and M. Reed. 2008. *Knowledge, Higher Education and the New Managerialism.* Oxford: Oxford University Press.

Deutsch, F. M. 2007. "Undoing Gender." *Gender and Society* 21 (1): 106–127.

Doherty, L., and S. Manfredi. 2010. "Improving Women's Representation in Senior Positions in Universities." *Employee Relations* 32 (2): 138–155.

Eagly, A. H., and S. Sczesny. 2009. "Stereotypes About Women, Men, and Leaders: Have Times Changed?" In *The Glass Ceiling in the 21st Century: Understanding Barriers to Gender Equality*, edited by M. Barreto, M. K. Ryan, and M. T. Schmitt, 21–47. Washington, DC: APA Books.

Ely, R. J. 1994. "The Effect of Organisational Demographics and Social Identity on Relationships among Professional Women." *Administrative Science Quarterly* 39: 203–238.

Ely, R. J., and D. E. Meyerson. 2000. "Theories of Gender in Organisations: A New Approach to Organisational Analysis and Change." *Research in Organisational Behaviour* 22: 103–151.

EU. 2012. "Structural Change in Research Institutions: Enhancing Excellence, Gender Equality and Efficiency in Research and Innovation." Accessed December 2, 2012. http://ec.europa.eu/research/science-society/document_library/pdf_06/structural-changes-final-report_en.pdf

Fitzgerald, T. 2014. *Women Leaders in Higher Education: Shattering the Myths.* London: SRHE.

Foucault, M. 1978. *The History of Sexuality, Volume I: An Introduction.* Translated by Robert Hurley. New York: Pantheon.

Gherardi, S. 1996. "Gendered Organisational Cultures: Narratives of Women Travellers in a Male World." *Gender, Work and Organisation* 3 (4): 187–201.

Glaser, B., and A. Strauss. 1967. *The Discovery of Grounded Theory: Strategies for Qualitative Research.* Chicago, IL: Aldine.

Grummell, B., K. Lynch, and D. Devine. 2009. "Appointing Senior Managers in Education: Homosociality, Local Logics and Authenticity in the Selection Process." *Educational Management, Administration and Leadership* 37 (30): 329–349.

Hammersley, M. 2008. "Assessing Validity in Social Research." In *The Sage Handbook of Social Research Methods*, edited by P. Alasuutari, L. Bickman, and J. Brannen, 42–53. London: Sage.

Harris, P., B. Thiele, and J. Currie. 1998. "Success, Gender and Academic Voices: Consuming Passion or Selling the Soul?" *Gender and Education* 10 (2): 133–148.

Hartmann, H. 1981. "The Unhappy Marriage of Marxism and Feminism: Towards a More Progressive Union." In *Women and Revolution: A Discussion of the Unhappy Marriage of Marxism and Feminism*, edited by L. Sargent, 1–41. Boston, MA: South End Press.

Hearn, J. 2001. "Academia, Management and Men: Making the Connections, Exploring the Implications." In *Gender and the Restructured University*, edited by A. Brooks and A. Mackinnon, 69–89. Buckingham: SRHE and Open University.

Hewlett, S. A., and C. Buck Luce. 2006. "Extreme Jobs: The Dangerous Allure of the 70 Hour Week." *Harvard Business Review* 84 (12): 49–59.

Huse, G. 2013. "Towards the Top: Advancing Women in the Workplace." Paper presented at women's economic engagement and the Europe 2020 genda, Irish presidency 2013 gender equality conference, Dublin Castle, April 29–30.

Husu, L. 2001. *Sexism Support and Survival in Academia: Academic Women and Hidden Discrimination in Finland.* Helsinki: University of Helsinki Press.

Hyvarinen, M. 2008. "Analysing Narratives and Story Telling." In *The Sage Handbook of Social Research Methods*, edited by P. Alasuutari, L. Bickman, and J. Brannen, 447–460. London: Sage.

Ibarra, H. 1997. "Paving an Alternative Route: Gender differences in Managerial Networks." *Social Psychology Quarterly* 60 (1): 91–102.

Kanter, R. M. [1993] 1977. *Men and Women of the Corporation*. 2nd ed. New York: Basic Books.

Kloot, L. 2004. "Women and Leadership in Universities: A Case Study of Women Academic Managers." *International Journal of Public Sector Management* 17 (6): 470–485.

Krefting, L. A. 2003. "Intertwined Discourses of Merit and Gender: Evidence from Academic Employment in the USA." *Gender, Work and Organisation* 10 (2): 260–278.

Leathwood, C., and B. Read. 2009. *Gender and the Changing Face of Higher Education: A Feminised Future?* Berkshire: McGraw-Hill, SRHE and Open University Press.

Lindholm, J. A. 2004. "Pathways to the Professoriate: The Role of Self, Others and Environment in Shaping Academic Career Aspirations." *Journal of Higher Education* 75 (6): 603–665.

Linehan, C., J. Buckley, and N. Koslowski. 2009. "Backwards … and in High Heels: Exploring Why Women Have Been Under-Represented at Senior Academic Levels 1987–2010." *Journal of Workplace Rights* 14 (4): 399–417.

Lukes, S. 2005. *Power: A Radical View*. 2nd ed. London: Macmillan.

Lynch, K. 1999. "Equality Studies, the Academy and the Role of Research in Emancipatory Social Change." *The Economic and Social Review* 30 (1): 41–69.

Lynch, K., B. Grummell, and D. Devine. 2012. *New Managerialism in Education: Commercialisation, Carelessness and Gender*. Basingstoke: Palgrave Macmillan.

Mabry, L. 2008. "Case Study in Social Research." In *The Sage Handbook of Social Research Methods*, edited by P. Alasuutari, L. Bickman, and J. Brannen, 328–343. London: Sage.

Mackenzie Davey, K. 2008. "Women's Accounts of Organisational Politics as a Gendering Process." *Gender, Work and Organisation* 15 (6): 650–671.

Mavin, S., and P. Bryans. 2002. "Academic Women in the UK: Mainstreaming Our Experiences and Networking for Action." *Gender and Education* 14 (3): 235–250.

Maxwell, J. A. 2012. *A Realist Approach for Qualitative Research*. New York, CA: Sage.

Meyerson, D. E., and M. A. Scully. [1995] 2011. "Tempered Radicalism and the Politics of Ambivalence and Change." In *Leadership: Volume 4, 2005–2009*, edited by D. Collinson, K. Grint, and B. Jackson, 177–120. London: Sage.

Mihelich, J., and D. Storrs. 2003. "Higher Education and the Negotiated Process of Hegemony: Embedded Resistance among Mormon Women." *Gender and Society* 17 (3): 404–422.

Morley, L. 2013. *Women and Higher Educational Leadership: Absences and Aspirations*. London: Leadership Foundation for Higher Education.

Neale, J. 2011. "Doing Senior Management." In *Gender, Power and Management: A Cross Cultural Analysis of Higher Education*, edited by B. Bagilhole and K. White, 140–167. Basingstoke: Palgrave Macmillan.

Nilsen, A. 2008. "From Questions of Method to Epistemological Issues: The Case of Biographical Research." In *The Sage Handbook of Social Research Methods*, edited by P. Alasuutari, L. Bickman, and J. Brannen, 81–94. London: Sage.

O'Connor, P. [1992] 2002. *Friendships Between Women*. Hemel Hempstead: Harvester Wheatsheaf/Pearsons.

O'Connor, P. 1998. *Emerging Voices: Women in Contemporary Irish Society*. Dublin: IPA.

O'Connor, P. 2001. "A Bird's Eye View … Resistance in Academia." *Irish Journal of Sociology* 10 (2): 86–104.

O'Connor, P. 2014. *Management and Gender in Higher Education*. Manchester: Manchester University Press.

O' Connor, P., and T. Carvalho. 2014. "Different or Similar: Constructions of Leadership by Senior Managers in Irish and Portuguese Universities." *Studies in Higher Education*. http://dx.doi.org/10.1080/03075079.2014.914909

O'Connor, P., T. Carvalho, and K. White. 2014. "The Experiences of Senior Positional Leaders in Australian, Irish and Portuguese Universities: Universal or Contingent?" *Higher Education Research and Development: Special Issue on Leadership* 33 (1): 1–14.

O'Connor, P., and A. Goransson. 2015. "Constructing or Rejecting the Notion of Other in Senior University Management: The Cases of Ireland and Sweden." *Educational Management, Administration and Leadership* 43 (2): 323–340.

OECD. 2012. "Closing the Gender Gap: Act Now!" Accessed December 19, 2012. www.oecd. org/gender/closingthegap.htm

Parry, K. W. 1998. "The New Leader: A Synthesis of Leadership Research in Australia and New Zealand." *Journal of Leadership Studies* 54: 82–105.

Ridgeway, C. 2011. *Framed by Gender*. Oxford: Oxford University Press.

Ridgeway, C., and S. L. Correll. 2004. "Unpacking the Gender System: A Theoretical Perspective on Gender Beliefs and Social Relations." *Gender and Society* 18 (4): 510–531.

Riordan, S. 2011. "Paths to Success in Senior Management." In *Gender, Power and Management: A Cross-Cultural Analysis of Higher Education*, edited by B. Bagilhole and K. White, 110–139. Basingstoke: Palgrave Macmillan.

Risman, B. J. 2004. "Gender as a Social Structure: Theory Wrestling with Activism." *Gender and Society* 18 (4): 429–450.

Shah, S., and U. Shah. 2012. "Women, Educational Leadership and Societal Culture." *Journal of Education* 2: 180–207.

Smircich, L. 1983. "Concepts of Culture and Organisational Analysis." *Administrative Science Quarterly* 28 (3): 339–358.

Thornton, M. 2013. "The Mirage of Merit." *Australian Feminist Studies* 28 (76): 127–143.

Tierney, W. G. 1998. "Organisational Culture in Higher Education." *Journal of Higher Education* 59 (1): 1–21.

Wajcman, J. 1998. *Managing like a Man: Women and Men in Corporate Management*. Cambridge: Polity Press.

Wharton, A. 2012. *The Sociology of Gender*. Oxford: Wiley-Blackwell.

Whitchurch, C. 2008. "Shifting Identities and Blurring Boundaries: The Emergence of Third Space Professionals in UK Higher Education." *Higher Education Quarterly* 62 (4): 377–396.

Wicks, D., and P. Bradshaw. 2002. "Investigating Gender and Organisational Culture: Gendered Value Foundations that Reproduce Discrimination and Inhibit Organisational Change." In *Gender, Identity and the Culture of Organisations*, edited by I. Aaltio and A. J. Mills, 137–159. Abingdon: Routledge.

Yancey Martin, Patricia. 2003. "'Said and Done' versus 'Saying and Doing': Gendering Practices, Practicing Gender at Work." *Gender and Society* 17 (3): 342–366.

Yancey Martin, P. 2006. "Practising Gender at Work: Further Thoughts on Reflexivity." *Gender, Work and Organisation* 13 (3): 254–276.

Yates, L. 2009. "'If it Can't Be Measured it Doesn't Count': Confronting Equity, Gender and Higher Education in the 21st Century." Paper presented at UPSI international conference on teaching and learning in higher education, Kuala Lumpur, November 23–25.

Executive power and scaled-up gender subtexts in Australian entrepreneurial universities

Jill Blackmore and Naarah Sawers

Center for Research in Educational Futures in Innovation, Deakin University, Geelong, Australia

Deputy Vice Chancellor and Pro Vice Chancellor positions have proliferated in response to the global, corporatised university landscape [Scott, G., S. Bell, H. Coates, and L. Grebennikov. 2010. "Australian Higher Education Leaders in Times of Change: The Role of Pro Vice Chancellor and Deputy Vice Chancellor." *Journal of Higher Education Policy and Management 32* (4): 401–418]. Senior leadership is the sphere where academic and management identities are negotiated and values around the role of the university are decided. This paper examines the changing and gendered nature of the senior leadership setting and its implications for diversity in and of university leadership. The analysis draws from a three-year empirical study funded by the Australian Research Council on leadership in Australian universities. It focuses on executive leaders in three universities – one which is research-intensive, the second, in a regional site, and the third, university of technology. The article argues that the university landscape and its management systems are being restructured in gendered ways. It utilises the notion of organisational gender subtexts to make explicit how gender works through structural and cultural reform.

The rise and rise of executive management in the Australian higher education landscape

During the new millennium, higher education as a social field, with all its gendered stratifications in terms of what knowledge is valued, its discourse and language, and its relative positioning of individuals, groups and disciplines, is again being restructured on a global scale. Neoliberal discourses, processes and practices of marketisation, managerialism and privatisation (King, Marginson, and Naidoo 2013) are constituted by and re/constitute specific institutional cultures and policy frames in gendered ways (MacKinnon and Brooks 2001; Blackmore and Sachs 2007). Women's underrepresentation in leadership historically has been attributed to women's individual choices about career, discriminatory recruitment and exclusionary cultures and practices, and thus primarily a human resource issue of leadership, talent management and/or equal employment policy. But such approaches ignore 'the functioning of universities as social institutions, where gender is "done" in a specific way', requiring the need to analyse how the 'structural, cultural and procedural arrangements of academic organising constitute gender relations' (Benschop and Brouns 2003, 194). As Benschop and Brouns (2003, 195) point out, 'Gender is part of organizing; it is an important element in the organization and division of labour.'

The issue of gender and leadership cannot be extracted from the wider context of global edu-capitalism and the increasingly ambiguous role of the university in terms of its public and commercial commitments (Marginson 2011). Hey and Bradford (2004, 696) write that:

> We think it increasingly important to map circuits of power between the state, its devolved (higher education) agencies and actors. Any ensuing explanation would need to account for relays of power that encompass public, professional, private, personal, and affective realms. It would require an appreciation of the material and discursive as well as intimate dimensions of the regulation of social experience.

The restructuring of the higher education sector during the 1980s and 1990s in many Anglophone countries was national, with the aim to produce unified seamless education systems directed towards national economic and social needs. For instance, in Australia, universities amalgamated with colleges of advanced education and Technical and Further Education institutes, and in 1992, in England, universities merged with polytechnics. It was a period marked by the increased participation of female students and academics, the former now a numerical majority. This has been seen as indicative of, and encouraging for, gender equity. In the performative university, equity, efficiency and effectiveness discourses jostled against each other uncomfortably as the system rapidly 'massified', although government investment in higher education in real terms, at least in Australia, reduced, intensifying academic labour (Currie and Vidovich 2009). New regulative regimes opened universities up to greater market competition, corporatised universities through managerialism and marketisation, introduced greater industry influence through partnerships, and intensified focus on outcomes in terms of performance management, quality assurance and research assessment as emerging measures of national and international reputation (Marginson and Considine 2000; Blackmore and Sachs 2007). It was a period in which women were encouraged to move into leadership positions in middle management (in roles such as Heads of School and Deans) through leadership programmes, mentoring and other formal strategies (Devers et al. 2006; White, Bagilhole, and Riordan 2012).

Post-2000, there has been scaling up of higher education globally. Universities have become multinational corporations. In Australian policy, education has increasingly been treated as an individual positional good, as an export earner and source of revenue to fund domestic expansion, and to be increasingly funded by individuals not governments (Marginson 2011). The entrepreneurial university is marked by its changing relationship with business (Mautner 2005, 96). In 2014, the nation state now expects universities to be a source of innovation to develop globalised knowledge-based economies through application in industry or the health sector (Peters, Marginson, and Murphy 2009). At the same time, and following the Bradley review (2008), equity discourses encouraged widening participation, as they did in the UK, of non-traditional users. Because a skilled technical and professional workforce is considered central to knowledge economies, the lack of women in science, technology, engineering and executive management is now viewed in higher education policy and business discourses as a 'waste of talent' (Burnell 2012, Blackmore 2014).

We argue that the re/structuring and re/culturing of the university sector is gendered on multiple fronts. Within the academy, and in response to changing policy environments, organisational power is being reconstituted in a number of ways. First, the education sector is becoming feminised, casualised and, some would argue, depro-fessionalised (Roberts and Donahue 2000). Second, university decision-making is becoming more centralised with greater executive prerogative being asserted with a focus on 'leaderism' (Morley 2013a) with men in 70% of university executive positions (Gordon and Whitchurch 2010; Fitzgerald 2012). Third, there is a shift away from aca-demic involvement in decision-making to managerial decision-making (Scott et al. 2010; Rowlands 2011, 2014). Fourth, there has been a reassertion of gendered knowl-edge–power relations around the dominance of discourses of science and technology linked to innovation around high-status 'hard' science dominated by males (Thornton, forthcoming; Blackmore 2014). Fifth, while there are more women in middle manage-ment, we illustrate, as others have illustrated (Grummell, Devine, and Lynch 2009a, 2009b; White, Bagilhole, and Riordan 2012), that there is at the executive level a gen-dered division of labour between the 'domestic' (internally oriented) roles of change management, teaching and learning and 'public' (externally oriented) organisational roles such as research, finance, partnerships and global engagement. Finally, the con-ditions of executive labour presume a particular capacity for flexibility and mobility, a 'careless' and 'carefree' individual, that discourages many women from taking up lea-dership (Devine, Grummell, and Lynch 2011).

Researching gender

The paper draws from a three-year study of three Australian universities located in metropolitan areas: one is a well-established research-intensive university (UMetro); the second, a University of Technology (Utech); and the third is regional (URegional). The cases were selected on the basis of their stated claims and reputations of being 'entrepreneurial'. Our study investigated how current leaders in management and research leadership positions viewed the nature and future of the university and leader-ship; questioned those academics who may (or may not) consider moving into research or managerial leadership in the future; and explored the aspirations of the next gener-ation of academics (early career and completing Ph.D.s) and how they understand their capacity and opportunities with regard to advancement into leadership in the academy. It was comprehensive, in that we interviewed academics and those in management pos-itions (Heads of School or Department, Deans, Pro Vice Chancellors (PVC), Deputy Vice Chancellors (DVC) and Vice Chancellors (VC)), male and female, across all dis-ciplines. We interviewed lecturers through to professors, from VC to completing doc-toral students ($n = 198$). For the purposes of this article, data are sourced from these interviews and focused predominantly on interviews with 16 executive members, including VCs, PCs and DVCs from the three case-study universities. A university-wide perspective was gained through interviewing key human resource, equal opportu-nity and union personnel. Our inquiry focused on how the changing nature of universities and academic work conditions impacted academic careers into leadership and the institutional support provided.

Gender was not foregrounded in the interviews, but a series of questions around the nature of academic work, the work/life balance and other pressures on leaders in research and management were asked. Questions also addressed ethno-cultural diver-sity (or lack of it) in leadership positions. A desktop and institutional analysis of each university mapped the extent and composition of senior management and research positions. A policy analysis of each university with regard to career development identified strategies that focused on building leadership capacity for and in research, teaching and management and whether interviewees were aware of and participated in any leadership programmes.

Due to the widening scope and scale of university activities in Australia as elsewhere, the trend has been for 'increase in abundance of PVCs' (Scott et al. 2010, 402) where males make up 70–74% of university executives in 2004 and 2006, respectively (Scott, Coates, and Anderson 2008, 7). While the number of female VCs has remained stable at 9 of 39 in 2004 and in 2013 (Universities Australia online), in 2014, women are increasingly present at the level of PVC and DVC, as could be expected with increasing numbers in middle management (from lists on the Universities Australia website, in 2014, they made up 75 of 245 executive positions). Gender was not seen to be an issue by both female and male executives at this senior management level. We recorded no instances of overt sexism or discrimination and women were relatively well represented at the case-study universities – in one instance, 50% of the executive committee. Indeed, across all universities, the discourse is pro-equity. Not having women in the top positions was understood in one male VC's words as a 'vulnerability' and something to 'be worked at'. The general consensus was that gender is no longer a problem and if it is, or is perceived to be, as Ahmed argues (2012), someone at the top will do something about it.

This paper argues that the evidence is that women at the DVC and PVC senior leadership level are still ambiguously located, as are those in middle management, within the entrepreneurial university (Blackmore and Sachs 2007). The social relations of gender with regard to power remain problematic, even where women are seen to exert greater influence over decision-making at the executive level. Knights and Kerfoot (2004) argue that embedded in the gender binary implicit in everyday organisational life and power/knowledge relations is a hierarchy in which the feminine is positioned as subordinate to the masculine. They remind us:

> While seeking to deconstruct the gender binary so as to disrupt its hierarchical implications, we also have to remain ambivalent about gender distinctions in order not to remove the very 'object' of critique. (Knights and Kerfoot 2004, 432)

Thus, we have to adopt a form of reflexive ambivalence towards the gender binary, treating it as a useful analytical tool.

Benschop and Doorewaard (1998) also identify the necessity to deconstruct the gendered practices and processes that render gender/power relations invisible. In organisational practice, 'gender equality is still persistent … while a dominant perception of equality occurs at the same time' (Benschop and Doorewaard 1998, 787). Benschop and Doorewaard's (1998, 788–790) concept of the 'gender subtext' to unpack processes of gender relations 'enables better understanding of the persistence of gender distinction in organisations, and, moreover, it provides insights into the organisational processes (re)producing this distinction'. Martinez (2011) uses this concept of gender subtext because:

> First, the textual reference underlines the symbolic and discursive character of the social production of meaning in organisations. Second, the concept implies a distinction between an apparent organisational reality, which is normally taken for granted and assumed to be neutral (the dominant texts), and a number of processes and arrangements that often remain tacit or unacknowledged (the underlying subtexts); the dominance of the former serves to conceal the workings of the latter, thus reinforcing an appearance of

normality and neutrality in organisational practices. Finally, the analysis of the gender subtext focuses attention on the power base of the gendering processes in organizations; that is, how gender is not a given attribute that is imported into the organisation, but it concerns both meanings and practices that involve the mobilisation of power resources.

A feminist perspective therefore considers the subtexts underpinning structural and institutional relations; the materialist conditions of labour; the procedural practices that render gender invisible and the epistemological claims embedded in seemingly gender-neutral concepts. Our research suggests that while there is a discourse of inclusion and diversity and sometimes a greater presence of women at the executive level, the turn towards hyper-managerialism and intensification of power in the executive is part of a wider gender restructuring of the field of higher education.

The nimble university

Universities, while always international, are now multinational corporations competing within globalised education markets. Much publicised reports, promoting discourses of insecurity in, and vulnerability of, the modern university, argue that they have to be more businesslike and academics, more entrepreneurial (e.g. Ernst and Young 2012). Yet, in our study, 18 VC, DVC and PVC at the executive level argued that Australian universities have been highly responsive to the external pressures confronting them. A DVC (Research) stated:

> I think we faced a major challenge in the early 1990s when there was a monetary shortfall ... we had addressed that by being more nimble and becoming more commercial and by moving into international education in a fairly big way ... I think of all the university sectors in the world we probably are actually very resilient. We have got a good brand ...

All the senior leaders agreed that funding constraints made flexibility in a global environment difficult, the main challenge being 'money money, money' (DVC). Australia in 2014 had the lowest level of Research and Development funding in 30 years (2.2% gross domestic product), lower than the significant investment by Asian and other Organization for Economic Cooperation and Development (OECD) countries. One DVC noted that 'the base funding is still under what we would want it to be' and it impacts their 'business model'. Other challenges mentioned included greater expectations around accountability, quality and relevance; changing international/domestic demographics; enhancing campus life; new private providers; and access and equity. A major priority was sourcing new funding not only from government but also from industry, alumni or philanthropic organisations. As one DVC Research argued, there is a 'mismatch between where our research investment is and where Australian industrial competitiveness lies'. The inability to capture the patents and commercial benefits from investment was due to lack of investors, regulations and infrastructure. But the economisation of the university also could conflict with their obligations to their students, the public and government, which, if neglected, de-legitimates their role (Marginson 2011).

The scaling up of universities from being nation-centric to global-centric was most evident in the executive fetish with the new global measurements of excellence in world rankings (e.g. Shanghai Jiao Tong, Times Higher Education and Subject Rankings) and achieving 'world-class' status. Universities have adopted strategic planning processes, benchmarking themselves against global competitors they seek to emulate. Largely based on reputation and research intensity, these rankings, most interviewees agreed, favoured established elite universities (Pusser and Marginson 2013, 554). Greater competitiveness for international students, demand-driven funding, quality assurance and global rankings had raised the status of teaching and learning as signified by its position at DVC status across the sector. DVCs responsible identified multiple competing pressures: capturing new student markets; best serving student diversity and equity; defining postgraduate attributes; addressing generic employability skills and E-learning. Academic pedagogies were expected to respond to the students' desire for multimodal provision and flexible forms of study. This was contingent on significant re-modelling of built environments to provide well-designed learning spaces (Blackmore et al. 2011). Massive open online course had heightened their focus on blended learning, considered to potentially facilitate a global repositioning of elite universities (Marginson 2012). As one DVC (Research) commented, 'Content is almost gone because the quality of content that will eventually become available … in a few years' time online will be superior to anything an average academic can produce'. Paradoxically, while universities were seeking to develop distinctive 'brands', the National Qualifications Framework was flattening the curriculum and standardising content, thus reducing differentiation in order to guarantee transferability (and supposedly quality) of credentials (e.g. Bologna). The rise of deregulation and outcomes-based funding had exacerbated tensions between excellence, equity and access (Lingard and Rawolle 2011).

Gender subtext 1: executive prerogative

The current phase of global restructuring is marked by the increased scope, scale, differentiation and intensity of leadership work. Being nimble, the VCs and executives argued, demanded rapid responses to changing policies and circumstances, thus requiring leaner (and meaner?) decision-making processes. This justified the creation of parallel managerial decision-making committees that effectively sidelined traditional formal academic procedures, thus reducing academic input (Rowlands 2014). In Utech, 17 members of the key decision-making committee included 8 Deans with 50% female members. UMetro had adopted the new position of Provost in addition to a Senior DVC (Academic) to undertake the internal leadership who, together with VC and DVCs (Research and Engagement), comprised the executive. In all three universities, as across the sector, small executive committees closest to the VC also included DVCs or Heads of finance, international and administration.

The increased scope and authority of line management that have marginalised academic voices is most evident in the changing make-up of University Councils and role of Academic Boards. In Victoria, new legislation excluded academic or student representation on Councils, although most retained these positions as good management practice. The role of Academic Boards and Senates in their varying forms is highly variable and dependent on the age of the university. At Utech, the VC or appointee chairs Academic Board. At UMetro, the Board was chaired full-time by a Professor, also on the executive, and comprised the full professoriate, most who generally attended for critical issues only. At URegional, as often in younger universities, there was a wider representation of senior and junior academics. The Chair (formerly held by a female PVC) had been upgraded from a part- to full-time (now held by a male professor) on the executive with administrative support. Thus, the Academic Board Chair, elected in most instances by academics, is incorporated in many instances within the executive committee, but has differing obligations to the academic community from those in line management whose responsibility is, given that they are on contract, to the VC. Rowlands (2014) argues that this constitutes a form of symbolic violence as the academic role is reduced to quality assurance within a corporate decision-making framework dominated by a committee system that imparts greater power to the executive members.

Furthermore, the ex-officio presence of DVCs and PVCs on key committees means that they provide the continuity of the leadership narrative and decide what information gets presented regarding decision-making outside the Board's quality assurance domain, a transmission rather than consultative model of governance. A female professor, a former chair, reflected: 'we don't have an active academic board anymore'. A male Head of School at UMetro considered Academic Board was itself a 'feminised space'. Rowlands (2011) depicts this trend, using Bourdieu, as a shift in power from intellectual capital (power that is earned through reputation with regard to scholarly work) to academic capital (managerial power that is bestowed through position within the organisational hierarchy). Executive prerogative is thus asserted through these additional layers and increased range of senior management.

Thus, there is a horizontal demarcation between those who do the core work of teaching, research and engagement, while the executive (PVC and above) has full control in terms of determining priorities and resource allocation, sometimes but not often, with academic input. This demarcation is most evident in the significant pay gap between professorial/academic salaries and executive management salaries (with Australian VCs receiving up to $1.5m) (Altbach et al. 2012). There is also a vertical separation with the shift in power to academic (managerial) and away from intellectual capital. Both processes are inflected by gender. The shifts in power across to line management and up to the executive have occurred at the same time there is greater diversification of, and changing social relations of gender in, academic work with an increasingly feminised academic and professional workforce (from 52.2% in 2004 to 55.6% in 2014, females being 36.9% of 71.3% full-time tenured staff and 9.7% of 12.5% staff on limited contracts) (Blackmore 2014; Department of Education and Training 2014). Men dominate senior positions making up 72.7% of senior lecturers, 67.7% of associate professors, and 72.7% of professorial roles in 2014 (Department of Education and Training 2014; Universities Australia 2014), whereas women 30–54 years old remain clustered at Level B in lecturer positions. At the same time, academic work is being unbundled with an increase in research-only and teaching-only positions (more women than men in the latter), and more men than women in the shrinking teaching and research category (Turner and Brass 2014). Meanwhile 'third space' professionals in E-learning are moving into teaching and learning (Gordon and Whitchurch 2010), and an increasingly feminised professional workforce is confronted with efficiency reductions in all three universities. Similar patterns are reflected internationally. Morley's (2013b) Stimulus paper, *Women and higher education leadership,* demonstrated that although there are slightly more women enrolled than men in higher education globally, this 'has yet to translate into proportional representation in the labour market or access to leadership and decision-making positions' (2013, 3; see also Altbach et al. 2012).

Subtext 2: branding and alignment

University compacts, intensified competition for shrinking research funds together with new regimes of research assessment with Excellence in Research in Australia introduced in 2010 meant that each university was repositioning itself. This meant sharpening their strategic direction and priorities and being distinctive relative to other Australian universities, but increasingly as quality providers internationally through branding (Blackmore 2013). Organisational restructuring has been undertaken to produce distinctive research and teaching concentrations resulting in greater specialisation across the sector. The trend has been to focus on science and technology as the best source of funding to counter shrinking government investment.

In response to, or in anticipation of, this agenda, each of the three case-study universities had undergone radical organisational restructuring during the previous 10 years, driven by strategic 'change' policies or blueprints. UMetro restructured its entire programme to develop a 'general' liberal undergraduate programme and professional fee-paying graduate programmes in order to align with US and European systems. The aim was to attract international students due to the flexibility and transportability of credentials, but also to distinguish itself from the other 38 Australian universities as 'world class'. The Utech under the previous and current VC, both male, developed a strategic blueprint to reposition the university as one that was closely linked to industry and to its urban environment. URegional had undertaken a lengthy review of its purpose over the first three years under its new female VC and led by the DVC (Research). It now focuses on 'the tropics' as a brand that reflects their regional location and research strengths in marine science. The agenda was for both teaching and research across all fields to refocus on how they related to the 'the tropics'. Being strategic means focusing on the male-dominated fields of engineering, marine science and, at the senior levels, health and biosciences.

Furthermore, there has been a national trend towards larger faculties or Divisions. At URegional, the DVC-led Taskforce collapsed 15 schools into 7 colleges and four faculties into 6 divisions. In the Utech, humanities and social sciences had been replaced by cultural, design and communication studies in a new Creative Industries Faculty while integrating individual sociologists, historians, anthropologists within interdisciplinary research and teaching programmes. The merging of humanities, arts and social sciences (HASS), for example, has reduced the diversity of disciplinary voices on both Academic Boards and executive committees, skewing the discourse and channelling debates towards entrepreneurialism and particular valued outcomes (e.g. commercialisation). HASS, even as a female-dominated field, is not necessarily feminist-friendly, with strong resistance to feminist approaches in political science and economics due to their 'disciplinary' logics (Johnson, forthcoming). The focus on partnerships, patents and products also restricts the possibilities of leadership for academics of a more critical disposition. Feminist research, which often requires a level of critique and advocacy as well as application, is often not palatable to many partners (Thornton, forthcoming). In effect, universities are becoming less comprehensive and more vocationally and instrumentally oriented, and academics in turn are expected to align their teaching and research with university priorities. Universities are arguably less favourable to voices challenging dominant epistemological and methodological paradigms.

Subtext 3 public and domestic labour

While all executive leaders are expected to understand and fulfil the mission statement, some positions are more oriented outwards and others inwards, creating a subtle division between public (performative) and institutional (domestic) labour. The VC and key executive roles are increasingly publically and politically oriented as the 'face' of the university. Most evident is that the DVC Research position is predominantly held by males from a science, technology, engineering and mathematics (STEM) background, a key position acknowledged as providing the strategic direction for the university with regard to application, commercialisation and 'income generation activities' (Fisher and Kingsley 2014, 53). As one DVC (research) describes it:

> I have to manage the context. I have to globally understand what's happening, not just in research, that's a fairly narrow thing, what's basically globally happening economically. Where the big demographic shifts are happening. What is happening in terms of the intra-play in society between technologies, the different challenges that are emerging.

The DVC Research role is now more overtly in the public domain, often appointing PVCs to undertake research management internally.

In another case, the male VC had assumed a high public profile in negotiating with government, state and federal, as well as industry and NGOs. The new position of Provost, held by a female, was responsible for the internal work of change management and quality. Teaching and learning are also a major measure of quality and central to recruitment strategies and funding, with DVCs in education, academic, engagement and participation. Working with DVCs and PVCs who head faculties and divisions, their role is to develop and implement policy in curriculum, assessment and e-learning, quality, including access and equity, more than global income-generating activities. Across the sector and in the three case studies, women executive leaders constitute two-thirds of the DVC (teaching and learning) roles in Australian universities with greater diversity of disciplinarity backgrounds (Universities Australia 2014). One DVC teaching and learning describes her role:

> I mean generally my responsibility lies in quality of learning and teaching and so I work with the associate deans in all the faculties to improve the quality of what we do. Also obviously play a significant role in curriculum generally at the university with policies and position papers around curriculum and then working with people to implement policies ... Much more an influence role actually, it's really about winning hearts and minds, and to do things that are within the institution.

Another DVC teaching and learning describes her role as having responsibility

> for the quality of learning and teaching at [the university] ... delivering the graduate certificates ... co-responsibility for all evaluation ... the development and accreditation of all our courses. And most of the professional development for sessional and academic staff ... student succession and retention rates ... and the awards and grants programs.

A third DVC Academic, had moved horizontally from the Registrar's role to be DVC Academic. This role was different, in that 'it's a bigger brief from the point of view [...] of the operations of the university and back to where I think of...like the mainstream of the university' and not previously 'back of house' when she had managed administration as the Registrar. Interviews with Heads of Schools and Deans showed this DVC academic's support was integral to negotiating with staff and unions, particularly during fractious times of transition. The domestic labour of change management meant using incentives and inducements to manage academics and reform curriculum while invoking notions of blended learning. It meant involved monitoring of 'quality' with regard to academic performance, student retention, teaching and learning, equity, curriculum, accreditation and accountabilities.

A further feature has been the unpacking into distinct roles of what were formerly under one division head of administration: student welfare and well-being (student life), finance, human resources, marketing and, most recently, international education and community engagement, representing the entrepreneurial face of the university. At Utech, for example, the focus on community engagement required a redefinition of roles at DVC and PVC levels and involved recruiting senior academics (Deans and above) with industry links into a multiplicity of positions such as 'Corporate Programs and Partnerships', 'International and Development' and 'Technology, Information and Learning Support'. Interestingly, international education, largely about recruitment and branding, has an internationalisation and marketing brief. As one female DVC (International) noted, her position involves a 'bigger brief in terms of the operations of the university', they are 'very much involved in our strategic position', 'work very closely with the DVC Research', and employ 'a fairly corporate approach'.

These women's biographical narratives demonstrate that change management was the most desirable leadership quality with a focus on curriculum, pedagogy, human resources and pastoral care. As PVCs, they had shown the ability to persuade and convince, important qualities, given their lack of personnel or financial resources. They also had to undertake difficult organisational restructuring to create better alignment and reduce costs internally. The task for a previous Dean of Science and Engineering recently promoted to PVC due to a university-wide restructure was to merge the schools of Mathematics and Physics into Engineering, an activity he described as 'fun'. He described his faculty as the 'powerhouse of the research for the university' and that his faculty 'own[s] the brand' of the university. Similarly, others discussed their success in change management as being critical to their upward mobility. A Dean of Business and Law, now PVC International, noted that in her previous job she had taken the

> Faculty from being…use to be known as the gangrenous limb that should be cut off and floated out to sea to being the prize of the faculties. I think I got rid of 70 staff while I was there. I did the first whole faculty change proposal they've ever done.

Being ambitious and asserting that the 'brand' was a common theme amongst the newly promoted executives. Devine, Grummell, and Lynch (2011, 632) refer to the seductive nature of possessing and exerting executive power in a purposeful manner within the entrepreneurial university that demands from their leaders 'flexibility, adaptability, self-empowerment and self-actualisation'. These leaders in our study, both male and female, identified as needing exciting challenges and thriving on change, including restructuring (merging schools), reviews, and reshaping faculties, or, as in the case of a new PVC, building university 'cottage industries' into 'corporate education business[es]'. At the same time, women who undertook such risky activities, challenging embodied and situated practices which linked masculinity to entrepreneurialism, were also viewed sceptically. Bruni, Gherardi, and Poggio (2004, 408) comment:

> The features of entrepreneurship reside in the symbolic domain of initiative-taking, accomplishment and relative risk. They therefore reside in the symbolic domain of the male and when these same features are transposed to the symbolic domain of the female they become uncertain. It is necessary to justify female entrepreneurship because it is not an immediately shared and self-evident social value. The symbolic order of gender assigns the sphere of activity and proactivity to the male, while it associates passivity, adaptation and flexibility with the female.

Our case studies reflected national patterns based on a gender binary at the executive level, where men largely dominate finance, administration and the 'hard' entrepreneurial labour of external strategic engagement of the university (e.g. research, finance and administration, partnerships, international education) while women are positioned as undertaking the 'soft' domestic (and emotional) labour of change management, teaching, equity, pastoral care and quality (Blackmore and Sachs 2007).

Subtext 4: leaderism

The dominant discourse at the executive level was that of excellence, entrepreneurship, market advantage and leaderism. Leaderism is where leadership is promoted as the solution to the complexity of issues confronting higher education. 'The cultural ideology of leaderism suggests that certain subjectivities, values, behaviours, dispositions and characteristics can strategically overcome institutional inertia, outflank resistance and recalcitrance and provide direction for new university futures' (Morley 2013b). Leaderism is one offshoot of 'new managerialism' and wider public sector reform. Deem and Brehony (2005, 223) agree writing that, 'new managerialism language asserts that the solution to all public service problems is management' (Deem and Brehony 2005, 223). The assumptions and values that inform the new managerial cultures in university executives are revealed through who gets recruited and on what criteria, a relatively underresearched area in higher education (Scott et al. 2010, 402).

Unpacking the subtexts of recruitment uncovers the tacit assumptions that underpin how different forms of social capital (research, teaching, leadership) are linked to a preferred leadership habitus in gendered ways at the top end. The VCs had clear ideas about the dispositions they look for in an executive manager: being positive, a '...glass half full not half empty type' (VC). One VC says that he wants a DVC to be 'someone who can throw themselves ahead...with any luck take others with them'. Another VC refers to how being a Dean is like a feudal lord and the DVC is 'like being a member of the Royal Court: You have a lot of influence but you don't have the armies'. Their job is to produce policy and persuade those lower down to follow. Despite such comments, DVCs do possess power, in that they are members of the executive group that plans, makes policies, and distribute resources accordingly.

A number of themes emerged. An emerging pattern is that there is increased mobility from different occupational sectors into the professoriate at the PVC and DVC levels, many now recruited from industry, business and government as well as NGOs, identified by Scott et al. as up to 40% (2010, 404). Evident in the interviews was the view that experience outside the university was indicative of entrepreneurial leadership and desirable for those in an executive position. Over 50% of the senior managers (including non-academic positions) we interviewed spent time either in industry or government, then returning to the university sector. While none of the VCs explicitly referred to the necessity for non-university experience, their own biographical narratives and career trajectories featured external experience, importing notions of how big business or government worked. One VC, for instance, noted that:

> when I came back I thought universities were in the dark ages and I was pretty sure I was right. [I] had a different view on a number of things. Not a radical, just a different, view. But it was a very important thing to do in terms of getting some perspectives

This became apparent in when he responded to why some academics were disengaged:

> What I do say to people who whinge is I say to them 'why don't you piss off for a semester and actually experience life somewhere else, then you can'…sorry to be blunt, 'but then you can come back and say this is a good place or not a good place'. And have some perspective about it. But it's often those people who have never been anywhere else who think the world is wicked.

Not surprisingly, their personal disposition, as that of their colleagues, was to select 'people like us' into leadership positions, a form of homosociability (Blackmore and Barty 2004). Moving from an executive administrative position horizontally into DVC (academic) was no longer an issue, one DVC commented, because 'you know the fact that you haven't got recent…very recent, academic experience probably doesn't matter. Most people who are here if they've come out of a dean role, haven't had it either'.

While at the level of middle management, academic (managerial) capital and intellectual capital were considered important in terms of gaining credibility, it was becoming less so at the executive level.

> I look for people who have to have in my view academic credibility, so they need to have teaching and research track record. It doesn't have to be the most stellar…but I want people who will have the esteem of their peers as being credible. (VC)

Academic record had to be balanced by managerial expertise, producing what the VCs recognised as the contradictions inherent in executive positions. For instance, one VC said that they are

> Janis-like, you know that's a double faced positioned, but the reality is that the job is a senior executive position, it is primarily an academic management position, but it is not just a general manager position, it's an academic management position.

Bringing a strong research record to a DVC position was less important than a commitment to the strategic positioning of the university and managerial capacities. Research leaders with accrued intellectual capital were less appropriate for university executive leadership. Their 're-alignment has to be affectively absorbed in order to demonstrate transferable leadership skills and attributes, for example, from leading research to leading whole or parts of HE organisations' (Morley 2013b, 3).

Recruiting for executive positions from those with non-academic background was not unproblematic as it was also about how the prospective employee will adhere to the academic culture of the university (as well as change it). As one VC said, 'if you go outside…you just have to be very careful that they can adjust to the culture and keep the culture'. The dominant theme was that the executive member will commit to the university branding and positioning. But for all at the executive level, the VCs were, as one stated, 'not interested in anybody who isn't prepared to be part of that vision, and isn't prepared to play that role'. The increased pressure for alignment (compliance?) intensifies at the executive level where all positions are on contract. The benefits were, another VC commented, that being in increasingly well-paid executive positions was excellent training for moving into corporate and consultancy positions outside the academy.

As women increasingly occupy middle management, our study also indicated a trend away from the traditional pathway up through line management from Head of

School, Dean and into executive positions as the search for industry and commercial links intensifies. Again, most of these external recruits are male (Scott et al. 2010). This questions pipeline theory which assumes that once a significant pool of women exists in middle management they will move into the executive level. Instead, imperatives are to recruit from outside not within, and then less so from middle management, increasingly privileging entrepreneurial over academic and intellectual capital.

Subtext 5 gender/knowledge binaries

There was a similar implicit preference (subtext) for candidates and appointees into particular executive positions (Research) to have a STEM disciplinary background (science, technology, engineering or mathematical) (Scott et al. 2010, 404). In our three case studies, all the DVC Research positions were held by men from STEM backgrounds, reflecting the sector 70% of DVC Research positions held by men, the far majority of 'outward looking' DVC roles also had STEM or management backgrounds, except one in international (Asian studies background). Australia wide, 83% of DVC Research is from the STEM fields, predominantly science but also engineering and IT (Universities Australia 2014). This gender/knowledge subtext was made explicit when it came to research management at the institutional and national levels. A key policy-maker in research commented:

> Unquestionably the skills that come with scientific training help in this game, there's no question about that. I think it's the numeracy…the kind of analytical skills. It's the capacity to understand and you know get your head around difficult concepts. So I've been asked a lot in the last few weeks whether they think you need to be a scientist to do this job. And I think it's…you know if you had someone from the humanities who had the kind of…those analytical skills and that numeracy, it wouldn't be a problem. And if Vice Chancellors ask me, they say they're having trouble recruiting a DVCR I say 'what's your dean of science like?' That would be my advice. I said 'just try up there 'cause usually that's the kind of route'.

These subtexts are also made explicit by recruitment firms, who in providing a 'diverse' field of applicants often seek to include female candidates. In reviewing potential candidates, their preference is for candidates who possess certain scientific dispositions and experience considered necessary to manage research. One VC responded to why this occurred with the comment: 'the big bucks are in the sciences in terms of ARC and other things…certainly for our university science is the engine room. Medicine and health are growing…'. Thornton (forthcoming) argues, the imperative in new knowledge economies is towards greater instrumentalism and 'value for money' from government and industry which means that

> applied knowledge is favoured, particularly in fields where it is patentable, such as technoscience. Theoretical, humanistic and critical knowledge of all kinds is regarded as marginal to knowledge capitalism.

At the same time, this VC was wary that at the PVC level, 'other experiences' such as 'leadership and management type experiences' are also significant.

This conjuncture of 'hard' science and masculinity exaggerates a similar emphasis in ERA that establishes science as the normative model of research and source of university funding if not survival. HASS Australian researchers contribute 36% of research outputs and only receive 16% of all research funding, a gap which cannot be explained by the relative 'cheapness' of research approaches (Turner and Brass 2014). The privileging of material and biological rather than social science and humanities in turn impacts on what knowledge and research are valued and how resources are allocated within the academy, with many in the social sciences and humanities feeling marginalised. One English professor commented that she felt that Literature was now considered to be 'recreational' relative to the more 'vocational' or applied science domains with commercial potential. As Benschop and Brouns (2003, 200) comment:

> Perhaps one of the most influential contributions to gender inequality in academia is made by the symbolic images of science and of the abstract, ideal academic. This image represents science as a voracious system, an ivory tower with very stringent rules for ascending within the tower that requires constant attention and does not tolerate part-time work, the distraction that children provide, or any other distraction for that matter. The ideal scientist then is the dedicated intellectual, who lives and breathes academia, and is engaged in his (naturally) studies practically 24 hours a day.

This dominance determines how 'scientific quality is defined, operationalized and put into practice' (Benschop and Brouns 2003, 195). It is difficult for a feminist and only PVC from humanities and social sciences at UMetro to be the only voice constantly reminding committees as to the effects of the privileging of science and particular measurements of quality research. Furthermore, while there are increased numbers of women in bioscience and health sciences, there is evidence that women are leaving rather than moving up the ranks in science as intensified competition requires longer and harder working days (Blackmore 2014). It therefore explains 'the slow progression of female researchers towards the top of academia', particularly if outside science or even within an increasingly competitive field (Benschop and Brouns 2003, 195). Despite the increased presence of women in executive positions, the subtext of the old science/humanities binaries and vertical division of labour between 'hard' and 'soft' executive leadership domains remains. Furthermore, the executive rarely represents the epistemological diversity that constitutes a vibrant university community, due to increasingly strong market, service and vocational mindsets.

Subtext 6 careless and carefree leadership work

The absence of reference to gender in the interviews was the norm in nearly all interviews with male academics at this level. Our probing around work–life balance and who does the housework or childcare, who moves with whom when career decisions are made, led to more nuanced discussions of the conditions of academic labour, making visible the invisible subtext of gender at work. In most instances, for example, families moved with the male academic. Contrarily, nearly all the female executives mentioned gender without prompting. Partners and children, or lack of, when tracking their life narrative, were critical factors in how female executives negotiated their career path and how they did their job. Not surprisingly, a major issue, as one DVC argues, is

> how do we make those [executive] roles a bit more attractive to those women…They are so time consuming and full on that you cannot…there's no way that you could keep a very active research profile. A couple of our deans do. It comes at great personal cost to them… And they've got a research assistant that helps them but basically all of their leave…all of

their long service leave, all of their spare time, is taken up to do that. So they actually never have a break.

Interviewer: And what happens if you have a family?
DVC: Well they don't. The ones who do it, don't have a family. The women that is.

Recent research indicates that work/life conflict are major factors in women's career choices within the academy and how they require particular entrepreneurial disposi-tions and require reconstituting identities (Devine, Grummell, and Lynch 2011). Devine, Grummell, and Lynch's (2011, 632) study of woman academic managers in Ireland applies to our study where women executives felt that the culture of new man-agerialism leads to the crafting of an 'elastic self':

> This requires a relentless pursuit of working goals without boundaries in time, space energy or emotion…the experience of this elasticity is gendered, deriving from the moral imperative of women to be primary carers, as well as the need for both men and women to manage 'otherness' and 'do' or 'undo' their gendered identities in line with organizational cultural norms.

The data do not suggest that we can reductively argue that only men benefit from, or women are limited by, the reconstituted identities seen to be necessary to lead the uni-versities. The expectations of leaderism impact both men's and women's work/life con-flict and the particular pleasures that come with the positions (Blackmore and Sachs 2007); the point is that these changes have broad, differential gendered impacts.

Conclusion

Whilst gender is not an issue for women in the top positions in terms of overt discrimi-nation in policy, discourses or practice, careful analysis demonstrates that the restruc-turing of both the sector and each university is gendered in its discourses, processes, priorities and effects. Educational restructuring (Blackmore 2010, Blackmore and Sachs 2007) mobilises gender subtexts that underpin organisational objectives (effi-ciency, standardisation, market position), processes (alignment of individuals to organ-isational aims, amalgamations), principles (gender-neutral notion of merit) and knowledge hierarchies (dominance of science and technology as key sites of inno-vation). In Australia, and across the European Union, 'women's academic careers remain characterised by strong vertical segregation' (Morley 2013b, 5) regardless of gender equity policy and legislation. Theories of choice that argue that women are opting not to apply for executive leadership in terms of self-selecting out of contention or are opting out due to rejection of corporate value system do not fully explain these gendered patterns.

Our study indicates how the shift in the locus of power from academics to manage-ment in regard to the repositioning of universities in new knowledge economies occurs with changing social relations of gender. Executive management has to be considered in the context of an increasingly feminised and casualised academic and professional administrative workforce, the concentration of women where access to tenured pos-itions and pathways into leadership is difficult, and the gender binaries evident in recruitment practices. Furthermore, internal restructuring to create a distinctive brand has led to a reduction of both the size and voice of the humanities and social sciences, dominated by female students and scholars. Gender subtexts underpin the changing organisational structures (membership of key committees), decision-making processes (definitions of role, selection processes) and normative images of what constitutes a good leader-manager (corporate loyalty).

While teaching and quality assurance have been leveraged to executive status, they, as institutional domestic domains are designated as fields of female leadership. The public face of the performative university is that of research and the hard sciences in the promotion of institutional reputations globally. Despite their presence in executive leadership, women continue not to be where key decision-making occurs (Morley 2013b, 4). Universities continue to be structured around both vertical and horizontal divisions of labour – horizontally with increased centralisation of executive power held by men; vertically based on power/knowledge with the privileging of science, technology and business experience and in terms of the public/domestic labour of the university. Furthermore, university leadership to this point has required a balance between accumulated intellectual and academic capitals. In a deregulated environment, leaders value significant entrepreneurial capital, suggesting a weakening of the value of intellectual capital in leadership and a move towards techno-scientific masculinist norms.

Disclosure statement

No potential conflict of interest was reported by the authors.

Funding

We did get funding to do this research from the Australian Research Council, project number [DP110103700].

References

Ahmed, S. 2012. *On Being Included: Racism and Diversity in Institutional Life*. Durham: Duke University Press.

Altbach, P. G., L. Reisberg, M. Yudevich, G. Androushchak, and I. F. Pacheco. 2012. *Paying the Professoriate: A Global Comparison of Compensation and Contracts*. New York: Routledge.

Benschop, Y., and M. Brouns. 2003. "Crumbling Ivory Towers: Academic Organizing and its Gender Effects." *Gender, Work and Organization* 10 (2): 194–212.

Benschop, Y., and H. Doorewaard. 1998. "Covered by Equality: The Gender Subtext of Organizations." *Organization Studies* 19 (5): 787–805.

Blackmore, J. 2010. "'More Power to the Powerful': Mergers, Corporate Management and their Implications for Women in the Reshaping of Higher Education." *Australian Feminist Studies* 7 (15): 65–98.

Blackmore, J. 2013. "Student Dis/Satisfaction and Academic Dis/Enchantment with Edu-Capitalism." *Access: Critical Perspectives on Communication, Cultural & Policy Studies* 32: 27–34.

Blackmore, J. 2014. "'Wasting Talent'? Gender and the Problematics of Academic Disenchantment and Disengagement with Leadership." *Higher Education Research & Development* 33 (1): 86–99.

Blackmore, J., and K. Barty. 2004. "Principal Selection: Homosociabillity, The Search for Security and the Production of Normalised Principal Identities." Paper presented at Australian Association for Research in Education Conference, Melbourne.

Blackmore, J., D. Bateman, J. Loughlin, J. O'Mara, and G. Aranda. 2011. *Research into the Connection between Built Learning Spaces and Student Outcomes*. East Melbourne, VIC: Department of Education and Early Childhood Development.

Blackmore, J., and J. Sachs. 2007. *Performing and Reforming Leaders: Gender, Educational Restructuring, and Organizational Change*. Albany: State University of New York Press.

Bradley, D. 2008. *Review of Australian Higher Education*. http://www.industry.gov.au/highereducation/ResourcesAndPublications/ReviewOfAustralianHigherEducation/Pages/default.aspx.

Bruni, A., S. Gherardi, and B. Poggio. 2004. "Doing Gender, Doing Entrepreneurship: An Ethnographic Account of Intertwined Practices." *Gender, Work and Organization* 11 (4): 406–429.

Burnell, J. B. 2012. *Tapping all our Talents: Women in Science, Technology, Engineering and Mathematics, a Strategy for Scotland*. Report for The Royal Society of Edinburgh.

Currie, J., and L. Vidovich. 2009. "The Changing Nature of Academic Work." In *The Routledge International Handbook of Higher Education*, edited by M. Tight, K. Mok, J. Huisman, and C. Morphew, 441–451. New York: Routledge.

Deem, R., and K. J. Brehony. 2005. "Management as Ideology: The Case of 'New Managerialism' in Higher Education." *Oxford Review of Education* 31 (2): 217–235.

Department of Education and Training. 2014. *Higher Education Statistics – Staff Data*. https://www.education.gov/selected-higher-education-statistics-2014-staff-data.

Devers, M., Z. Morrison, B. Dalton, and S. Tayton. 2006. *When Research Works for Women*. Melbourne: Monash University.

Devine, D., B. Grummell, and K. Lynch. 2011. "Crafting the Elastic Self? Gender and Identities in Senior Appointments in Irish Education." *Gender, Work and Organization* 18 (6): 631–649.

Ernst and Young. 2012. *University of the Future: A Thousand Year Old Industry on the Cusp of Profound Change*. http://www.ey.com/Publication/vwLUAssets/University_of_the_future/$FILE/University_of_the_future_2012.pdf.

Fisher, V., and S. Kingsley. 2014. "Behind Closed Doors! Homosocial Desire and the Academic Boys Club." *Gender in Management: An International Journal* 29 (1): 44–64.

Fitzgerald, T. 2012. "Ivory Basements and Ivory Towers." In *Hard Labour? Academic Work and the Changing Landscape of Higher Education*, edited by T. Fitzgerald, J. White, and H. M. Gunter, 113–135. Bingley, UK: Emerald.

Gordon, G., and C. Whitchurch, eds. 2010. *Academic and Professional Identities in Higher Education*. New York: Routledge.

Grummell, B., D. Devine, and K. Lynch. 2009a. "The Careless Manager: Gender, Care and New Managerialism in Higher Education." *Gender and Education* 21 (2): 191–208.

Grummell, B., D. Devine, and K. Lynch. 2009b. "Appointing Senior Managers in Education: Homosociability, Local Logics and Authenticity in the Selection Process." *Educational Management Administration and Leadership* 37 (3): 329–349.

Hey, V., and S. Bradford. 2004. "The Return of the Repressed? The Gender Politics of Emergent Forms of Professionalism in Education." *Journal of Education Policy* 19 (6): 691–713.

Johnson, C. Forthcoming. "Hard Heads and Soft Hearts: The Gendering of Australian Political Science." In *Markets, Managers and Mandarins: The Modern University and the Social Sciences*, edited by M. Thorton and G. Withers. Canberra: ANU Press.

King, R., S. Marginson, and R. Naidoo, eds. 2013. *The Globalisation of Higher Education*. Cheltenham: Edward Elgar.

Knights, D., and D. Kerfoot. 2004. "Between Representations and Subjectivity: Gender Binaries and the Politics of Organizational Transformation." *Gender, Work and Organization* 11 (4): 430–454.

Lingard, B., and S. Rawolle. 2011. "New Scalar Politics: Implications for Educational Policy." *Comparative Education: An International Journal of Comparative Studies* 47 (4): 489–502.

Mackinnon, A., and A. Brooks, eds. 2001. *Gender and the Restructured University*. Buckingham: Open University Press.

Marginson, S. 2011. "Higher Education and Public Good." *Higher Education Quarterly* 65 (4): 411–433.

Marginson, S. 2012. "Online Open Education: Yes, This is a Game Changer." http://theconversation.com/online-open-education-yes-this-is-the-game-changer-8078.

Marginson, S., and M. Considine. 2000. *The Enterprise University: Power, Governance and Reinvention*. Cambridge: Cambridge University Press.

Martínez, J. M. L. 2011. "'Feminising' Middle Management? An Inquiry into the Gendered Subtexts in University Department Headship." *SAGE Open* 1. http://classic.sgo.sagepub.com/content/1/2/2158244011414731.full.pdf+html.

Mautner, G. 2005. "The Entrepreneurial University. A Discursive Profile of a Higher Education Buzzword." *Critical Discourse Studies* 2 (2): 95–120.

Morley, L. 2013a. "The Rules of the Game: Women and the Leaderist Turn in Higher Education." *Gender and Education* 25 (1): 116–131.

Morley, L. 2013b. *Women and Higher Education Leadership. Absences and aspirations*. University of Sussex. http://www.lfhe.ac.uk/en/research-resources/publications/index.cfm/Morley.

Peters, M. A., S. Marginson, and P. Murphy. 2009. *Creativity and the Global Knowledge Economy*. New York, NY: Peter Lang.

Pusser, B., and S. Marginson. 2013. "University Rankings in Critical Perspective." *The Journal of Higher Education* 84 (4): 544–568.

Roberts, K. A., and K. A. Donahue. 2000. "Professing Professionalism: Bureaucratisation and Deprofessionalisation in the Academy." *Sociological Focus* 33 (4): 365–383.

Rowlands, J. 2011. "Academic Boards: Less Intellectual and More Academic Capital in Higher Education Governance?" *Studies in Higher Education* 38 (9): 1274–1289.

Rowlands, J. 2014. "Turning Collegial Governance on its Head: Symbolic Violence, Hegemony and the Academic Board." *British Journal of Sociology of Education* 1–19. doi:10.1080/01425692.2014.883916

Scott, G., S. Bell, H. Coates, and L. Grebennikov. 2010. "Australian Higher Education Leaders in Times of Change: The Role of Pro Vice-Chancellor and Deputy Vice-Chancellor." *Journal of Higher Education Policy and Management* 32 (4): 401–418.

Scott, G., H. Coates, and M. Anderson. 2008. "Learning Leaders in Times of Change: Academic Leadership Capabilities for Australian Higher Education." Study for Australian Council for Educational Research. http://research.acer.edu.au/cgi/viewcontent.cgi?article=1001&context=higher_education.

Thornton, M. Forthcoming. "Feminist Research in a Politics Context of Uncertainty." In *Markets, Managers and Mandarins: The Modern University and the Social Sciences*, edited by M. Thornton and G. Withers. Canberra: ANU Press.

Turner, G., and K. Brass. 2014. *Mapping the Humanities, Arts and Social Sciences in Australia*. Canberra: Australian Academy of the Humanities.

Universities Australia. 2014. *Selected Inter-Institutional gender Equity Statistics-Australia Wide-2011*. https://www.universitiesaustralia.edu.au.

White, K., B. Bagilhole, and S. Riordan. 2012. "The Gendered Shaping of University Leadership in Australia, South Africa and the United Kingdom." *Higher Education Quarterly* 66 (3): 293–307.

Faculty peer networks: role and relevance in advancing agency and gender equity

KerryAnn O'Meara and Nelly P. Stromquist

College of Education, University of Maryland, College Park, USA

Organisational efforts to alter gender asymmetries are relatively rare, yet they are taking place in a number of universities. In the USA, sponsored by the National Science Foundation, ADVANCE programmes implement a number of interventions to improve the recruitment, retention, and advancement of women faculty. This study focused on one common intervention, faculty peer networks, and the role they play in gender equity reform. Longitudinal and cross-sectional qualitative data indicate that such peer networks function as catalysts for women's career agency, and challenge gendered organisational practices. Two key features of the peer networks, their structure and internal dynamics, facilitate these outcomes. At the same time, peer networks are limited by design in promoting structural change and must be implemented in concert with other forms of policy and structural change to be effective mechanisms for gender equity reform.

Despite gains in gender equity in doctoral programmes and early career hiring (Trower 2012; Ward and Wolf-Wendel 2012), women faculty remain under-represented in the more senior ranks (Valian 1998; Trower 2012; Ward and Wolf-Wendel 2012), experience lower salaries (West and Curtis 2006), and enjoy less decision-making power in research universities (Clark and Corcoran 1986; Acker 1990; Glazer-Raymo 1999). Pre-tenure women disproportionately resign and many women feel 'stuck' at associate professor levels (Valian 1998; Glazer-Raymo 1999, 2008; Modern Language Association 2009; Misra et al. 2011; Terosky, O'Meara, and Campbell 2014). Many forces influence gender inequality in universities, including divisions of labour where women faculty complete more campus service and men spend more time on research (Winslow 2010; Misra et al. 2011; Pyke 2014), as well as the disproportionate amount of time women spend on family care and housework (Misra et al. 2011), the tendency for women to be recognised less often through awards for their accomplishments (Lincoln et al. 2014), and women's isolation in the academic workplace (Kemelgor and Etkowitz 2001; Smith and Calasanti 2005).

Government efforts to improve the conditions of women in higher education are increasing in many parts of the world. In an effort to accelerate movement towards greater gender parity among faculty in higher education in the USA, the National Science Foundation (NSF) created the ADVANCE Institutional Transformation (IT programme) in 2001. ADVANCE programmes have been prominent in research universities over the past 10 years (e.g. Columbia University, Purdue University, University of California, University of Michigan, and Syracuse University). Though focused on the recruitment, retention, and advancement of women in the natural and social sciences (National Science Foundation 2006; Sturm 2006; Cantor 2011), the broader goals of IT ADVANCE grants have been defined as 'planned alterations in the core elements of the institutions: authority, goals, decision-making practices, and policies' (Fox 2008, 83).

There is a growing literature on the implementation and outcomes of ADVANCE IT programmes (Stewart, LaVaque-Manty, and Malley 2004; Rosser and Chameau 2006; Bilimoria, Joy, and Liang 2008) and analysis of the goals, challenges, and possibility for success among feminist scholars (Bird 2011; Morimoto and Zajicek 2012; Morimoto et al. 2013). Most of this literature begins from the premise, as we do here, that higher education organisations are gendered, with organisational practices, structures, and cultures that favour men and devalue women in critical ways (Acker 1990, 2006; Dean, Bracken, and Allen 2009). Thus, any effort at improving gender equity must target core operating procedures that disadvantage women faculty and their sense of agency to succeed in their careers. ADVANCE programmes implement many different kinds of interventions, including but not limited to reform of search practices, leadership development, research seed grants, campus climate surveys, and department chair training on unconscious bias (Morimoto et al. 2013). Research has explored the larger challenges and successes of culture change through ADVANCE programmes (Stewart, LaVaque-Manty, and Malley 2004; Bilmoria and Liang 2012; Morimoto et al. 2013). However, less work has examined what occurs within specific ADVANCE IT interventions to alter the nature of gendered organisations for their participants.

In this study, we examined the role of one common ADVANCE IT intervention, peer networks, in enhancing participant agency in career advancement and in disrupting gendered organisational logics and patterns. We asked: What aspects of peer networks seemed most influential in enhancing participant agency in career advancement? Did these peer networks disrupt gendered organisational practices and logics, and if so, how?

'Inequality regimes' (Acker 2006), including the lesser retention, advancement, and career satisfaction of women faculty when compared to men, are complex problems; they involve 'interlocked practices and processes' (Acker 2006, 441). By looking inside one of the most common NSF ADVANCE interventions – peer networks – we can see the gendered logics and patterns of isolation that perpetuate inequality and, importantly, the kinds of programme structure and internal dynamics that can change gendered norms and experiences. Understanding the contributions and limitations of ADVANCE peer networks in furthering gender equity is important for women's advancement in these settings.

The university we focused on (Progressive University, PU hereafter) is a large research-intensive institution with a budget of about $500 million in research funds and some 38,000 students. This institution received an ADVANCE grant to focus on issues of gender equity in the retention and advancement of women faculty. Our data comprise participant observations of three ADVANCE peer networks of faculty (year-long, cross-campus programmes – involving faculty at each of three career stages: assistant, associate, and full professor levels), programme evaluations of the peer networks, and interviews and focus groups with participants in the programmes. We examine these data to understand the contributions and limitations of faculty peer networks embedded within gendered organisations in catalysing gender equity and career advancement.

Guiding perspectives

Our study begins from the premise that all research universities are gendered organisations wherein organisational practices favour men and devalue women in critical ways (Acker 1990, 2006; Dean, Bracken, and Allen 2009). Acker's (1990, 2006) research outlined five ways in which all organisations to greater or lesser degrees have embedded gendered organisational practices. These include (1) a division of labour with low representation of women in higher positions; (2) symbols, language, and images that reinforce labour division; (3) interactions that foster dominance and submission; (4) gendered ways of thinking about work that seep into identity; and (5) organisational logic, systems of evaluation, and management that favour male preferences and characteristics. Acker's (1990, 2006) conceptualisation of gendered organisations has been applied to understand how women faculty experience barriers to success in gendered universities (Lester, Sallee, and Hart 2013), and on ideal worker norms and how they influence graduate student and faculty balance of work and family (Sallee 2011, 2013).

We assumed that women participants in ADVANCE peer networks were socialised through, and were living out their academic careers in, fields and departments with explicit and implicit practices that constrain their agency in career advancement. Agency has been studied in many social science disciplines and fields including sociology, psychology, human development, organisational behaviour, cultural, standpoint, and realist. By agency we refer to perspectives and actions taken by participants to achieve meaningful goals (Campbell and O'Meara 2014; Terosky, O'Meara, and Campbell 2014; O'Meara 2015). Our definition recognises the need for both individual and collective action. Agency is area specific (e.g. agency undertaken for career advancement or for securing work–life balance) and is enacted in specific social contexts (e.g. fields, departments, and gendered universities). Agency in career advancement emerges from and is facilitated by organisational environments. Organisational structures and cultures play powerful roles in shaping agentic possibilities (Giddens 1979; Bourdieu 1985). Acker (1990, 2006) observes that in gendered organisations interactions between members display dominance and submission. This might take the form of talking over or ignoring the opinions of women faculty or crediting their ideas to others. Women faculty might not see other women faculty being successful in balancing career and family, might not find mentors and sponsors for their research, and might consider resigning. Each of these contexts constrains women's agency in career advancement. Alternatively, women faculty could experience interventions – as intended by ADVANCE – that interrupt these gendered dynamics to present strong role models, intellectual and social support, and strategies to handle interactions and situations where women's voices are not being heard.

We chose to study peer networks because they are a common ADVANCE intervention, intended to interrupt gendered organisational norms. The structure of peer networks brings together a group of faculty (such as women assistant professors) on a regular basis (such as monthly) for knowledge sharing and peer support. The online meetings and conversations that take place between face-to-face meetings are organised around various topics relevant to their group (such as preparation for promotion, time management, and life–work balance) and typically organised by a facilitator, who herself serves as a role model and has achieved the advancement the members seek. Such groups typically involve an initial open call for participation, but then confirm a cohort to participate as regular members for one year. As scholars who study social networks have observed, 'Relationships matter to enacting change' (Daly 2010, 2). Peer networks that have been found to develop strong ties include those where individuals within the network have frequent interactions, mutual confiding, and sharing of information (Tenkasi and Chesmore 2003; Kilduff and Krackhardt 2008; Kezar 2014). Kezar (2014) observes that there is an embedded 'lack of trust, conflict, autonomy, and/or disconnection of faculty and siloed units' (109) that make the creation of on-campus peer networks a challenge. Peer networks, like the ones created in ADVANCE programmes among women faculty, can be critical to change efforts because of their ability to simultaneously support individual faculty navigating gendered work environments while also creating new norms and logics (Tenkasi and Chesmore 2003; Hart 2007, 2008; Kezar 2014). Yet little work has considered the specific programme structures or dynamics of such networks that matter to the outcome of enhanced faculty agency and gender equity reform.

Because we were interested in the structures of and dynamics inside peer networks, we turned to two conceptual approaches: critical theory and third spaces. Critical theory asserts that concepts such as justice, equality, and emancipation are nurtured through the intersubjective construction of meaning that occurs primarily through language (Habermas 1992). Although people are deeply embedded in historical contexts and may even live under democratic regimes, they constantly experience social and institutional practices that constrain their identity and autonomy. Critical theory, therefore, 'seeks to provide a dialectical method of discovering and rediscovering "better ways" to develop people and transform society in always fluid ways' (Abel and Sementelli 2004, 80; see also Gaventa and Tandon 2010). Dialogue among oppressed persons is indispensable to share experiences of powerlessness and injustice and to create new collective meanings. It is an important way that people strengthen their sense of agency. A critical mechanism by which peer networks might deliver on the promise of enhancing women's agency is dialogue among peers who have experienced similar gendered challenges and their subsequent actions to advance as a result of new awareness and confidence.

Critical theorists argue that despite the pervasive oppressive power operating in society, people can emancipate themselves through new discourses and practices. On the other hand, critical theory underscores an inherent contradiction between bureaucracy and emancipation and between agencies and agency. In this respect, original thinkers, such as Marcuse (1970), argued that 'all domination assumes the form of administration' (1–2). Under this assumption, it would be difficult to envisage institutions that would provide spaces where they would be open to critique of their own performance. Can this ever be reversed? New contributions from the field of public administration, after considering various case studies, argue that not all administration is oppressive and that, under certain conditions and certain leaderships, 'right kinds' of bureaucracies can emerge and foster enabling dialogue – and subsequent practice – towards the emancipation of individuals. Abel and Sementelli (2004) call this form of critical theory 'evolutionary critical theory'. We apply this concept to understand how the process that occurs within peer networks (i.e. dialogue, practices, and inter-actions) might enhance participant sense of agency in career advancement.

The concept of third spaces posed initially by Oldenburg (1989, 1991) builds up on the notion of a space where dialogue can take place and argues that a third space (or place) separate from home and workplace was important for community building and civil society. Such an environment, which might include churches or women's knit-ting circles, enhances a sense of belonging and place, and becomes an anchor of com-munity life. Key characteristics of third spaces are that they are free or inexpensive, highly accessible, involve regulars but welcome newcomers, are welcoming and com-fortable, and ideally involve some connections over food and drink (Oldenburg 1991; Putnam 1995, 2000).

Cantor (2011) described the formation of third spaces for women faculty via peer networks in the Syracuse University ADVANCE programme. Cantor observed peer networks for women that were interdisciplinary and cross-campus and were:

> especially good environments to nurture women faculty in STEM, as they quite naturally override the typical barriers of a chilly climate. In them, women are less isolated and less likely to feel like tokens than in their departments (as a critical mass can form from par-ticipants across departments and disciplines). They can build richer social/professional networks (with instrumental support coming from a wider variety of colleagues in differ-ing positions), and in the process see a somewhat more flexible array of career models (such as those pursued in industry). (Cantor 2011, 9–10)

Although faculty peer networks technically occur at work, they can be built structurally as third spaces: these move faculty from their immediate work environment (the depart-ment or college) to spaces devoid of competition and evaluation, and free from any vig-ilance by administrators. Such spaces focus on mutual knowledge sharing, provide new role models, and initiate dialogue that challenges, defies, and transcends gendered logics (Bird 2011; Cantor 2011).

In summary, we were interested in how the creation of safe and autonomous spaces fosters dialogue to create peer networks, and how the dynamics that occur within peer networks facilitate agency in career advancement and promote gender equity by chal-lenging and disrupting gendered organisational norms and structures.

Methods

Study context

In this article, we examine three peer networks implemented by ADVANCE at PU. These include the following:

(1) 'Keeping Our Faculties'. This peer network (KOF hereafter) enables pre-tenure assistant professor women faculty to come together with a facilitator to gain knowledge and skills that will aid them in their career advancement. The key areas of focus are preparation of the tenure dossier and personal narrative, net-working, external funding, managing large classes and research labs, work–life balance, time management, managing service obligations, strategic communi-cations training, and personal branding.

(2) 'Advancing Together'. This peer network makes it possible for associate pro-fessor women faculty to come together with a facilitator to gain knowledge and skills that will help them advance to full professor. The key areas of

focus are preparation of the promotion dossier and personal narrative, networking, ramping up external funding, managing large classes and research labs, work–life balance, time management, managing service obligations, strategic communications training, and personal branding.

(3) 'ADVANCE Professors'. This peer network brings together full professor women faculty who agree to mentor assistant and associate women faculty in their college. There is also a professional development aspect for the women full professors themselves. They work together as a cohort to transform college and university structures and cultures to better retain and advance women faculty. The key areas of focus are mentoring, workload, recognition, teaching, research and publishing, work–life policies and awareness, implicit bias, and management of conflict and service responsibilities.

Early on in this project, we reviewed internal and external evaluator reports on all three networks over the first three years of the PU ADVANCE programme. Evaluators concluded that these three programmes enhanced participants' agency in career advancement. Post-evaluations showed improvements in agency in career advancement using the same survey items asked of each candidate before they began the programme. Qualitative data showed that participants themselves attributed the programme with having enhanced their sense of agency in career advancement. Thus, we approached this study with the assumption that these programmes positively influenced women's agency in career advancement. We sought to understand *how and why* the peer networks enhanced women's agency in career advancement. Specifically, we wanted to understand the aspects of peer networks that seemed most influential in enhancing participant agency in career advancement. Beyond individual agency in career advancement, we also wanted to understand if the ADVANCE peer networks were disrupting gendered organisational practices and logics present within PU.

Research design

The primary method used for this study was a qualitative mixed-methods design of concurrent triangulation (Creswell 2003; Johnson, Onwuegbuzie, and Turner 2007; Creswell and Plano Clark 2011). In concurrent triangulation, different kinds of data are collected simultaneously, with the goal of confirming or substantiating findings within a single study. Creswell (2003) observed that in such studies, one offsets the weakness of one method or set of data with another, and findings are integrated and interpreted together.

We engaged in participant observations of the three peer networks at PU. We also analysed programme evaluations of the same peer networks and conducted interviews with faculty who had participated in these ADVANCE programmes.

The research design of this project has several strengths. A mixed-methods approach allowed the researchers to create a panoramic view of the three peer networks, with data that could be triangulated. The fact that data were collected over three years and included multiple cohorts of several peer networks created an opportunity to study the outcomes from multiple interventions and detect the degree of consistency in outcomes. Also, the sheer number of participant observations and evaluations completed increased our ability to achieve saturation in the kinds of peer network characteristics (e.g. programme structure and internal dynamics) that were most influential in supporting faculty agency in career advancement and in countering the negative effects of gendered organisational practices for women faculty. Table 1 provides a description of each of the three peer networks, the number of participant observations completed, the number of participants in the peer network each year, and interviews and focus group interviews conducted.

Interview and focus group questions relevant to this study focused on participant experiences in the ADVANCE peer networks. We asked what aspects of participating in the peer network were most relevant and helpful to their careers, how, and why. We asked women faculty participants if they had experienced any challenges in their careers at PU. Participants were asked to reflect on whether and how participation in the peer network changed their way of viewing certain career situations or obstacles, and/or actions that they took to advance in their career.

During participant observations, we took both descriptive and reflective notes using an observation protocol (Creswell 2007). The protocol for note-taking allowed us to listen to and observe aspects of the programme that previous research has shown to be relevant to supporting faculty agency in career advancement, but was open-ended enough to allow other themes that emerged from discussions also to be recorded. For example, our literature review suggested there might be aspects of the physical setting and structure of the programme that might influence the outcome of agency, such as a comfortable room, set aside from typical work activities and devoid of evaluation. Our literature review cued our attention to how dialogue between peers who were likely to have experienced similar challenges (as women in a research university) might reveal gendered logics and experiences of dominance and submission and at the same time provide women strategies to overcome such challenges or ameliorate their effects. Thus, observations were informed by the literature review. However, there was also an

Table 1.   Peer network description and data collected.

Cohort	Number of participants	Number of observations	Programme evaluations	Interviews and focus groups
KOF: Programme description: year-long network of pre-tenure assistant professor women created to enhance agency in career advancement (meets monthly for 2 hours)				
2011–2012	11	5 of 8 meetings	Pre and post	
2012–2013	18	7 of 10 meetings	Pre and post	12 interviews
2013–2014	16	8 of 10 meetings	Pre and post	
Advancing Together: Programme description: two-day workshop for women associate professors created to enhance agency in career advancement to full professor				
Winter 2012	16	All of the workshops for all three runs of the programme	Pre and post	Two focus groups, 75 minutes each. 12 total participants
2013	12		Pre and post	
2014	12		Pre and post	
Advance Professors: Programme description: year-long network of women full professors created to enhance their agency as college leaders and mentors as well as provide a set of mentors for junior faculty				
Spring 2011	13	5 of 5 meetings	Pre and post	
2011–2012	13	6 of 9 meetings	Pre and post	21 interviews
2012–2013	13	6 of 9 meetings	Pre and post	
2013–2014	10	7 of 9 meetings	Pre and post	

open-ended aspect of observations wherein additional influences, not previously considered, could be recorded and later examined.

Corbin and Strauss (2008) note that 'observations put researchers right where the action is, in a place where they can see what is going on' (29–30). A potential drawback of observations is that the observer will misinterpret comments. Therefore, observations are often best used alongside other data sources from the same participants (Corbin and Strauss 2008). Accordingly, we triangulated observations with interview, focus group, and programme evaluation data. Confidentiality was provided to faculty by avoiding the use of names and disciplines and masking other identifiable comments.

Data analysis

The coding process for the analysis of programme evaluations, interviews, and observation notes was iterative and involved 'thematic memoing' (Rossman and Rallis 2003). We went through all three peer network meeting observations, interviews, and all programme evaluation material, and used Acker's (1990, 2006) conceptualisation of gendered organisational practices to identify gendered organisational experiences faced by women faculty at PU. We then went through and coded the same observations, interview/focus groups, and programme evaluations for aspects of peer networks that seemed to be enhancing faculty agency in career advancement. Very quickly, two themes emerged. There were aspects of the programme structure itself that were influencing the outcome of enhanced agency and there were aspects of the dynamics between individuals within the groups that were influencing agency in career advancement. Finally, we went through meeting observations, interviews, and programme evaluation material to see if there were any ways in which aspects of the peer networks were disrupting or challenging gendered organisational practices and norms at PU. Although it could be argued that if peer networks enhanced the agency of women faculty in career advancement, the networks were in fact challenging gendered organisational cultures and norms, in this last round of coding we were interested in more than individual agency. Rather, we sought evidence of collective changes in thinking, influences on operating structures, and patterns of interactions that might disrupt or challenge more systematic gendered organisational structures and cultures.

Trustworthiness was strengthened by collecting data from multiple sources (Lincoln and Guba 2000), member checking the transcripts with participants, and being transparent with participants about the purposes and reporting of results (Maxwell 2012). We engaged in member checking by sharing transcripts with participants and giving them an opportunity to correct any part of their initial comments. Only three participants responded with clarifying statements, which were added to transcripts. All participants were provided anonymity, and we further masked the identity of participants by not noting their discipline next to their name in the text.

Internal validity was strengthened by each of the author's separate analysis of transcripts to develop themes, and then joining them to compare these conclusions.

As with all research, there were limitations to this research design. Although the data for this study were collected over three years, this is not long enough to know if the peer networks achieved their long-term goals of influencing faculty retention and advancement. Also, our data collection was only able to capture interactions within meetings and not the many connections that occurred outside as participants connected by email, over lunch, or at committee meetings.

Findings

ADVANCE peer networks supported women's agency in career advancement. Specifically, peer networks enhanced women faculty's sense that they could be successful at PU in earning tenure, promotion, and advancement to leadership positions. Likewise, ADVANCE peer networks encouraged women faculty to take actions that helped them advance in their careers. ADVANCE peer networks also challenged gendered organisational logics and practices.

Two key aspects of peer networks facilitated these outcomes. First, the structure and design of peer networks as third spaces supported agentic perspectives and actions towards career advancement. Second, internal dynamics within peer networks, wherein participants engaged in dialogue, shared challenges, brainstormed solutions, and affirmed and recognised members, supported career agency and challenged gendered organisational logics. In this section, we describe how the structure and internal dynamics of the peer networks (a) enhanced agentic actions and agentic perspectives of individual women faculty and (b) challenged gendered logics. We also consider the strengths and limitations of peer networks in disrupting the gendered nature of universities.

How peer networks influenced women's career agency

The structure of ADVANCE peer networks as women-only, third spaces and the interactions that occurred within the networks fostered agentic perspectives and agentic actions in women's career advancement. The design of the peer networks and internal dynamics had this effect because they disrupted at least three gendered organisational practices that constrained agency in career advancement: isolation within gendered divisions of labour, interactions of dominance and submission, and gendered evaluation logics. As noted earlier, the gendered division of labour in most research universities means that there is a low representation of women in higher ranked faculty positions, and in some fields, only one woman, or woman of colour, in a department or college. The design of the peer networks as including women of similar rank, from all different departments across the university, decreased the isolation women faculty experienced inside departments. Also, this design expanded women's networks and connected them to a potential set of allies.

Within network sessions, the internal dynamics of women of similar rank sharing similar experiences and offering resonance, affirmation, strategies, and support further strengthened women's career agency. For example, for associate professors, the peer network was most helpful in finding women colleagues dealing with similar career constraints and affirming that these conditions were unfair but could be overcome. As one associate professor noted, 'It was comforting to be in an environment of women facing the same struggles and challenges that I face'. Another associate professor said, 'This job, while surrounded by people, can be very isolating, so knowing that I am not alone and that other people have the same concerns/issues as my own [was useful]'. Another associate professor noted that the ADVANCE programme was helpful in order to:

> talk to some people about this without getting anyone in trouble or hearing people's stories about when someone grabs onto you and publishes over you and being a sidekick. I don't want to be a sidekick; that is not going to help me become full.

Finally, an associate professor new to the university explained: 'Coming from an agency where all my mentors were senior women, women of colour, this [coming to

Progressive University] was a big change. ADVANCE has been instrumental in helping me adjust. Has helped me feel like I fit in' (Advancing Together participant).

In each of these reflections, women faculty noted that being in a group with women of similar rank, sharing common challenges and ways in which they might overcome these challenges, changed the way they felt and thought about their own career possibilities. The structure and dynamics of peer networks made women feel less isolated, and caused them to adopt perspectives for new pathways to tenure and promotion, and that collaborative working relationships were possible. In other words, the peer networks facilitated agentic perspectives towards career advancement.

Women full professors also felt that the design of peer networks and the interactions within them made them feel less isolated and encouraged them to think and act in agentic ways. Because of ADVANCE, women full professors noted they felt that they now had an 'inner circle' of professional relationships. One full professor said the ADVANCE programme has 'put me in contact with women across campus who I definitely would never have encountered before. Certainly having a professional community of senior faculty women is something new for me completely'. Women full professors felt they had more power by virtue of their connections, similar to Hart's (2007, 2008) findings related to women's groups organising to create gender equity. One full professor noted that an ADVANCE colleague had asked her to be on the university senate to which she replied, 'I want no part of walking down the [campus] hill and sitting at a table with 20 other people, 18 of them being men and acting like it isn't a problem – which has happened to me in previous years. And she said to me, "I guarantee that won't happen here and if it does I will help you out." And I like the power of that. Whereas before I wouldn't have known, you know?' Another ADVANCE professor noted that because of her new network of senior colleagues she did not need to go alone to the ombudsmen again for problems she was having with colleagues. Instead she could get well-informed, savvy advice from other ADVANCE professors who had been through similar situations. ADVANCE professors also mentioned advice and support they had received from each other on salary negotiations, chairing major committees, and mentoring junior faculty in difficult departments. They also described actions they took to advance in career as a result of this strategic advice and information. Thus, the design of bringing women full professors together in a third space devoid of hierarchy and evaluation, but full of insider information and allies, facilitated women full professors' sense of control over gendered challenges.

While full professors emphasised the importance of allies and the relief of being in a group of women full professors, assistant professor women stressed the importance of receiving critical career information in an environment that was non-threatening. For example, one assistant professor explained:

> Before I attended the KOF program, I only heard how hard the tenure process is from my senior colleagues, which makes me worry about it a lot. After attending these sessions offered by the KOF program, I started to figure out what I should do to pass the tenure process. Right now, I know what I should work hard for, so the pressure accumulated in my mind releases a lot. (KOF participant)

This faculty member felt as if the way career information had been delivered before was threatening and inaccessible. Both the information provided and its delivery constrained her sense that she could succeed. However, the structure of ADVANCE sessions, which always occurred in the same room, around a large, round table over coffee and bagels or lunch, with similar-rank women faculty, felt intimate. In fact, it was striking how often women participants in ADVANCE programmes discussed sessions as 'comfortable' and 'a relief', and observed that they felt like they could ask questions in ways they could not in other venues.

Likewise, another assistant professor noted that her ADVANCE sessions were helpful and informative:

> For example, we had one about grant writing, and I was so inspired by the workshop that I applied for a seed grant shortly after that and got the grant! It also gives us an opportunity to get to know our colleagues outside of our area of research. (KOF participant)

Another assistant professor learned skills related to negotiation and followed up her ADVANCE session with a request to her department chair for space for her research. In both cases, women faculty received information in a way that felt accessible, and left the session feeling greater possibility (i.e. agentic perspective) for negotiation or grant-writing; they then followed up with an agentic action to advance in career. Although topics of grant-writing or negotiation are career issues faced by all faculty, not just women faculty, during observations we also heard many issues raised that would likely not have been raised if men were present: bias in teaching evaluations, work–life conflict, chilly climates for collaboration, and unequal pay. For example, a KOF participant noted that she appreciated the chance to discuss teaching strategies and graduate students who did not treat her with the same respect as they did male colleagues. Regardless of topic though, ADVANCE peer networks enhanced agency in career advancement by creating rooms of allies, norms of open communication and exchange, and examples of how challenges might be overcome.

In a similar vein, Acker (2006) observes that interactions in gendered organisations tend to enact dominance and submission. Being spoken over in meetings, asked by a senior colleague to do more than one's fair share of work, or being discouraged from sharing one's opinion are all forms of domination. The third space nature of ADVANCE networks, wherein women faculty were not at home, not in their primary workplaces, but in a space where hierarchy and the threat of evaluation did not silence their voices, facilitated women faculty sharing experiences of bullying, and vulnerability based on rank. Facilitators, and women faculty themselves, provided resources for their peers to respond to sexist, racist, bullying behaviours; they gave people strategies for how to resist, navigate around, and ignore such behaviours. Many women faculty reported in programme evaluations that they used these suggestions to avoid or challenge situations where they previously felt constrained and dominated by colleagues.

Dialogue between participants in peer networks also helped participants see how their own agency in career advancement might have been constrained by the internalised ideal worker, or 'I can't' narratives. Through exchange of experiences, women identified gendered evaluation logics and ideal worker norms and discussed strategies and it choices to change or ignore those norms. For example, women associate professors shared stories of department colleagues who convinced them that they did not have 'the right stuff' to go up for promotion in their department. An associate professor said, 'I came to the ADVANCE workshop and I ended up talking to people involved in the ADVANCE program or related to it in my discipline who said, "You should really consider going forward. You've got a case". And my department is kind of like, "No, no, you need 150–200 papers. And you're not publishing in

Science ... ", despite the fact that is not an easy place period, but I'm [also] not doing something that necessarily fits in there very well.' When participants heard stories from other women faculty who had found other ways out of the same situation in which they had felt stuck, they saw more choices and strategies than they had originally realised. Feeling that one has choices and control in a situation is a form of agency (O'Meara, Campbell, and Terosky 2011). This associate professor followed up after participation in the Advancing Together peer network by preparing her case materials. In other words, she began taking agentic actions towards her goal of career advancement.

In sum, the design of these networks as women-only, with faculty from across the campus but of the same rank decreased a sense of isolation that had constrained women's agency before. Furthermore, the quality of dialogue, resonance, affirmation, information, and strategies exchanged between women in ADVANCE peer networks disrupted gendered organisational logics that had constrained women's sense of agency in career advancement. This logic conveyed that the gendered organisational practices they had experienced were not (a) something that happened just to them or (b) the way it is for everyone and (c) nothing could be done about it. Participation in ADVANCE peer networks allowed women to see gendered situations as a pattern and assume agency in perspective, and in action, to overcome these patterns, at least in their own careers.

How peer networks challenged gendered organisational practices and contributed to gender equity reform

Before examining how the structure and internal dynamics of these three peer networks contributed to gender equity reform, it is necessary to consider two important contexts. First, these three networks are nested inside an overall ADVANCE programme at PU, which has many other structural and policy-related components. For example, the PU ADVANCE programme was a major catalyst behind PU's adoption of parental leave for men and women academic parents in 2012, and it created a Dashboard project to make salary, career, and faculty workload data more transparent. The Dashboard project developed data tables that showed tenure track and tenured faculty whether their salary was in the 25th, 50th, 75th, or 100th percentile for their rank in their respective college. The same Dashboard also provided the average number of years between promotion to associate and full professor and the demographics of faculty within the college by rank as well as provided average campus service commitments.

Elsewhere in the ADVANCE programme, there were efforts to increase department chair awareness of implicit bias, provide seed grants to junior women faculty for interdisciplinary (two or more disciplines collaborating) and engaged research (research aligned with public good projects), and examine teaching and service workloads for gender equity. Thus, the three peer networks examined in this study were not the only efforts underway to disrupt gendered organisational practices and supports; moreover, their emphasis was on individual career agency and support. Many participants in the three peer networks discussed here were also benefitting from other ADVANCE programmes (e.g. a participant could be receiving a seed grant for research, be in one of our three peer networks, and have access to Dashboard data).

Second, the three programmes run annually for about 15 faculty members in each network, so their overall impact towards gender equity reform must be considered for scale, in comparison to the size of the institution (over 1200 tenure-line faculty, roughly 33% women faculty). Within that context, we found several ways in which the structure and internal dynamics of the peer networks worked towards collective action and structural or cultural gender equity reform.

As noted by Acker (2006), symbols, language, and images reinforce divisions of labour in gendered universities. The structure of the peer networks challenged the gendered organisation and everyday practices of PU in several ways. First, women were brought into a third space where they were no longer in the minority as women, and/ or were no longer in the minority at their rank – which was true in their departments and colleges for two-thirds of participants. This is stated recognising they still could have been in the minority by another identity such as race or sexual orientation. Second, the design of the peer networks brought women faculty into spaces not organised by disciplinary expertise and hierarchy. Membership in each peer network was not contingent on performance and involved no surveillance. Third, the ADVANCE professors not only served as a peer network among themselves, but also served in a structural role of mentor to other women in their colleges, thus formalising an ongoing role for recognition of gender issues and strategic sharing of information.

To build on this last point, ADVANCE professors were in visible, recognised positions. In this way, ADVANCE provided role models of successful women countering the norm of full professors and leaders as white men, with traditional male behaviours. The establishment of senior women talking to each other about gendered practices and interacting with leadership about such practices in their colleges meant the establishment of a key piece in the structure at the college level to promote change in the university. This type of established leadership role with clear responsibilities attached to a prestigious person who had the specific assignment to support assistant and associate professors opened an unprecedented space for interaction and support.

These positions, embedded in organisational structures, provided concrete support and mentoring in an ongoing way to women faculty – and often in ways that challenged structural norms and realities. For example, one participant said:

> I wanted to let you know that the data on the Advance [Dashboard] site helped me successfully make a case about the inequity of my salary. After making my case and also hearing from other colleagues (especially my ADVANCE Professor) that this was an issue, [my dean] chose to request an equity raise on my behalf from [the president of the university]. I was awarded almost a 10% equity raise in addition to a merit raise I received for being in the top one-third tier of productive faculty in the school. My salary is still not quite where it should be but this is a big improvement. (Advancing Together participant)

Additionally, the internal dynamics of peer networks, the dialogues, and interactions were at times revelatory enough to provoke subsequent collective action and structural change. For example, an ADVANCE professor said:

> We discussed a wide variety of challenges faced by women faculty and faculty of colour, and we considered various strategies for responding to those challenges. There was a strong consensus in favour of creating a Dean's ADVANCE Advisory Council to investigate the widespread feeling that women and faculty of colour bear a heavier burden of service. The Dean was very supportive of this idea, and we are currently working to make it happen.

New understandings gained through dialogue and through sharing of experiences also challenged previous assumptions and practices, such as tendencies on the part of women participants in the networks not to ask for or negotiate for lab space, course release for major service assignments, Teaching Assistants, and peer reviews of teaching. By virtue of participation in ADVANCE network programmes, women began taking steps in their departments to ask for more support and negotiate in different ways, which changed some of those procedures for themselves and others in the future. The high academic reputation enjoyed by the ADVANCE professors enabled them to attract other women faculty to engage in peer networks. In turn, participation in peer networks enabled the junior faculty to make connections across campus, breaking down previous experiences of isolation.

As is the case for a number of practices, gains also accrued to actors providing and receiving services. The ADVANCE professor position gave women in the ADVANCE professor role knowledge about major policy developments on campus. While ADVANCE professors saw themselves making a difference, many of the tasks they engaged in led to eye-opening experiences. Being an ADVANCE professor gave the women in that role an enormous opportunity to develop contacts with 'like-minded women'. The ADVANCE professor learned many details about the university, an institution often characterised by a concentration of research and teaching efforts in one's own field and thus with limited communication across colleges and disciplines. One ADVANCE professor made remarks widely shared by other peers in the same role:

> A couple of the junior faculty in my school who never thought about writing for grants came to the workshop; they wrote a grant, and they got it and they were so delighted. So you see you have these little wins and there's been a lot of enthusiasm for what ADVANCE is doing in my school so that's very encouraging to see. I love getting together with the ADVANCE professors and finding out what's happening, what issues they are facing, because I would never [have] had the opportunity to do it if it wasn't for the ADVANCE initiative.

In addition to providing a structural position and creating a communication network among ADVANCE professors, all three ADVANCE networks hosted many visitors who provided alternative models of success, beyond normative models. This was particularly important in disrupting dominant expectations about excellent faculty and their work as in the following examples:

> It was great to get a chance to ask these three successful women how they run their very successful labs! (KOF participant)

> The two scholars with kids that presented after the lunch break were great. I liked how they talked about squeezing in stuff like answering emails on their smartphones while waiting for appointments or reading a paper while waiting to pick up their kids at an activity. That was really useful. (KOF participant)

In these cases, high-profile women full professors acted as role models in a very accessible way to more junior women faculty, revealing the strategies they had and were using to succeed. Related to this, women associate professors who had not been on the fast-track since promotion to associate professor adopted an agency outlook after hearing very successful women full professors who also had not followed very traditional trajectories, as in these examples:

> After hearing what [well-known successful STEM woman faculty member] went through and didn't get [promoted], but went back again and did, I thought I am going to go back and see. I thought her speaking was just inspirational, a nontraditional trajectory. (Advancing Together participant)

153

As noted by Acker (2006), a key gendered practice is that organisational logic and systems of evaluation and management favour male preferences and characteristics. Participation in ADVANCE peer networks, especially at the associate and full levels, countered organisational logics about what one must do to be promoted, obtain resources, get a higher salary, or get a fairer workload. Women in these networks were from all across campus and things were done very differently in different colleges. They shared how they had shifted their thinking on promotion, requested resources, and otherwise overcame challenges in ways that challenged dominant narratives and gendered understandings that there was nothing they could do. Thus, the structure and design of the ADVANCE peer networks as third spaces, and ADVANCE professors as alternative role models and intermediaries challenged gendered organisational norms and practices. Interactions of resonance, shared experiences and strategies, affirmation, and increased awareness challenged gendered organisational practices by creating spaces where collective action could be imagined, considered, and initiated.

There was also a strong sense among ADVANCE network participants that simply the presence of the networks and the discussion of gender issues on campus were creating greater accountability on campus around them. One full professor said ADVANCE has built a 'cohort of women who know each other and are thinking hard about problems at the University'. An associate professor remarked that ADVANCE is 'opening the eyes of women or giving them connections and in-roads they wouldn't have had'. One full professor who had been on the campus a long time said, 'I think that people will get that they cannot do things unnoticed and, yes, there will be a bunch of women that may end up making life crazy and a little more difficult [laughs] because, sorry, somebody is watching'. Another full professor observed that the ADVANCE programme was acting as a sort of 'sidewalk cut-out' system for women in the research university who did not quite fit:

> Like you cut out the sidewalk [curb] so people with wheelchairs can get up on the sidewalks, but you also have able-bodied people pushing strollers, that are biking, that use the sidewalk cut-outs too. I think that's what the ADVANCE Program could be, is sidewalk cut-outs for all of us.

In this way, peer networks encouraged gender equity by increasing awareness and sense of accountability that there were actors interested in and trying to reform gendered organisational practices and norms.

The limitations of women-only peer networks to gender equity reform

Now we consider ways in which the design and internal dynamics of peer networks were limited and might not facilitate gender equity reform. The key finding here was that while peer networks enhanced awareness of structural problems, they were often not the right place to address them. For example, the ADVANCE networks created a safe space for women faculty to discuss gendered organisational practices such as unfair workloads, develop skills to negotiate better workloads, and prioritise service requests. However, this did not change gendered practices within departments wherein many women faculty continued to feel that they were asked more often to engage in service than men faculty, did more than their fair share, or held more time-consuming teaching and advising assignments. For example, one ADVANCE professor discovered that in her college 20 male faculty were mentoring 20 Ph.D.

students, while 10 women faculty were mentoring 60 Ph.D. students. This is an example where recognition of the need for a critical service was also contrasted with unequal burdens carried out by women professors. The ADVANCE professor reporting on this remarked, '[Mentoring] for many of us is the most satisfying part of the job but also tends to be one of the unrewarded parts of the job'. The ADVANCE networks offered greater awareness of these structural problems and even agentic career strategies to confront them, but not long-term structural solutions to lessening them. Both cultural and structural interventions with department chairs and department cultures on transparent, equitable workload practices would establish more lasting and targeted change for these issues. An example of such a strategy would be an analysis of faculty activity reports to reveal gender and race differences if they exist, and then constructing solutions together through department faculty consensus; in other words, by separating women faculty from the specific spaces where many of the gendered organisational practices were happening, and placing them in an environment with only other women – the peer networks removed them from many of the spaces where structural problems needed to be fixed.

In a second example, ADVANCE peer networks created a forum to share information about available work–life policies such as parental leave and stop-the-tenure-clock. In peer network meetings, participants discussed strategies they were using to balance work and life demands. However, discussion of policy options and strategies did not significantly reduce the stress women faculty felt in balancing work and life priorities, or provide long-term solutions to 'ideal worker norms' in their departments. In one observation of a network meeting for assistant professors, the stress women faculty expressed was palpable. There were tears as three assistant professors described their stress over rising expectations for productivity, and spouses who did not understand why they worked all of the time.

As participants in the workshops shared experiences, it became obvious that most women faced similar problems; the recognition of common problems gave them confidence to act to secure better conditions to balance work–life issues and to demand more transparency through a better dissemination of family and leave policies. However, this did not do much to change the overall work ethic and normative ideal worker culture of their departments and colleges which had expectations that made the balance of work and life challenging, especially with children. There were times when women faculty affirmed each other's concerns in meetings, noting their need to sometimes prioritize family over work, and carve out time for exercise and loved ones. However, the cultural narrative of working as hard as one could was strong (especially for pre-tenure faculty) and difficult to disrupt, especially since many of the senior role model women brought into the ADVANCE peer networks as role models admitted they themselves worked countless hours to advance.

Finally, participants in each of the ADVANCE peer networks found allies and peer support within networks. However, as women helped each other brainstorm solutions to gendered practices and specific problems women faced within their departments, the focus was more often overcoming a specific instance or problem. Rarely did the conversation turn to systemic problems and collective strategies that the group of women together might instigate for institutional change. One exception to this was collective action taken on the part of ADVANCE professors (full professor women) to recommend a change to the instructions external reviewers for promotion applications receive regarding how to evaluate candidates who had taken a parental leave or a stop-the-tenure-clock year. Here, they advocated together for an institutional policy that might be applied to all faculty so as to reduce the stigma and bias associated with individuals adding a year to their tenure clock. However, more often, women faculty discussed creative solutions for getting around, ignoring, or side-stepping bullying colleagues or unfair practices, rather than confronting them in any collective way. There were a number of reasons for this, not the least of which was that two of the three networks studied here were focused on the women's own professional career advancement and agency – not collective organising or change. There were other programmes within ADVANCE focused on structural change – such as policy reform, transparent data, and awareness of unconscious bias. However, it was striking that most of the women in the peer networks discussed how to overcome problems individually – with the help of colleagues – rather than as patterns to be addressed collectively. The peer networks served as excellent forums to increase awareness that there were global problems, provide affirmation and resonance of experience, and devise individual strategies, but rarely did discussions turn towards collective change, and when they did, they were more often among the more senior women professors, and out of their concern as mentors of other women.

Discussion and implications

We found two key features of peer networks, their structure and design, and the internal dynamics promoted within them, essential to promoting women's career agency and challenging gendered organisational practices. These findings are consistent with those of previous studies that found that women-focused social networks and organising groups can be important spaces of self-awareness, agency, and collective efforts at gender equity reform (Hart 2007, 2008). Likewise, our findings are consistent with those of Kiyama, Lee, and Rhoades (2012) and Kezar (2014) that emphasise the role of personal and professional relationships in enacting organisational change and inspiring critical agency, especially around equity.

The ingredients in these peer networks were critical to their success in achieving identified outcomes. That is, their design as cross-campus networks of women of similar rank, with no performance or evaluation component, mattered to their ability to enhance women's agency. Likewise, the fact that the structure and internal dynamics within the sessions were non-hierarchical and set outside everyday department organisational practices provided relief from gendered organisational norms and empowerment. In addition, as critical theory suggests (Abel and Sementelli 2004), the dialogues within sessions promoted sharing of information, awareness, examples, role models, resonance, and a sense of allies, all of which worked against the constraints placed on women's careers by gendered organisational cultures and practices.

At the same time, the design of these activities limited their utility in long-term gender equity reform. Women faculty conducted most of their academic work inside their departments and in their disciplinary fields. Participation in the network was thereby structured to help women navigate department and field challenges better, but did not directly change the structural challenges in their departments and fields that they would have to face. It could be argued that if these networks are successful, and retain and promote an increasing percentage of women, organisational change will occur by virtue of the changing division of labour and norms of faculty work life. For example, each time a woman full professor is appointed and each time an assistant professor renegotiates her lab space or workload for equity reasons, gendered organisational norms are challenged and shift. However, these programmes are small and, while critically important, will usually not serve the majority of the women faculty at any one research university. Compared to the strength of norms they are facing, impact will be limited. For this reason, it is important that peer networks be one part of institutional efforts at gender equity reform, but not the only one. Ideally there needs to be greater integration between peer networks and other structural efforts at change.

ADVANCE programmes might consider merging individual professional growth and advancement programmes such as those explored here with action-oriented, collective efforts used by many women activists, women's commissions, and women's equity legislation programmes. For example, early career assistant professor women might be encouraged not only to meet to support each other's individual career advancement, but also to collectively consider the culture of impediments to women's advancement and retention and publish their concerns in a white paper or blog, authored by the collective group but without any one name on the author line. Such efforts could inform administration and policy change.

Women full professors meeting together in a peer network might work with administrators and ADVANCE programmes to develop unconscious bias trainings for their colleges and improve university-wide awareness of gender bias in student evaluations, workload allocation, and pay. There is untapped potential in the design of peer networks as a collective voice. Rather than individuals fighting battles alone, these groups could utilise shared experiences and advocate together as a stronger voice for campus-level awareness, policy reform, transparency, and accountability for gender equity outcomes.

This account of the achievements of ADVANCE peer networks at a research-intensive university gives hope for considerable improvement of women's conditions, even in highly competitive and individualistic environments, such as the twenty-first century university. At the same time, analyses of peer networks as mechanisms for gender equity reform reveal the need for coordination of individual support and structural reform. Such strategies will need to focus on persons trying to navigate gendered organisational environments, and on their successes, as well as on changing those environments structurally, so they will enable inclusive excellence.

Disclosure statement

No potential conflict of interest was reported by the author.

Funding

This article is based upon work supported by the National Science Foundation under Grant No. HRD-1008117.

References

Abel, C., and A. Sementelli. 2004. *Evolutionary Critical Theory and Its Role in Public Affairs.* Armonk, NJ: M.E. Sharpe.
Acker, J. 1990. "Hierarchies, Jobs, Bodies: A Theory of Gendered Organizations." *Gender and Society* 4 (2): 139–158.
Acker, J. 2006. "Inequality Regimes, Gender, Class and Race in Organizations." *Gender and Society* 20 (4): 441–464.

Bilimoria, D., Joy, S., and Liang, X. F. 2008. "Breaking Barriers and Creating Inclusiveness: Lessons of Organizational Transformation to Advance Women Faculty in Academic Science and Engineering." *Human Resource Management* 47 (3): 423–441.

Bilmoria, D., and X. Liang. 2012. *Gender Equity in Science and Engineering: Advancing Change in Higher Education*. New York: Routledge.

Bird, S. R. 2011. "Unsettling Universities' Incongruous, Gendered, Bureaucratic Structures: A Case-Study Approach." *Gender, Work and Organization* 18: 202–230.

Bourdieu, P. 1985. "The Genesis of the Concepts of Habitus and Field." *Socio-criticism* 2 (2): 11–24.

Campbell, C. M., and K. O'Meara. 2014. "Faculty Agency: Departmental Contexts that Matter in Faculty Careers." *Research in Higher Education* 55 (1): 49–74.

Cantor, N. 2011. *Gender Equity in the Sciences: Forging a 'Third Space'*. Office of the Chancellor, Paper 42. Syracuse, NY: Syracuse University. http://surface.syr.edu/cgi/viewcontent.cgi?article=1044&context=chancellor.

Clark, S. M., and M. Corcoran. 1986. "Perspectives on the Professional Socialization of Women Faculty: A Case of Accumulative Disadvantage?" *The Journal of Higher Education* 57 (1): 20–43.

Corbin, J., and A. Strauss. 2008. *Basics of Qualitative Research: Techniques and Procedures for Developing Grounded Theory*. Thousand Oaks, CA: Sage.

Creswell, J. W. 2003. *Research Design. Qualitative, Quantitative and Mixed Methods Approaches*. 2nd ed. Thousand Oaks, CA: Sage.

Creswell, J. 2007. *Qualitative Inquiry and Research Design: Choosing Among Five Approaches*. 2nd ed. Thousand Oaks, CA: Sage.

Creswell, J. W., and V. L. Plano Clark. 2011. *Designing and Conducting Mixed Methods Research*. 2nd ed. Thousand Oaks, CA: Sage.

Daly, A. 2010. "Mapping the Terrain: Social Network Theory and Educational Change." In *Social Network Theory*, edited by A. Daly, 1–17. Cambridge, MA: Harvard Education Press.

Dean, D., S. Bracken, and J. Allen, eds. 2009. *Women in Academic Leadership: Professional Strategies, Personal Choices*. Sterling, VA: Stylus Publishing.

Fox, M. F. 2008. "Institutional Transformation in the Advancement of Women Faculty: The Case of Academic Science and Engineering." In *Higher Education: Handbook of Theory and Research*, Vol. 23, edited by J. C. Smart, 73–103. New York: Springer.

Gaventa, J., and R. Tandon, eds. 2010. *Globalizing Citizens: New Dynamics of Inclusion and Exclusion*. London: Zed Books.

Giddens, A. 1979. *Central Problems in Social Theory: Action, Structure and Contradictions in Social Analysis*. Berkeley: University of California Press.

Glazer-Raymo, J. 1999. *Shattering the Myths: Women in Academe*. Baltimore, MD: Johns Hopkins University Press.

Glazer-Raymo, J. 2008. "The Feminist Agenda: A Work in Progress." In *Unfinished Agendas: New and Continuing Gender Challenges in Higher Education*, edited by J. Glazer-Raymo, 1–34. Baltimore, MD: Johns Hopkins University Press.

Habermas, J. 1992. *The Structural Transformation of the Public Sphere: An Inquiry into a Category of Bourgeois Society*. Cambridge: Polity.

Hart, J. 2007. "Creating Networks as an Activist Strategy: Differing Approaches Among Academic Feminist Organizations." *Journal of the Professoriate* 2 (1): 33–52.

Hart, J. 2008. "Mobilization Among Women Academics: The Interplay Between Feminism and Professionalization." *National Women's Studies Association (NWSA) Journal* 20 (1): 184–208.

Johnson, R. B., A. J. Onwuegbuzie, and L. A. Turner. 2007. "Toward a Definition of Mixed Methods Research." *Journal of Mixed Methods Research* 1 (2): 112–133.

Kemelgor, C., and H. Etkowitz. 2001. "Overcoming Isolation: Women's Dilemmas in American Academic Science." *Minerva* 39: 239–257.

Kezar, A. 2014. "Higher Education Change and Social Networks: A Review of Research." *The Journal of Higher Education* 85 (1): 91–124.

Kilduff, M., and D. Krackhardt. 2008. *Interpersonal Networks in Organizations: Cognition, Personality, Dynamics, and Culture*. Cambridge: Cambridge University Press.

Kiyama, J. M., J. J. Lee, and G. Rhoades. 2012. "A Critical Agency Network Model for Building an Integrated Outreach Program." *The Journal of Higher Education* 83 (2): 276–303.

Lester, J., M. Sallee, and J. Hart. 2013, May. "Beyond Gendered Universities? Implications for Research on Gender in Organizations." Paper presented at the meeting of the American Educational Research Association, San Francisco, CA.

Lincoln, Y. S., and E. G. Guba. 2000. "Paradigmatic Controversies, Contradictions, and Emerging Confluences." In *Handbook of Qualitative Research*. 2nd ed., edited by N. K. Denzin and Y. S. Lincoln, 163–188. Thousand Oaks, CA: Sage.

Lincoln, A. E., S. Pincus, J. Bandows Koster, and P. S. Leboy. 2014. "The Matilda Effect in Science: Awards and Prizes in the US, 1990s and 2000s." *Social Studies of Science* 42 (2): 302–320.

Marcuse, H. 1970. *Five Lectures*. Boston, MA: Beacon Press.

Maxwell, J. A. 2012. *A Realist Approach for Qualitative Research*. Thousand Oaks, CA: Sage.

Misra, J., J. H. Lundquist, E. Holmes, and S. Agiomavritis. 2011, January/February. "The Ivory Ceiling of Service Work." *Academe* 97 (1): 22–26. http://www.aaup.org/aaup/pubsres/academe/2011/jf/feat/misr.htm.

Modern Language Association. 2009. *Standing Still: The Associate Professor Survey*. New York: MLA. http://www.mla.org/assocprof_survey.

Morimoto, S. A., and A. Zajicek. 2012. "Dismantling the 'Master's House': Feminist Reflections on Institutional Transformation." *Critical Sociology*: 1–16. doi:10.1177/0896920512460063

Morimoto, S. A., A. M. Zajicek, V. B. Hunt, and R. Lisnic. 2013. "Beyond Binders Full of Women: NSF ADVANCE and Initiatives for Institutional Transformation." *Sociological Spectrum: Mid-South Sociological Association* 33 (5): 397–415. doi:10.1080/02732173.2013.818505

National Science Foundation. 2006. *ADVANCE: Increasing the Participation and Advancement of Women in Academic Science and Engineering Careers*. Arlington, VA: National Science Foundation. http://www.nsf.gov/funding/pgm_summ.jsp?pims_id=5383.

Oldenburg, R. 1989. *The Great Good Place*. New York: Marlowe & Company.

Oldenburg, R. 1991. *The Great Good Place*. Berkeley: University of California Press.

O'Meara, K. A. 2015. "A Career with a View: Agentic Perspectives of Women Faculty." *Journal of Higher Education* 86 (3): 1–26.

O'Meara, K. A., C. M. Campbell, and A. Terosky. 2011, November. "Living Agency in the Academy: A Conceptual Framework for Research and Action." Paper presented at the annual meeting of the Association for the Study of Higher Education, Charlotte, NC.

Putnam, R. 1995. "Bowling Alone: America's Declining Social Capital." *The Journal of Democracy* 6 (1): 65–78.

Putnam, R. 2000. *Bowling Alone: The Collapse and Revival of American Community*. New York, NY: Simon and Schuster.

Pyke, K. 2014. "Faculty Gender Inequity and the 'Just Say No to Service' Fairytale." In *Disrupting the Culture of Silence: Confronting Gender Inequality and Making Change in Higher Education*, edited by Kris De Welde and Andi Stepnick, 83–95. Sterling, VA: Stylus Publishing.

Rosser, S. V., and J. L. Chameau. 2006. "Institutionalization, Sustainability, and Repeatability of ADVANCE for Institutional Transformation." *Journal of Technology Transfer* 31: 335–344.

Rossman, G. B., and S. F. Rallis. 2003. *Learning in the Field: An Introduction to Qualitative Research*. Thousand Oaks, CA: Sage.

Sallee, M. W. 2013. "Gender Norms and Institutional Culture: The Family-Friendly Versus the Father-Friendly University." *The Journal of Higher Education* 84 (3): 363–396.

Sallee, M. W. 2011. "Performing Masculinity: Considering Gender in Doctoral Student Socialization." *The Journal of Higher Education* 82 (2): 187–216.

Smith, J. W., and T. Calasanti. 2005. "The Influences of Gender, Race, and Ethnicity on Workplace Experiences of Institutional and Social Isolation: An Exploratory Study of University Faculty." *Sociological Spectrum* 25 (3): 307–334.

Stewart, A., D. LaVaque-Manty, and J. Malley. 2004. "Recruiting Female Faculty Members in Science and Engineering: Preliminary Evaluation of One Intervention Model." *Journal of Women and Minorities in Science and Engineering* 10: 361–375.

Sturm, S. 2006. "The Architecture of Inclusion: Advancing Workplace Equity in Higher Education." *Harvard Journal of Law and Gender* 29 (2): 248–333.

Tenkasi, R., and M. Chesmore. 2003. "Social Networks and Planned Change: The Impact of Strong Ties on Effective Change Implementation and Use." *Journal of Applied Behavioral Science* 39 (3): 281–300.
Terosky, A. L., K. O'Meara, and C. Campbell. 2014. "Enabling Possibility: Women Associate Professors Sense of Agency in Career Advancement." *Journal of Diversity in Higher Education* 7 (1): 58–76.
Trower, C. A. 2012. *Success on the Tenure Track: Five Keys to Faculty Job Satisfaction.* Baltimore, MD: Johns Hopkins University Press.
Valian, V. 1998. *Why So Slow? The Advancement of Women.* Cambridge, MA: MIT Press.
Ward, K., and L. Wolf-Wendel. 2012. *Academic Motherhood: How Faculty Manage Work and Family.* New Brunswick, NJ: Rutgers University Press.
West, M. S., and J. W. Curtis. 2006. *AAUP Faculty Gender Equity Indicators 2006.* Washington, DC: American Association of University Professors.
Winslow, S. 2010. "Gender Inequality and Time Allocations Among Academic Faculty." *Gender & Society* 24 (6): 769–793.

Index

161

INDEX

For Product Safety Concerns and Information please contact our EU
representative GPSR@taylorandfrancis.com
Taylor & Francis Verlag GmbH, Kaufingerstraße 24, 80331 München, Germany

www.ingramcontent.com/pod-product-compliance
Ingram Content Group UK Ltd.
Pitfield, Milton Keynes, MK11 3LW, UK
UKHW051831180425
457613UK00022B/1202